NAIL IT THEN SCALE IT: THE ENTREPRENEUR'S GUIDE TO CREATING AND MANAGING BREAKTHROUGH INNOVATION

Nathan Furr and Paul Ahlstrom

D0940347

First Edition, June 2011

ISBN: 0983723605
ISBN-13: 9780983723608

CONTENTS

Preface...i

About the Authors... iii

Chapter 1: The Entrepreneur's Paradox..1

Chapter 2: The Mystery of Market Winning Innovation 21

Chapter 3: Nail It then Scale It—Fundamentals 35

Phase 1: Nailing the Customer Pain...65

Phase 2: Nail the Solution 93

Phase 3: Nail the Go-to-Market Strategy 135

Phase 4: Nail the Business Model..159

Phase 5: Scale It..171

Chapter 9: Context Matters!...197

Chapter 10: Crisis and Focus 211

Appendix: Nail It then Scale It Checklist 231

Appendix: Nail It then Scale It Sample Interview Guide.......................241

End Notes...245

PREFACE

Entrepreneurship is changing. A fundamental paradigm shift is sweeping the field from the bottom up as successful entrepreneurs reflect on their experience and begin to recognize the disconnect between what they thought would make them successful and what actually led to their success. Entrepreneurs and investors alike are dissatisfied with the time and money required to launch a successful startup.

In our real-world laboratory over the last 20 years we have researched thousands of companies and directly invested more than $400 million dollars into 100+ startup companies which have gone on to raise an additional $900 million from co-investors and generated billions of dollars in exits and value. In watching the winners and losers, we have noticed patterns of success and failure. For example, we have noticed how many entrepreneurs spend immense sums of money without ever discovering a real opportunity, or how the lack of alignment between investors and entrepreneurs leads to distorted outcomes. These and other problems come from a mistaken commitment to the traditional startup process. Through research and trial-and-error we have discovered that there is a better way— a consistently effective way that leads to entrepreneurial success. We packed up our learning into this book and call it *Nail It then Scale It*.

We are not alone in our observations and as this grassroots movement takes hold of the entrepreneurial community, entrepreneurship educators are becoming increasingly dissatisfied with the results of traditional educational programs that focus on writing business plans. The reasons for this disconnect have to do with the underlying evolution of management education and the lack of understanding of the innovation process. The outcome of the paradigm shift will profoundly reshape how entrepreneurs and innovators launch disruptive products and start new businesses, whether as stand-alone businesses or corporate ventures.

The evidence of the change can be seen sprouting in numerous places around the world. Steve Blank's Customer Development philosophy has been followed by others, such as Eric Ries and the Lean Startup; and John Mullins and Randy Komisar in their Getting to Plan B approach.

Similarly, the methodologies underlying successful seed funds such as Kickstart or incubators such as Y Combinator or Tech Stars all point to an emerging belief that there is a better process to succeed than what many people are following. Nail It then Scale It represents the best ideas that have come from more than two decades of observing hundreds of world-class entrepreneurs drive positive outcomes. For entrepreneurs and product managers who want additional ideas on the product-development and startup process, we recommend Steve Blank's book *Four Steps to the Epiphany*.

Together, we have applied our experience and research in this emerging field to create what we see as the entry point for entrepreneurs and innovators who want to launch innovative products and build successful businesses. Whether you are designing a disruptive new product, starting a corporate venture, starting your own business or rescuing your business, applying the principles of the Nail It then Scale It process will dramatically change the way you view a startup and significantly improve your chances of success. We are always looking for customer feedback and case studies. Please send feedback to us at info@nailthenscale.com. Best of luck and stay committed to the process. We have seen it save entrepreneurs years and transform their businesses. It will do the same for you.

–Nathan Furr and Paul Ahlstrom

ABOUT THE AUTHORS

Nathan Furr, Entrepreneurship Professor

Nathan Furr earned his PhD from the Stanford Technology Ventures Program at Stanford University and is currently an entrepreneurship professor at Brigham Young University (recently ranked in the top five entrepreneurship programs nationally). Professionally, Nathan has acted as the founder or advisor to startups in web 2.0, clean technology, professional services, retail and financial services industries. Nathan also sits on the investment board of the Kickstart Seed Fund, an innovative early-stage venture fund and is an expert contributor to Forbes. Nathan also worked as a consultant at Monitor Group, a premiere international strategy consulting firm, working with senior executives on a range of strategic and market discovery initiatives.

Nathan's research focuses on market development and early stage entrepreneurship, including leading the Lean Startup Research Project and the "e-school" approach to rethinking how we teach entrepreneurship. His current research examines how both startups and existing firms successfully adapt to enter a new market. Nathan has co-authored papers on the process by which firms develop innovative business models, the determinants of success for firms changing industries, and the impact of organizational learning on international entry. In addition to his doctoral studies, Nathan has a BA, MA, and an MBA.

Paul Ahlstrom, Managing Director and Founder

Paul Ahlstrom is an entrepreneur and investor who focused most of his career on the early-stage startup process. Paul has founded multiple high-technology startup companies and investment funds in the United States and Mexico.

Paul's current focus is opening up capital sources to Mexican entrepreneurs and supporting the vibrant entrepreneurial ecosystems of Mexico and Latin America. As a leader of Mexico's venture capital industry, Paul and his partner, Rogelio de los Santos, have launched Alta Venture Mexico located in Monterrey, Mexico. (www.altaventures.com)

Prior to founding Alta Ventures Mexico, Paul co-founded vSpring Capital (www.vspring.com) and Kickstart Seed Fund (www.kickstartseedfund.com) in the Rocky Mountain region and Alta Growth Capital (www.agcmexico.com) in Mexico City. As an entrepreneur and through his venture funds, Paul has directly invested more than $400 million dollars in more than one-hundred startup companies. Some of these companies include Ancestry.com (www.ancestry.com, NASDAQ:ACOM); GlobalSim (www.globalsim.com), sold to Kongsberg Maritime (KOG - Oslo Stock Exchange); Senforce, sold to Novell (www.novell.com, NASDAQ: NOVL); and Altiris (NASDAQ:ATRS), which went public and then sold to Symantec (NASDAQ: SYMC); Rhomobile (www.rhomobile.com); Aeroprise (www.aeroprise.com), sold to BMC (NASDAQ: BMC). Paul has also served on the boards of many successful venture-backed startups including: Public Engines (www.crimereports.com); 7degrees (www.mypeoplemaps.com); The American Academy (www.TheAmericanAcademy.com); and FamilyLink (www.familylink.com).

In addition to fund creation and investment experience, Paul has direct entrepreneurial and operating experience, having personally founded multiple startups, including Knowlix (1997), a knowledge management IT company which raised venture capital financing and sold to Peregrine Systems in 1999 which in turn sold to Hewlett Packard (www.hp.com) (NYSE: HPQ). Paul was a founding advisory board member of Brigham Young University's Rollins eBusiness Center, and he is listed as one of the Founders of Brigham Young University's Center for Entrepreneurship and Technology. Paul also serves on the executive committee and board for the University of Utah's Technology Commercialization Office (http://www.tco.utah.edu), which is ranked number one in university-generated spinouts in the United States. Paul previously served as trustee for the Utah Technology Council and other community boards and has also served multiple years as a member of Motorola Corporation's Visionary Research Board (NYSE: MOT). Paul earned his BA in Communications from Brigham Young University. He has also received an honorary doctorate from the Netanya Academic College in Netanya, Israel.

Chapter 1: The Entrepreneur's Paradox

It was the *process*. Doing everything right was killing his business. It all started several years earlier when Greg's apartment building had been robbed. Frustrated and feeling a need to do something about it, he joined a neighborhood watch group and offered to map crimes that were happening in the area. As Greg continued, he came to believe that mapping the locations of crimes would align and empower the efforts of citizens and police to reduce crimes in each neighborhood.

With real motivation and passion, Greg did what all good entrepreneurs are supposed to do—he wrote a business plan and developed a website to report crime statistics (with an underlying revenue model built on advertising). Website in hand, he contacted a friend at the Washington DC police department and together, Greg and his friend convinced the police chief to commit to a trial run. Excited by his success, Greg took the next step and presented to venture capitalists, who were impressed by Greg's vision and provided seed capital to grow the business. Capital in hand, Greg continued building CrimeReports.com and hired developers and sales people to expand before competitors could catch up. But then something perplexing began to happen. Despite all his efforts, the business didn't take off. New deals with police departments seemed to hover in a state of limbo, never closing; and despite moments of hope and seeming progress, CrimeReports.com remained stuck in a purgatory that had now lasted for several years without producing any new customers. After investing the first two tranches of venture funding, Greg began to dig deeper and ask himself why. Why, when he had done everything right, had things gone so wrong? It was during this crisis that Greg began to apply the principles behind the Nail It then Scale It process—a significant departure from traditional methods most entrepreneurs are taught to follow. Greg stopped developing, stopped selling, and started listening to the customer and the market. What he learned shocked him and led him to change course. Within one year he went from one customer to signing up 200 new police departments with 2,000 new customers total signed by the third year, while also building one of the first successful Gov 2.0 business models. What was the difference between failure and success? It was the *process*, but not the intuitive one he had been taught his whole life. No, the lifelong ideas he had been told about how to be an entrepreneur were leading him down the road to failure. Using the principles, processes and tools described in this book, Greg was able to correct his course and build the leading crime-mapping company in the world.

We have seen entrepreneurs like Greg fall into this same trap over and over—entrepreneurs who seem to do everything right end up stumbling. Although statistically most startups fail, the dirty secret is that these startups aren't failing because they couldn't make the product or the founders lacked talent. Indeed less than 10% of businesses fail because the technology or product didn't work, and we've met thousands of smart, talented entrepreneurs who struggled despite their great ideas.[1] In reality, these businesses fail because the entrepreneurs who started them had passion and drive, they wrote a business plan, they raised money to build the business, they developed a product, and they successfully executed on their plan. Why, then, did they fail? Because the very fact that they believe and take action reinforces their initial belief—which is really only a guess—while decreasing their options to correct that guess in the future. When entrepreneurs fail for doing exactly what they were taught to do, it seems bewildering. As a result, many people feel that the secret to being a successful entrepreneur is a mystery, and so great entrepreneurs must simply be born great ... right? We disagree. There is a better way.

> *The entrepreneur's paradox: entrepreneurs only act when they believe they have a real opportunity but this belief can lead them to fail.*

So why do so many entrepreneurs fail? Is there a way that entrepreneurs and innovators can successfully and repeatedly innovate? The answer to these questions is the focus of this book, but it also represents our collective passion and research. Twenty years ago, in the late 1980's, Paul Ahlstrom started his quest as a young entrepreneur recovering from a failed startup. During the past 20+ years, he read dozens of books, hired many consultants, raised more than $500 million, and participated in the investment or founding of more than 100 companies. Paul's observations were that companies that followed certain principles had a much higher success rate and were also very efficient with their cash. What was startling was that these principles were 180 degrees opposite of conventional wisdom.

In a parallel universe, Nathan Furr began studying these questions as a Ph.D. at Stanford University in the Stanford Technology Ventures Program. During his research on successful and unsuccessful new ventures, Nathan also observed that successful entrepreneurs acted in ways very different from those described in the popular press. Furthermore, through his interaction with hundreds of entrepreneurs, investors, and companies in Silicon Valley, Nathan recognized that the most successful entrepreneurs followed a unique pattern very different from a traditional business-planning process or product-development process.

Although we both independently arrived at the same realization, we felt compelled to work together to help entrepreneurs by describing our discovery. Over the years we have both examined several hundred successful and unsuccessful entrepreneurial companies. Together we took what we discovered and applied it to over a dozen new ventures, either from founding or in midstream, to validate our findings. The more we applied what we discovered, the more success we had with the process.

Innovators, entrepreneurs, and even product managers fail precisely because they believe in their idea and then follow conventional wisdom about how to build a new product or a new business. In so doing, they tackle the wrong tasks, do good things in the wrong order, and in the end fall prey to their own strengths. The solution is a remarkably simple process that successful entrepreneurs and new ventures, from Edison to Intuit, Cisco to Google, have applied to successfully and repeatedly innovate. It is a process we have used to help new startups, struggling ventures, and large businesses leap forward. For example, from the ashes of a struggling corporation, one startup applied these principles to sift through the confusion to literally dominate their market, generating more sales than all their competitors combined and exiting the market for tens of millions of dollars. Another startup used this process from the start to discover how to extend online education to the over six billion people in the world without access to university education. As yet another example, one startup was struggling to close customers, despite having made all the right partnerships and developing an incredible product. Using this process, the startup developers discovered that they had to change their business, fire their partners, and refocus, all of which led them to beat their annual sales target by the end of the first quarter of the 2009 recession. Another startup learned how to move from a struggling product to a 100% close rate on deals worth over $100k each. All of these successes were due to following the Nail It then Scale It process.

At its core, the Nail It then Scale It process flips the conventional wisdom about how to build a company on its head and helps entrepreneurs do the right things in the right order. The process discussed here is based on both extended experience and research—dozens of personal examples, case studies and quantitative research. It represents the process that successful entrepreneurs and companies have already discovered. It can be applied by product managers, entrepreneurs, and innovators of all kinds who are trying to bring a new product to market. Whether you are someone with just an idea or an entrepreneur in a startup or corporation; whether you are a product manager or a high-growth entrepreneur, the process can transform your business. But before we describe the process, we need to provide some motivation for why what you already know about entrepreneurship might lead you astray.

THE THREE MYTHS OF ENTREPRENEURSHIP

Earlier we asked why so many talented, well-intentioned entrepreneurs fail. One reason is that there are three core myths about entrepreneurs, or traps, which snare entrepreneurs: the hero myth, the process myth, and the money myth.

THE ENTREPRENEUR HERO MYTH: WHY BELIEVING IN YOUR PRODUCT LEADS TO FAILURE

One of the most surprising myths about entrepreneurship surrounds what it takes to be a successful entrepreneur. Whenever we talk to students, executives, and entrepreneurs about what it takes to be an entrepreneur, we always hear the same list of qualities: passion, determination, vision, and so forth. In many ways they are right—entrepreneurship does require all these qualities, and these qualities are part of the formula we have all been taught. For example, in the press, entrepreneurs are depicted as larger-than-life individuals, committed at all costs, passionate about their vision, and determined to walk through brick walls to achieve their vision. Similarly, we have heard entrepreneurs say that the secret to their success was determination in the face of all odds or that the one quality entrepreneurs must have is passion.

The problem is that when we actually look at startups, we find that passionate, determined, visionary entrepreneurs lead startups to failure more often than passionate, determined, visionary entrepreneurs lead startups to success. In fact, despite our collective belief in passion, determination and vision, decades of research trying to tease out the personality qualities of successful entrepreneurs has come up empty-handed.[2] Why does this happen? Although passion, determination, and vision are important, they can also be extremely dangerous. For entrepreneurs who have risked their time, reputation, and cash, passion can quickly become dogmatism, determination can become commitment to a failing course of action, and vision can lead one down a dead-end road. All too often, entrepreneurs fall in love with their product or technology, they ignore negative feedback from customers, and they spend years building a product based on a vision that no one else shares.

> *All too often, entrepreneurs fall in love with their product or technology, they ignore negative feedback from customers, and they spend years building a product based on a vision that no one else shares.*

If you don't believe that passion and determination can lead you into a trap, take the example of Einstein, the most well-known scientist of our generation. When Einstein published his general theory of relativity in 1916, he believed that the universe was static, so he incorporated a "cosmological constant" to make his theory work. Einstein stood doggedly by his theory for several years, rejecting the work of Alexander Friedmann in 1922 and Georges Lemaître in 1927 which suggested that the universe is expanding. Finally, in 1929, when Edwin Hubble demonstrated that the universe is expanding, Einstein realized that in fact his general theory of relativity actually implied that the universe was dynamic. Admitting that the cosmological constant was wrong, he called his dogged determination the "greatest blunder" of his life. In the end, Einstein's conviction that he had all the answers cost him the discovery of a groundbreaking insight—the universe *is* expanding!

Despite the tendency to be trapped by your drive and passion, it is possible to follow a process that allows you to adapt and succeed. As an example, consider the case of entrepreneur Mike Cassidy and his company Ultimate Arena. Prior to cofounding Ultimate Arena, Mike had successfully exited his second startup for $532 million and was searching for a new idea to try out. During this period Mike met Thresh, the world champion of a popular first-person shooter video game. Thresh had the idea to create an online "arena" where gamers could come together, put in a few dollars, and then fight for a winner-take-all cash pot. Although Mike wasn't much of a gamer, the idea was intriguing, and the two raised some initial money from venture capitalists to build Ultimate Arena. For almost a year, Mike and his team worked diligently to build Ultimate Arena; and at the time of their launch, the future looked promising. Thresh was out generating attention with his video game celebrity status, and over the next few months, users joined rapidly and the site began to push close to a half a million unique users per month. This all looked like strong evidence of success on the outside. However, when he really dug into the data, Mike started to notice a disturbing trend. Although new users were joining daily, those users weren't staying. Many users stayed for a few games but then never returned. In fact, once Mike put a number to it, he found that 50% of new users tried the site once and then never returned.

Concerned, Mike decided to investigate by personally calling users who had left the site to ask why they hadn't returned. Mike discovered that although Ultimate Arena players might participate in other games of chance, such as poker, the games were played typically among friends where the individual had a decent shot at winning. In contrast, on Ultimate Arena the player was always having her or his money taken by someone better—kind of like having a bully at school steal your lunch money. What the users highlighted was that Ultimate Arena lacked two critical ingredients: a social component and a fighting chance to win your money back.

A storm was brewing. The venture money couldn't last forever, and users couldn't keep churning in and out if the site was going to be successful. Mike brought the team together and showed them the cold, hard data—users were dropping rapidly, and the company was on the path to failure. Despite this threat, many of the company's most passionate and committed employees desperately wanted to keep trying to make it work. These team members were good people and good entrepreneurs: they were passionate, determined, and even visionary people. But because they were passionate and determined, many team members couldn't see the need to change. They argued that if they simply changed the fee scheme, or improved the ranking system, users might be happier and stay. Mike took a much more clinical view, applying the principles we will discuss, and determined that Ultimate Arena was not meeting customers' needs. After about a month of brainstorming and talking to customers about what to do, Mike dropped development of Ultimate Arena and began laying the framework for what became Xfire—an instant messaging service that allowed gamers to meet online and then play their favorite game. Xfire satisfied gamers' needs for a social element and quickly became successful. In the end, Xfire was sold for over $100 million to Vivendi—but not without a critical crisis along the way that required something different than passion, determination, and vision. Indeed, these very qualities would have led the company to persist into oblivion.

The fact that passion, determination, and vision sometimes lead to success and sometimes to failure raises an important question at the heart of what we like to call the *entrepreneur hero myth*. The entrepreneur hero myth is a common problem: whenever we see a successful entrepreneur who is passionate, determined, and visionary, the natural response is to attribute any success to the personal qualities of the individual. But there is a problem with explaining success by simply saying that someone is a great leader or a great entrepreneur. In social psychology this phenomenon is called the *Fundamental Attribution Error*.[3] This error argues that people often attribute far more success and far more failure to the individual than the individual actually deserves, when in fact other, more difficult to observe, factors often play a critical role in successful outcomes. In his book *Outliers*, Malcolm Gladwell illustrates this effect in the lives of highly successful individuals, such as Bill Gates, and highlights how other factors, such as Gates' co-location to early computing resources, shaped his highly successful future.

The fact that we are all subject to the Fundamental Attribution Error, particularly in entrepreneurship, means that if we take a closer look at the entrepreneur hero myth, two important insights emerge. First, attributes of great entrepreneurs that we talk about are actually neither the key to success nor the path to failure—they can play either role depending on how you approach the world and the problem. However, one of the things we will do in this book is show you how to focus these qualities so that they can become tools of success. Specifically, we will show you how to transform dangerous "passion" into positive passion to understand the customer's needs; how to turn "commitment" to a failing course of action into commitment to intellectually honest learning; and how to leverage blinding vision into vision that leads you to success. Second and more important, what the Fundamental Attribution Error suggests is that there may be another explanation behind successful entrepreneurs other than their personal qualities. Indeed, we discovered that the factor that makes entrepreneurs successful is not just their personal qualities but more importantly the process they use.

THE PROCESS MYTH: WHY BUILDING A PRODUCT LEADS TO FAILURE

The second myth is perhaps the most dangerous because it has to do with the actual process of entrepreneurship. Whenever we ask people, "What should you do if you have a great idea?" the answer is always the same: raise some money, hire a team, build the product, test the product, and, when the product is finished, go out and sell it. This answer isn't a surprise. In fact, it represents our collective wisdom about how to develop a product and is based on the product development model that came into popularity in the early part of the 20th century. In the product-development model, a new product proceeds through a series of stage gates from initial specification, to development, to testing, through production, and then into sales (Figure 1).

Figure 1: The Traditional Product Development Model

What we intuitively think of as the standard entrepreneurial process is almost an exact copy of the product development process, just with different words. Specifically, according to the traditional entrepreneurial model, an entrepreneur has an idea, gathers resources to build the product, develops the product, perfects the product, then produces and sells the product. Quite simply, the standard entrepreneurial process is the product-development model applied to the realm of innovation (Figure 2).

Figure 2: The Traditional Entrepreneurship Process Model

Why the Traditional Model Will Lead You to Failure

The problem with applying models for managing large firms is that while these models, like the product-development model, might produce good results for established companies in markets that have dominated for years, these models work very poorly for entrepreneurs because entrepreneurs are doing something very different than large companies. Specifically, most often large companies *execute* on relatively *known* problems. When you tackle known problems you focus on planning and executing; therefore, using the product development model—a planning-based model—can improve your chances of success. The process can work for large companies in known markets primarily because they already know what to build and who their customers are. In addition, it helps that large companies working on known problems have massive resources and deep knowledge they can apply to planning and executing. In contrast, entrepreneurs and innovators tackle *unknown* problems often with an *unknown* solution. All the planning in the world won't do anything to change the fact that entrepreneurs start out with a guess at the right problem and solution. That means that instead of executing, entrepreneurs must *search* for the right problem and the right solution! And searching requires a very different set of activities than execution! Indeed, when you need to search, planning can be the fastest way to failure—it wastes time, wastes resources, and commits you to a course of action that is no more than a guess.

Therefore, it doesn't make sense to use the same processes for a startup to *search* which large firms use when they *execute*. Even for large firms, it may not always make sense to use the product-development model. When a large firm is faced with a disruptive innovation or needs to grow into new territory, then they have a search problem, not an execution problem. In essence they have an entrepreneurial problem! In these situations, large firms and the product managers there should apply the NISI approach.

The problem for entrepreneurs is that in the absence of an alternative process to guide their search, entrepreneurs fall back on planning and execution. As a result, entrepreneurs believe that if only they write a business plan or build the product, they will succeed. The result is what we call the *Field of Dreams Myth*. In the popular movie *Field of Dreams*, Kevin Costner, who plays the main character, plows his cornfield under to build a baseball diamond. Miraculously, cars come from miles around to watch a team of baseball stars play a game on the farmer's land. Although the plot may sound crazy, the movie touts the power of believing in a dream even when it seems illogical to everyone else. Interestingly, many people see entrepreneurship the same way—as an act of faith: "if you build it they will come…" As a result, many entrepreneurs we meet believe that the process to become a successful entrepreneur is to have an idea, invest their time and resources to build a product, and then go sell it. This process intuitively seems right to most people because it is based on the product-development model—that you can plan your way to success and that the real obstacle is just to build it. The problem is that unless you are Kevin Costner, this will almost always lead to failure. Here is why. Below is the traditional model that most entrepreneurs follow, what we will rename *the product-based model of entrepreneurship* because entrepreneurs build a product based on their faith that customers will buy what they develop (Figure 3).

Figure 3: The Traditional (Product-Based) Entrepreneurial Process Model

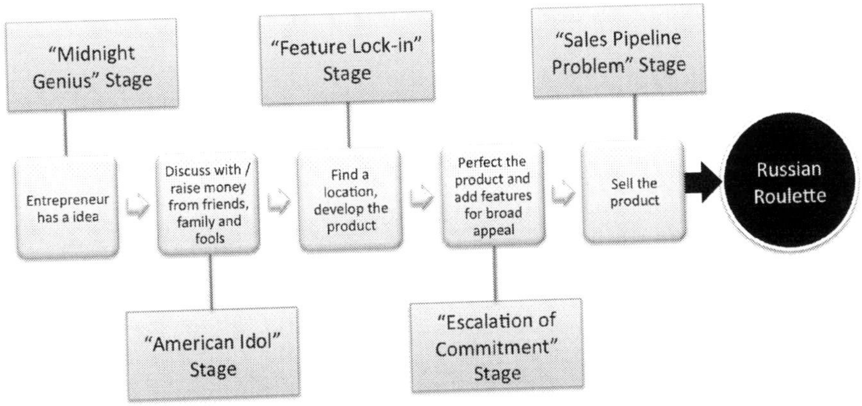

In the first stage of the traditional, product-based entrepreneurial model, the entrepreneur has an idea for what he or she thinks will be a great product or service. This "Midnight Genius" stage resembles the common experience of waking up in the middle of the night with an absolutely brilliant idea, only to discover later (usually in the morning, when reality hits) that the idea wasn't so great after all. This stage can be exciting, because it involves creative imagination, but it can also be dangerous. Remember, whatever the entrepreneur believes really only exists in the entrepreneur's head. The "flash of genius" is only a *guess* about what customers want, no matter how brilliant it may feel.

Next, the entrepreneur often looks for feedback from trusted friends and family. This feels logical, but it's actually a major tactical error—we've confused our social circle with our customer base. Far too often, bad ideas that sound good are encouraged by our intelligent but unqualified friends, and terrible ideas are encouraged by our kind mothers. As a result of this common error, too often the entrepreneurial landscape begins to resemble the popular television show *American Idol,* where some absolutely terrible singers (armed with delusions of grandeur) make their way to the competition among many good singers. Similarly, with biased feedback in hand, entrepreneurs take the leap of faith, and on the basis of their best guess begin building a company. Unfortunately, the very act of building the product has the effect of increasing an entrepreneur's belief that customers actually want the product features the entrepreneurs are developing. The features then begin to proliferate and get locked in, even when customers may not need them. As the product nears completion in the next stage, entrepreneurs escalate their commitment even more, trying to perfect the product and add more features to increase the appeal to a broader audience.

Finally, the great day comes when the product is ready to sell. But here comes the killer: whether customers actually buy the product or not has little to do with how hard the entrepreneur worked, how brilliant the technologist is, or how charismatic the salesperson. Why? Because the entire product was built on a guess about what customers wanted, and so whether customers actually buy is more of a random probability—a kind of entrepreneurial Russian roulette. It is the reason that most entrepreneurs fail—not because they couldn't make the product but because they didn't build what the customers wanted.

We've seen this pattern repeated so many times that it is tragic. But the real tragedy is that in many ways it wasn't the entrepreneurs' fault. The entrepreneurs were following the collective wisdom about how to be entrepreneurs—believing in themselves and acting on faith. Indeed, the entire time, they were doing many good things. But here is the key. The problem is that they were acting on faith about what customers wanted, and although doing good things, the entrepreneurs were doing them out of order. In contrast, successful entrepreneurs followed a very different process. If we were to redraw the traditional model as simply as possible, it might look something like Figure 4 below.

Figure 4: The Customer-Based Model of Entrepreneurship

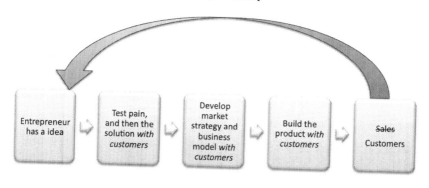

NAIL IT THEN SCALE IT

By changing the order and content of the steps in the process, the most successful entrepreneurs were able to turn their assumptions (which were almost always wrong) into facts that could be used to build a successful business. More important, rather than wasting hundreds of hours and thousands of dollars to find out an idea was wrong, entrepreneurs were able to develop a product that was a near perfect fit for what your customers wanted. Throughout the rest of this book we will demonstrate how you can use this same process to nail your product.

THE MONEY MYTH: WHY HAVING TOO MUCH MONEY LEADS TO FAILURE

The final myth is actually good news for entrepreneurs who don't have much money. The money myth is the belief that an entrepreneur needs to have a large amount of money to start a successful business. Although there is an old saying that "it takes money to make money," for entrepreneurs the formula isn't so simple. While most entrepreneurs believe that they could be successful if only they had more money, we studied entrepreneurs who start businesses with less than $1000 and entrepreneurs who receive several million dollars in investment. We found that although we all assume that more money is better, in fact, too much money at the wrong time can kill you. In a formal study, researchers found that having too much money can lead to extreme distortions.[4] The reason is that while capital is necessary to start a new business, it introduces a unique set of problems that can hinder a startup.

To illustrate the danger of the money myth, consider the early blowout success and then the later abysmal failure of the 3D Realms video game studio. When the studio started out, the two entrepreneurs, George Broussard and Scott Miller, built a successful business with only a few dollars to start. With such sparse resources, not only did they invent the shareware model of software distribution, which became a major movement in early software distribution, but in the short space of a year and a half they developed Duke Nukem 3D, an innovative video game that was ahead of its time and ultimately became one of the most financially successful video game titles of the era. With tens of millions of dollars in the coffers, the founders announced the sequel to their hit title, Duke Nukem Forever. Then something puzzling happened. Although the team now had enough money to hire developers, construct a new building, and do everything right for once, things started to go downhill. Development dragged out, expenses soared, and after a whopping twelve years of development, the Duke Nukem Forever project shut down without having even produced the game.[5] Unfortunately, entrepreneurs at 3D Realms are not unique but rather representative of the many, many entrepreneurs who have fallen prey to the money myth.

There are several reasons why more capital for a startup can actually increase failure rather than assure success. One reason is that, in the early days, entrepreneurs need to focus obsessively on finding out what customers want. When investment money comes in the door it creates some fundamental changes. For one, although the entrepreneur has been acting on assumptions (or guesses about what customers want), when investment money arrives it feels like a validation of those assumptions and an endorsement to go execute on the plan. The problem is that, as we highlighted in the traditional product-based process, the business plan is almost always based on faith, rather than facts, about what the market wants. This problem wouldn't be so bad if entrepreneurs were going to be forced by hunger to go talk to customers (at which point they would find out that their plan needed to be adjusted), but the money provides a cushion against the cold, hard world. Entrepreneurs can spend a long time executing on their plan before they discover they were wrong. This was the case with 3D Realms as well as with such high-profile failures as Eclipse Aviation and Webvan, which each burned through over a billion dollars in capital before failing.

> *"I believe that too much money in a startup is not only unnecessary, it's actually toxic."*
> *—Mike Maples Jr.*

In each case, the money allowed the entrepreneurs to execute their flawed business plan rather than to stay laser focused on the market so that they could find the facts about what customers wanted and adjust accordingly. Mike Maples Jr., a well-known angel investor, puts it another way:

I believe that too much money in a startup is not only unnecessary, it's actually toxic. It causes you to pursue losing strategies for too long to the detriment of the winning strategies. ... If you look at the truly great startups, ... they've been hyper frugal. Cisco, Google in the early days, Yahoo! in the early days, Microsoft. I mean, the list goes on and on. I think that there's an inverse correlation between the amount of money an entrepreneur requires and the potential chaotic success of a startup.[6]

Similarly, well-known lecturer Guy Kawasaki suggests, "If you get the money, I wouldn't spend it [because] it warps you."[7] Too much money warps entrepreneurs because it gives them the leeway to persist in what may be wrong rather than listening to customers to discover what is actually right. At the core, too much money at the wrong time encourages entrepreneurs to develop an internal focus on the product and fall back into the traditional product-based model when they really need to develop an external focus on customers and employ the new customer-based model.

The second danger of money is that it is easy to spend, and spending it increases the distractions and reduces flexibility at a critical time in the company's life. Quickly, the shabby green chairs in the office need to be replaced with Aero chairs, the five-year-old desktops are replaced with supercharged laptops, and subsistence salaries are replaced with the type of "market" salaries paid by large firms. Unfortunately, spending all this money doesn't increase your chances of success; it actually lowers them. The reason is that the entire goal of the startup is to discover something that customers want and how to deliver that to them, as quickly and inexpensively as possible. As entrepreneurs try to discover what customers want, they will inevitably discover insights they couldn't have seen in advance and will need to adjust. To do this, the startup needs to be nimble and flexible. But when money comes in the door, the extra expenses, the higher burn rate, the extra employees decrease the flexibility to make these changes. Worse yet, as the extra salaries and expenses draw down the entrepreneur's bank account, the runway to make changes gets shorter and shorter, and there simply isn't time to try again when the entrepreneur discovers that he or she needed to make a change. We've heard many entrepreneurs lament that their burn rate got so high that although they discovered a way to be successful, it was too late to make the change because of all the baggage the company is carrying around. For example, this was the case for a close friend who was the CEO of a high-profile Silicon Valley failure. Behind closed doors he lamented that they actually had the team and capabilities to capture a promising new market, but by the time they discovered it, they had wasted tens of millions trying to capture the market described in the business plan but which never materialized.

Last, having too much money early on leads to the temptation of *prematurely scaling* which is the number-one cause of startup death. Often when entrepreneurs get more money, they expand the team, hiring more engineers, VPs of sales, and other team members. The big team not only increases the burn rate but it also creates other problems for an early-stage company, such as increased communication friction and politics. The more money we invest in a company early on, the more people are hired, and the longer the company takes to get its product and go-to-market strategy right. Indeed, there seems to be an inverse relationship between a large investment up front and success, because as a company scales, employees begin to specialize and focus on their own job rather than worrying about the success of the entire startup. If the company has not nailed the core value exchange with its core customer, this specialization or compartmentalization process is counterproductive. In the early days, when the startup needs to focus on finding out what customers want and adjusting to provide a solution to their needs, such internal communication and political obstacles can be a major problem. For example, the sales team may bring a message from the field to the product manager, who might pass it along to the CTO. But the marketing team has a different message, which might or might not get passed to the product manager; and if it does, the CTO may just ignore it anyway. As the communication and politics get more complicated, the crucial facts about the customer get lost in the machine, and the startup misses the market it's trying to capture.

The dangers of money led one entrepreneur to state that "raising money for your startup is the root of all evil!" The entrepreneur, Jeremy Hanks, realized this only after spending months raising and then spending capital that nursed a business that ultimately couldn't succeed. Fortunately, at the moment he stood on the brink of mortgaging his family farm to keep the business alive, he realized that the fundamental business hypothesis was broken and he was blindly throwing away his inheritance to chase it down. Many entrepreneurs have not been so lucky as to have the same realization and have thrown away savings, careers, and even marriages by chasing a failure down the drain. Instead, Jeremy cut the apron strings, let the business die, and has since gone on to build a very successful business by avoiding all the mistakes that come from having too much money.

The truth is having less money can help you focus on the external market—on your customers—and increase your ability to develop creative solutions for those customers. Relying on customers to pay the bills creates a natural, intense focus on their needs. But it can also increase your creativity. One of the insights emerging from recent research is that constraints can actually increase your creativity. For example, Marissa Mayer, vice president at Google over search and user experience, highlights how constraining projects has produced better, more creative results.[8] Similarly, Tina Seelig, Executive Director of the Stanford Technology Ventures Program, illustrates this in her teaching. When teaching a class about creativity, Seelig decided to illustrate the power of constraint by giving students five dollars and a few hours to make as much money as possible. Initially, students found some creative ways to make a little money, often more than $100. However, when Tina made the problem more challenging by giving students a handful of paperclips, many students' perspectives shifted, and they realized that the real constraint was not the money, but their time. These students creatively found ways to turn a handful of paperclips into close to $1000 in a just few hours' time.[9] In like manner, when entrepreneurs face constraints, they often stay more focused on their customers and discover better, more useful solutions than those that can be purchased with an excess of investment capital.

DISTILLING ENTREPRENEURIAL SUCCESS

The three myths of entrepreneurship lay the foundation for the entrepreneur's paradox: if you have the right personality, follow the pattern we all know, or raise money too early, you are actually increasing the chance that you will fail. The entrepreneur's paradox may be one reason why the secret to entrepreneurial success seems somewhat mysterious, even to entrepreneurs themselves. Bob Metcalfe, inventor of the Ethernet, stated that "most successful entrepreneurs I've met have no idea about the reasons for their success. My [success] was a mystery to me then, and only a little less so now."[10]

But entrepreneurship should not be a mystery or a paradox. After studying hundreds of successful and unsuccessful companies, we discovered that successful entrepreneurs followed a pattern that was very different from conventional wisdom. To validate the process, we tested it in multiple startups—some from the very beginning and in others as a rescue effort midstream in the life of the company. The resulting methodology is not rocket science in and of itself—many talented entrepreneurs have described aspects of the process. But by pulling it together into a single model that describes the entire process from beginning to end, we offer something that is clearly a radical departure from the established pattern of entrepreneurship. This process can help you turn your passion into facts, your determination into wisdom, and your idea into a successful business. It can provide a shortcut to success before you have spent years or thousands of dollars finding out that you were wrong. Most important, this method can be used for all types and stages of a business that are dealing with entrepreneurial problems, whether a brand-new idea, a local startup, a university technology, or a struggling company facing a downward spiral. We have used it to turn around existing businesses as well as provide a head start to new businesses. We have used it in established organizations that look to launch new products and for startups going down the tubes. Depending on the circumstances, the process may need slight modification (see the chapter "Context Matters!"), but in each case, the process can help an entrepreneur or a business change direction and be successful.

THE NAIL IT THEN SCALE IT METHODOLOGY

In the following chapters we begin by describing some foundational principles that apply to the Nail It then Scale It process. Specifically we redefine innovation and then ask you to begin thinking like a scientist in a laboratory: seeing your entrepreneurial venture through an objective lens while looking for the facts. But your laboratory won't be inside a building, it will be in the real world in front of customers. In fact, you must get up from your desk and get out into the field with customers if you are going to succeed. You must learn to either change or fail fast. Indeed, failure will be perfectly acceptable—that is, if you fail fast in the process of testing your ideas, iterating, and moving on to something that will succeed. Be ready to make changes. Successful startups make changes, and so will you.[11] Also, we will discuss the importance of intellectually honest learning; the use of simple, inexpensive prototypes to rapidly experiment; and a small, focused team to work your way through the Nail It then Scale It Process.

The Nail It then Scale It Process

Once we have laid the groundwork, we then describe the phases of the Nail It then Scale It process itself. On the surface, these phases may appear simple, but entrepreneurs forget, skip, or bungle them. Really engaging these five steps, rather than assuming you have already completed them, will literally save you years and millions of dollars.

Figure 5: The Five Phases of the Nail It then Scale It Process

After completing these steps, described in more detail later, you will have a product or service that will be the foundation for a robust business. As you continue to validate your product, you may have to cycle back through some of the steps. Although we describe the Nail It then Scale It process in phases in order to make it simpler to understand, you will often need to go back to a previous phase to something you may have missed. By the end of the process you will have validated your market, developed a product customers desperately desire, and be ready to scale a successful business!

LIONS, TIGERS AND BEARS: CHALLENGES ALONG THE ROAD

Although we have proven that the Nail It then Scale It process works in many companies, that does not mean that you can apply the process without facing challenges. While the process itself is simple, it can be very hard for companies or entrepreneurs to have the discipline to go through the entire process. We all face numerous demands, pressures, and incentives that can distract us. Entrepreneurs have an extra dose of urgency. The old joke about entrepreneurs is that they "ready, fire, aim." Although a dose of urgency is critical, taking the time to run the Nail It then Scale It process can actually save you much more time than you invest, even years. But to do that, it will take buy-in from the leaders of the company, including the founders, the team, and investors. The process takes time, it takes commitment, and it may require seeing the world in a new way. It also requires going through the process without sabotaging it by shortchanging the process. We discuss how to create the commitment to run the Nail It then Scale It process, even when it comes from a company crisis. You may also have to adapt your approach, depending on the context in which you operate, which we describe at the end of the book. But despite the challenges, if you have patience and adhere to the steps in the process, you will succeed. Many of the most successful startups in the world have used these principles to nail their markets or to turn around struggling enterprises. If your team applies these principles, tools and processes, it can do the same for your business.

WHERE TO GO NEXT

At this point you may find yourself antsy, saying, "Let's get to it." Before you jump too far ahead in the book, understanding the principles in the next chapter will help you establish a more solid foundation upon which to build. These principles may also be helpful in establishing a common vocabulary with your team and help you as an entrepreneur reset your thinking about what it means to be an entrepreneur as you identify and overcome the three myths of entrepreneurship. First, we are going to help you establish a common understanding to think about what innovation means. Second, we need to break down some common barriers and introduce you to the fundamentals that will guide you through the NISI process. Then we will walk you through each of the phases of the NISI process. Finally, we will describe how the process differs depending on the type of market you are in, as well as highlight how to create the commitment in your team to successfully finish the process. By the end, you will have a better understanding of the principles and process that can dramatically change your business.

Chapter 2: The Mystery of Market Winning Innovation

If he hadn't failed, Thomas Edison might not have become America's most well-known and prolific innovator. Like most entrepreneurs, when Edison first started his career, he was certain he had observed a fundamental problem he could solve. Specifically, Edison noticed that whenever Congress voted on an issue, each senator would stand one by one and call out his vote. To Edison, the inefficiency of such a system was absolutely stunning, and he realized that he could invent a system to quickly tally all the votes and skip the unnecessary and wasteful step of calling out votes. Like any good entrepreneur following the traditional product-based model, Edison jumped right in, built the system, and then brought his automatic vote-tally system to Congress. Imagine Edison bounding up the steps to the congressional offices eager to demonstrate how he had solved such a significant problem and excited for the payoff at the end of his hard work. Now picture his outright surprise when the Senators listened and then bluntly rejected his invention—they didn't want it. Like most entrepreneurs, Edison was sure he had observed a real market need, and he must have been incensed at the inability of his "customers" to understand how he had saved them hours and hours by changing an inefficient and silly voting process. But the truth was that Edison hadn't validated his assumption that the Senators actually wanted an automatic voting system. In fact, as it turned out, there was a great deal of politics and posturing in the calling of votes, and the Senators weren't about to give up that system.

Fortunately, rather than letting the failure destroy him, Edison recovered and in the process discovered two very important principles that allowed him to become one of the most famous serial innovators of all time. First, he learned the crucial need to understand your customers—specifically the job they are trying to get done and why. After that experience, Edison reframed all his future efforts with one simple phrase, "I never want to build something that nobody wants to buy." Second, Edison learned the value of rapidly iterating to get to the solution customers needed. For example, in developing a commercially viable light bulb, Edison actually went through over ten thousand prototypes before getting it right. Had Edison followed the traditional model of product-development model of writing a product specification, building a product, then trying to sell it, his competitors would have beat him by decades. Edison's approach in understanding customer needs and rapidly iterating are at the core of the Nail It then Scale It (NISI) process and give us clues to a challenging mystery for most individuals and corporations: How can I repeatedly innovate?

Most people would agree that innovation is important and that understanding how to repeatedly innovate is crucial for global, regional, and individual prosperity. In a breakfast meeting with David McCullough, the Pulitzer Prize winning historian, I asked him what defines America's sustainable competitive advantage. David McCullough responded that America is the land of "opportunity and innovation."[12] Alan Greenspan, former Federal Reserve chairman, argued that technological innovations have contributed more than any other single factor to growth in America's economic history, and that further growth depends on innovation.[13] And Steve Jobs is famous for his saying that "innovation distinguishes between a leader and a follower." Throughout the world, governments, businesses, and individuals have come to recognize the power of innovation to solve intractable problems, provide jobs, and create wealth. Not only is innovation the fundamental driver of how new value is created, but understanding and empowering the innovation process is key to a sustainable advantage for any business or economy.

> *"Innovation distinguishes between a leader and a follower."*
> *—Steve Jobs*

Despite the importance of innovation, how to repeatedly innovate remains somewhat a mystery. Even though Edison had both failures and successes, he is famous because he was one of the few individuals who succeeded in repeatedly innovating. Although we clearly believe that it is possible to repeatedly innovate, most people truly struggle to innovate once, let alone several times. One of the purposes of this book is to demystify innovation and show readers how to repeatedly innovate. To do this, we first define innovation, and then map the process by which customers adopt new innovations. With this information as background you will have a stronger sense of how to approach the NISI process. However, if you are burning to get to the process, skip ahead and come back to this chapter later.

DEFINING INNOVATION THAT WINS

What is innovation? It seems like a basic question, but it has a surprising number of answers. For example, innovation has been defined based on the *scale* of change: radical, disruptive, or "brave-new-world" innovations that represent a significant improvement or change over existing products, whereas incremental, sustaining, or "better, faster, cheaper" represent a smaller scale of change. Alternatively, innovation can be defined based on the *target* it affects: innovations can be defined as innovations in revenue model, technology, service, process, product, or supply-chain innovation.[14] Similarly, innovations have also been defined based on the *process* by which the innovation occurs, such as redefining the market, compressing the supply chain, mass customization, product bundling, consolidating markets, and so forth.[15] While all these definitions are useful to categorize innovation, they do not actually describe what separates successful from unsuccessful innovation.

The first step to defining successful innovation is to separate out the ideas of "new" and "invention" from the idea of innovation. Typically when people think of innovation, they think of the creation of *new* things, whether ideas, technologies, products or services. Universities push faculty members to innovate by developing new ideas and inventions. Entrepreneurs and students rack their brains trying come up with a new idea or product. But the truth is that inventing something new may be the least important part of innovation. In fact, many great innovations are not new inventions at all but instead are simply borrowed or repackaged ideas from other areas. For example, although he became famous as the father of mass production, Henry Ford's success as a manufacturer was based on three principles already being used in other industries: 1) interchangeable parts used by the sewing machine, arms, and watch industries; 2) continuous-flow manufacturing used in the flour, canning, and cigarette industries; and 3) assembly-line techniques from meat-packing plants and breweries.[16] It wasn't that Henry Ford came up with something new—an invention—it was that he applied the existing inventions to solve a market problem, which made his approach to manufacturing cars an innovation. Professor Gary Rhoads and his coauthors, in their book *BoomStart*, argued that entrepreneurial R&D should be "Rip Off and Design," to emphasize that entrepreneurs too often focus on dreaming up something new to the world when instead they may be more successful by finding a way to apply something old in a different way.

To properly define innovation, the first critical distinction to make is the difference between invention and innovation. To illustrate this point, take a quick glance at the following products and ask yourself, are these innovations (Figure 6 below)?

Figure 6: Innovations?

All the items pictured (a solar car, the Apple Newton, and the Segway) represent an invention of something new but are not necessarily innovations because the inventions were not combined with a validated customer need. Invention is the discovery of a new technology, product, or service. Innovation is the combination of an invention (whether new or old) with insight about a market need. In other words, innovation lies at the intersection of invention and market insight (Figure 7).

Figure 7: Definition of Innovation

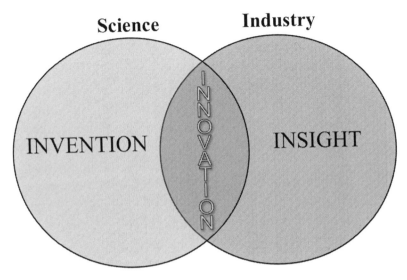

Without market insight, invention is just a novel technology, product, or service. A new discovery that sits on the shelf may be an interesting invention, but it is not yet an innovation. In contrast, market insight without invention is just imitation, a "me-too" business.

Take a second look at the "inventions" pictured above, and you will see how these inventions, when combined with market insight, led to actual innovations. That is, when targeted and packaged for the right market need, these inventions became innovations (Figure 8).

Figure 8: Inventions Turned Into Innovations

In contrast to the earlier examples of invention, solar panels applied to newly constructed houses, a convergent device combining a

PDA and phone, and Segways for police navigating crowded spaces are all innovations because they combine an invention with a market need. Similarly, Flash memory was an invention that had merits, but it also solved the need for much more rapid, reliable computer storage. As a result, it was quickly adopted and has become a multibillion-dollar industry. Alternatively, Howard Schulz took the high-end coffee products emerging from Peet's Coffee and the original Starbucks (which only sold coffee beans) and combined it with the market insight that people craved: a café setting where they could relax or work. The result was a customer-experience innovation—the combination of a product and insight that created a "coffee company" with a market valuation of $25 billion at the end of 2010. In summary, a simple definition of innovation, a first step toward understanding how innovations succeed, is the intersection of 1) an invention with 2) a market insight.

RECOGNIZING THE TWO TYPES OF RISK IN INNOVATION

As you think about the two components of innovation (innovation and market insight), recognize you have also uncovered the two fundamental risks you face when innovating: technology risk (can we make it) and market risk (will customers buy it). For example, making a drug that cures heart disease has limited market risk and plenty of technology risk. In contrast, the next big website probably has no technology risk and plenty of market risk. Reducing and overcoming these two types of risk is critical to successfully innovating. However, most entrepreneurs act as if they face technology risk and so start building their product. But the truth is that over 90% of businesses fail because they couldn't get anyone to buy it, not because they couldn't build it. As a result, in the NISI process we focus primarily on market risk and teach you the principles to overcome these risks. But if you face technology risk as well, be certain that you pay attention to this risk and use the right tactics to manage the risk. These tactics are the subject of a separate book but include things such as parallel development, assumption identification, simulation,

The two fundamental risks you face when innovating: technology risk (can we make it) and market risk (will customers buy it).

26

rapid prototypes, borrowing solutions in adjacent industries, prioritizing risks, managing the timeline, and taking an ecosystem level view of innovation. You will notice that many of these principles overlap with the NISI process and there is a good reason why. When you face the unknown in one area of risk, the tactics to conquer the unknown in another area of risk are similar. In fact, sometimes people criticize the NISI process by asking "does it only apply to software or Web 2.0?" The answer is, of course not, it applies to any problem with market risk but don't confuse market risk with technology risk or vice versa as you try to tackle your business.

WHERE DO WINNING INNOVATIONS COME FROM?

If innovation is the combination of invention and market insight, where do invention and market insight come from? Invention may come when you get deeply involved with an industry. For example, Sam Walton spent well over a decade experimenting with thrift stores, such as Franklin Five and Dime, before coming up with Wal-Mart.[17] Similarly, Ingvar Kamprad, who founded IKEA, spent years selling furniture before the day when, during a photo shoot, he and his partners asked themselves why they shipped tables with the legs on: voilà, the birth of the flat-pack furniture concept, which revolutionized furniture delivery.[18] At the same time, invention can come because you are an outsider and bring a fresh perspective. This was the case with Charles Schwab, who applied a supermarket analogy to the mutual fund industry to create a supermarket for mutual funds—an innovation that changed the industry and earned Schwab billions. Similarly, the founders of Google were working on a library text-search tool when they realized it could also be applied to Internet search.

Finally, inventions may also come from purposefully throwing together different ideas and knowledge. For example, the design firm IDEO uses physical artifacts to recombine old ideas to create new ones. Team members might use props, like bicycle parts or Japanese toys, and try to apply these ideas to products such as skin staplers and computer monitors.[19] At the same time, entrepreneurs don't necessarily have to invent their own solutions—in fact, inventing has its dangers. Although many entrepreneurs spend a great deal of time trying to come up with a new idea, in the course of inventing they fall in love with their idea. There are many, many inventions lying around that can be picked up and applied to a market problem. These include inventions that can be licensed from companies or universities, inventions from other industries or geographies that can be applied in a new market, old ideas that can be applied in new ways, and many other sources. As an example of how much invention is available, university patents have increased by 1600% in the last thirty years, but less than 30% of these patents have been licensed or commercialized.[20] And inventions need not come from patents alone—entrepreneurs can draw on many sources of inventions, most of which come from nearby or adjacent industries. For that reason, the greatest mystery to entrepreneurs is not the invention—it is the market insight that leads to innovation and market adoption.

If market insight is the most challenging part of innovation, where does market insight come from? It comes from customers, but not from asking them directly. Somewhat counter-intuitively, if you simply ask customers what they would like, they tend to describe what they already know or incremental improvements on the status quo. Henry Ford stated "If I had asked customers what they wanted, they would have said faster horses." The reason is that human beings have a hard time seeing past the status quo. In one study, researchers gave subjects a problem that required a wire to solve. When subjects were given a paperclip, often they could solve the problem; but if they were given a stack of papers, held by a paper clip, far fewer subjects could solve the problem.[21] Furthermore, customers often ask for contradictory things. For example, when Huggies customers told researchers they didn't want their toddlers to wear diapers but also didn't want them to wet the bed, the solution may have seemed intractable. But Huggies came up with Pull-ups, which solved both these problems at the same time.[21]

The key difference in this early stage of innovation is not to just ask customers what they want but to deeply understand the customers—their motivations, their needs, and most important, the job they are trying to get done. The job customers are trying to do may not fit neatly into existing product categories. As an example, Clayton Christensen highlights how customers have used baking soda for deodorant, toothpaste, and cleaning—uses that Arm & Hammer originally overlooked but which eventually became the basis for new products. Looking deeply at what your customer is trying to accomplish—or the purpose for which they purchase a product—can yield surprising results. For example, Christensen describes how his team of consultants re-examined why customers purchased milkshakes and discovered an entirely unknown job—food/entertainment for morning commutes which led them to offer a narrower straw (to lengthen the experience), as well as fruit to go along with the shake.[22] Market insights come from actually interacting with customers and deeply understanding the problems they are trying to solve. However, it is usually not something that customers will just up and tell you; it comes from deep observation of customer pain and the outcomes customers are trying to achieve. Although this sounds simple enough, it can be difficult for entrepreneurs because usually entrepreneurs already have a belief about what the market needs. The challenge for entrepreneurs then becomes how to find their customers, how to really listen, how to discover their needs, and then how to re-see their own approach honestly in the light of those needs. In contrast, many entrepreneurs fail because they observe a general need and then convince themselves that somehow their product solves that need.

ENTREPRENEURS INNOVATE, CUSTOMERS VALIDATE

The key then is to remember that customers don't innovate. Entrepreneurs innovate and customers validate. Although we argued earlier that market insights come from understanding customer needs—and we will repeatedly emphasize the importance of interacting with customers—we also argued that customers can't innovate for you. Ultimately it is the job of the entrepreneur to do the hard work of innovation. Thomas Edison stated that "I find out what the world needs. Then I go ahead and try to invent it." If you rely on your customers to innovate, they will most likely suggest solutions that are only incrementally better than what is already in the market or that are simply an amalgamation of features that competitors already have. In either case, the resulting solution most likely won't be compelling enough for customers to overcome the switching costs involved in adopting your product. Therefore it is the entrepreneur's job to observe a customer pain and then connect that with an invention to solve a market problem. Often the invention that solves a customer pain can be simple, for example, when the inventors of the Spin Pop® (a lollipop that has a battery-operated spin mechanism) applied the same spin device to create electric toothbrushes that appealed to children.[23]

It is the entrepreneur's job to think in new ways to solve a customer pain. But don't be discouraged if you feel like you aren't the best at thinking big or dreaming up solutions. The good news is twofold. First, just the very act of going through the Nail It then Scale It process will lead you to sudden insights that you couldn't have foreseen in advance. Most entrepreneurs don't dream up solutions in the abstract—they do it when they are working in an industry, talking to customers, and experiencing problems firsthand. In fact, an entire group of economists, known as the Austrian School of Economics, believed you actually couldn't have insight into what a market needed until you jumped in and started participating in that market.[24, 25] In other words, you will be much more likely to innovate if you immerse yourself in a market—read about it, work in it, talk to customers, talk to suppliers, and get your hands dirty.

> *It's an entrepreneur's job too think in new ways to solve a customer pain. Entrepreneurs innovate, customers validate.*

The second piece of good news is that you can actually increase your ability to innovate through your actions. While some people believe that innovative capacity is simply genetic, research does not support this belief. In fact, even something as fundamental as intelligence, which many people believe is predetermined at birth, can actually be changed dramatically based on one's actions. Carol Dweck, at Stanford University, was one of the first to demonstrate that "intelligence" can be increased or decreased based on a person's work and attitude.[26] The same is true for innovation and creativity. For example, Jeff Dyer, Hal Gregersen, and Clayton Christensen researched innovators and found that innovation capacity is determined primarily by the choices we make, not by our birth. These researchers identified five activities that individuals employed to be more innovative: questioning, observing, experimenting, networking, and associating ideas.[27] In summary, if you don't feel innovative now, you can be. Get involved in the market and adopt the habits that can make you more innovative.

Although it is the job of entrepreneurs to innovate, never forget the importance of having customers validate that innovation. If you come up with an innovation that solves a customer pain, customers will then fill the vital role of being able to tell you very concretely whether that solution actually does the job. The mistake most entrepreneurs make is that once they do discover an invention, they either fall in love with their invention or they follow the traditional product-focused model to build it and then sell it. In either case, the unvalidated invention is most likely not quite right and thus ultimately fails in the market. You can avoid this by testing the invention with customers. If entrepreneurs go out and show their invention to customers, customers will validate whether the entrepreneur is right or wrong. One of central tenants of Nail It then Scale It is the process of validating the invention with customers.

HOW ARE WINNING INNOVATIONS ADOPTED?

In the spirit of our brief discussion of innovation, it is essential to understand, from an industry-level perspective, how innovations are adopted. From a 30,000-foot view, the most well-known explanation comes from the early work of Everett Rogers and his study of Iowa corn farmers. Rogers, studying the spread of a new invention—hybrid corn seeds—among farmers, found that the spread of that innovation followed a pattern which he described using a bell curve, segmented into different groups who shared similar characteristics in the technology-adoption process.

Figure 9: The Diffusion of Innovation

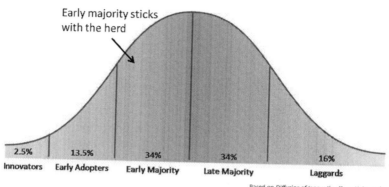

Based on *Diffusion of Innovation* (Everett Rogers)

Rogers found that innovators and early adopters implemented the new seed technology very early and with fairly little evidence of its value, whereas other groups, such as the early and late majorities, waited until the seeds were proven and they felt comfortable that they were safe in adopting the new seeds. These later groups waited because they had a very different set of requirements to adopt a new technology than did the early adopters—the vast majority of users wanted to feel safe that adopting the new innovation would be beneficial and that the source of the innovation was legitimate.[28]

Geoffrey Moore, drawing on Rogers' research, applied the pattern to technology startups in his books *Crossing the Chasm* and *Inside the Tornado*. Moore argued that although technology adoption followed the pattern described by Rogers, there was a gap between the needs of each group. More important, the gap between early adopters and the early majority was actually a chasm.

32

Figure 10: Moore's Adaptation of Innovation Diffusion

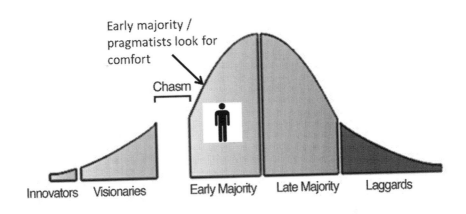

Moore highlighted that although many technology companies get early traction with the early adopters and innovators, they then struggle to move to the next segment of customers: the early majority. The reason is that early-majority customers have very different needs and purchasing requirements than the early adopters, who were willing to take an early risk for increased benefit. Instead, the early majority, who are defined as pragmatists, want to make a safe purchase decision and tend to follow the herd. The early majority look left and right for their opinion and gain comfort in what they see others doing. The inability to establish market credibility creates a chasm between a startup and the mass-market adoption of its products. To cross the chasm, Moore suggests focusing on a single industry vertical, leveraging all your resources to win early-majority reference customers in that segment (by convincing them you are a safe, legitimate choice), and then dominating that segment before moving on to the next industry vertical.

THE GREAT BLACK HOLE OF INNOVATION

Although we have provided an overview of innovation and the pattern by which innovations are adopted, don't overlook the very motivation for this book: the great black hole of innovation. The truth is that most new ventures die before they ever reach the chasm, and little has been written on this stage between idea and the chasm. Business schools tend to focus either on writing business plans or high-level strategy issues. Business books tend to focus on low-level tactics, such as getting a business license, or just a slice of the process, such as gathering customer input. Little material covers the process from the beginning to the end, from developing an innovation and then taking it to market. When I sat down with Geoffrey Moore and asked how to get a new business to the chasm, Moore's frank answer was, "I don't know." His honesty was a catalyst to study how entrepreneurs successfully cross get past the black hole, where most businesses go in and never come out, as well as how to cross the chasm. The ideas in this book will help you move from idea to the chasm and then over the chasm so that you too can build a successful business.

Chapter 3: Nail It then Scale It— Fundamentals

Nail It then Scale It: An Evidence-Based Approach to Entrepreneurship

Although virtual worlds such as Second Life, Sims Online, and World of Warcraft are a multi-billion dollar business today, few people have heard of the first virtual world, There.com. Early in its history, There.com seemed to be doing everything right according to conventional wisdom in Silicon Valley. The company had a gifted team of entrepreneurial founders who handed over the leadership reins to an experienced CEO. The CEO crafted a strategy, with the blessing of the board, to raise venture funding and "go big." To that end, There.com executives raised over $40 million from venture capitalists to develop the product and then launch a massive blitzkrieg of PR and advertising that would drive users to join in droves.

With the money in hand, the team turned to perfecting the product, carefully developing a list of "required" features based on what the team believed was an intimate intuition about customer desires. In the end, developing the first virtual world proved more challenging than expected, and leadership felt that releasing a faulty online world with bugs and glitches would turn away important early customers. The management team did what seemed reasonable—they delayed launch until the product was perfect. Finally, after several years in development, There.com launched with a flashy PR campaign and features in *The Wall Street Journal* and *The New York Times*. What was the result of their flawless execution? In the first month a few thousand users signed up for the service, but the resulting revenues of $20,000 were far below expectations. The following months showed little growth, and over the rest of the year the plateau continued. In the end, There.com's launch was a massive disappointment. They had spent millions building a product customers just didn't want. By the time they discovered this fact, it was too hard to change. At the time, Eric Ries, one of the lead developers, wondered why

35

they failed when they had done everything right according to conventional wisdom.[29]

Frustrated with his experience, Eric Ries moved on and founded IMVU with Will Harvey, There.com's original founder. The founders determined that if they did everything right the last time and failed, they needed to try a new approach. Ries and Harvey decided that they would try a dramatically different approach to development. Rather than follow the traditional product-development model, they would instead try to test their assumptions about what customers wanted by quickly releasing the bare bones of the product (what Ries later called a *minimum viable product*, a term first coined by Frank Robinson and popularized by Ries). In a few months, Ries and Harvey released IMVU (IMVU hosts virtual interactions between people by combining instant messaging with avatars), but it was so bad it frequently crashed users' computers. Many of the board members were skeptical and even warned against the approach—developers wouldn't be able to attract users with such a terrible product or might even offend them. In some ways they were right: almost no one paid attention, with the exception of a handful of early adopters who picked up the product and began providing feedback. This information in hand, the team rapidly cycled through countless rapid iterations of the product. In a fraction of the time it took There.com to launch and fail, IMVU was generating revenues in excess of $40 million.

After the experience, Ries asked himself why There.com failed when they did everything right, whereas IMVU succeeded when they did everything wrong. The answer lay not in the quality of the original idea but in the startup process itself. The Nail It then Scale It (NISI) methodology relies on transforming the guessing and planning in the traditional product-based process into an evidence-based approach where you rapidly test your assumptions in the market so that you understand exactly what you need to build and how exactly to communicate with customers so that they will buy your product. In this chapter, we discuss fundamental principles that apply throughout the process. The following chapters will focus on each stage of the process.

NISI FUNDAMENTAL: GET INTO THE FIELD

To set the stage for running the Nail It then Scale It (NISI) process, it is useful to think about your venture as an experiment and think about your efforts in the light of a creative but unemotional scientist trying to test whether your assumptions are right or wrong. When we think of a laboratory, what usually comes to mind is an orderly, sterilized place where expert scientists conduct experiments. A quick tour of many corporate headquarters turns up many similarities—most office buildings are clean, air-conditioned, and optimized for work. And not surprisingly, most work is performed inside the building—in offices and cubicles, or on factory floors. As a result, when most entrepreneurs want to start a business, they find an office, even if it is in their basement, and start plugging away.

But the NISI laboratory is not a quiet, private office where the entrepreneur can work uninterrupted. It is the complete opposite. Instead you need to get out among your customers—you need to get into the field. Think of yourself as a farmer—you can't harvest anything till you've spent time in the field. Indeed, when it comes to entrepreneurship, as Steve Blank, serial entrepreneur and author, argues, "The first thing you should do is get the hell out of the building."[30] Getting outside the building, outside the company, even outside the circle of friends, is crucial because by fact of our human nature

> *"The first thing you should do is get the hell out of the building."*
> *–Steve Blank*

we gradually become absolutely convinced we understand the outside world when in fact we do not. This is because our cognitive processes are structured to reassure us that we understand reality, but the truth is we almost never really do. Our understanding of the world is at best a representation, simplified so that we can process it, and most often inaccurate in some ways which don't matter much for everyday life but which are critical for entrepreneurship.[31] It is only when we stop, get out of our comfort zone, get outside, and start talking to customers, suppliers and competitors that we begin to understand what the world is really like. For every entrepreneur we have ever worked with, the results of getting into the field are always surprising.

You can't really test your assumptions or know what the truth is until you get into the field and sending the junior hire in marketing or the intern outside isn't going to cut it. The founders themselves need to leave the building and talk to customers, because it turns out that the people who have the deepest investment in the business—those who feel they understand the product and the customer the most, the ones who have drunk the proverbial Kool-Aid—they are the very ones who most need to leave the building but are the least likely to do so. We call this phenomenon the *inverse Kool-Aid law*: the team members who most need to get outside and be shocked by reality are the ones who usually believe they actually understand reality. They are also often the founders and the CEO. Everyone, most especially the founders and CEO, need to test their hypotheses in the real world, and by so doing have their perspective shifted or even shattered. It seems disarmingly simple, but by taking a "road trip" and talking to real customers, you will find that the truth can be surprisingly different than you imagined it from within the four walls of your office.

This was precisely the case at There.com. The company believed that virtual worlds would revolutionize online interaction. Because many of the engineers at There.com were also future users, many of the initial insights regarding what customers desired came from the founders and early engineers. As engineers and product managers began to develop the product, they became more confident about the value of what they were building. As the There.com management segmented the potential market based on demographics and Internet-use habits, the team became even more convinced that they "understood" how their customers acted and what they desired. Layered on top of this, There.com was operating in stealth mode, purposely trying not to give away information about their plans. The result was a comfortable but insular development culture in which the company developed a product for a customer they felt certain they understood. The reality was that despite their best intentions and their collective intelligence, the founders and engineers didn't understand the customer very clearly. The result was a product that fizzled rather than launched into orbit.

Contrast this with IMVU: the founders purposely spent as much time as possible in the field, talking to customers early and often, as well as throughout development. Getting into the field revealed many important facts to the IMVU team. For example, although the team thought they understood their target customers, they found that in fact two different customer segments emerged: an older group of online professionals and a younger group of teenage instant-message users. A typical startup might never recognize this or try to serve both segments. Alternatively, most entrepreneurs without deep information would focus on the customers who could pay: the older professionals. In fact, even IMVU was tempted to go this direction, but because the IMVU team was focused on interacting with customers and observing their behavior, they realized that teenage users had an unusual passion for the product. In fact, the teenage users were so enamored with IMVU that although they couldn't make credit card payments to buy virtual goods for their avatars, they regularly sent hand-written notes with checks or cash attached. This kind of intense customer devotion signaled to IMVU where the real growth opportunity lay.

The fundamental practice of getting into the field and talking to customers is not new. In fact, this practice is at the heart of many innovative and successful businesses. Take Sam Walton of Wal-Mart as an example. Walton was famous for getting into the field to observe both customers and competitors. Part of the inspiration for Wal-Mart came from getting out in the field and noticing a local business breaking with the traditional variety store approach and instead adopting a "stack it high, sell it cheap" mantra—an idea that became the core of the Wal-Mart high-volume, low-cost model. As another example, when Walton began developing the Wal-Mart concept, most stores were full-service, meaning that a salesperson on the floor helped customers. Walton heard about a "self-service" store in a nearby state, so he got on a bus, rode to the neighboring state, and with his famous notepad in hand jotted down every single detail of the new store. He observed how customers reacted to coming in the door, and how check-out clerks were positioned near the exits; he even interviewed customers after they came out the door. This experience led Walton to develop self-service for Wal-Mart stores, which turned out to be a critical component of their low-cost strategy. In all of his interactions, Sam Walton embodied the idea of "getting into the field," and it transformed his business as a result.[17] Ultimately, his open-laboratory approach was wildly successful, and Wal-Mart is one of the world's largest corporations today.

What Walton's example and that of other successful entrepreneurs demonstrate is that although it is often unimaginable that our understanding of customers and the world is imperfect, it always is! The only solution is to get into the field, in front of customers, competitors, and partners, getting laughed at, ignored by, or lectured to but always listening.[32] Indeed, the only way to run the NISI process is to get into the field and have your worldview shaken. Start in the field and stay there.

The Guardrail to Guardrail Trap of Customer Interaction

Earlier we emphasized that entrepreneurs innovate and customers validate. Getting into the field is the key to doing this but entrepreneurs need to be careful to avoid the "Guardrail to Guardrail Trap." If you think of a meeting with customers, at one extreme—or guardrail at the edge of the path you are trying to follow—is walking into the meeting and hard-selling the customer. If you walk in and try to sell the customer you won't be able to really hear what customers need—you will spend your entire time selling your vision and you will fail. But the other extreme—or guardrail—is to go into a customer meeting completely unstructured so that in asking the customers for feedback you are asking customers to innovate for you. As we discussed in the chapter on innovation, if you ask your customers to innovate for you, you will also fail. So the key is to avoid either extreme and instead when you go into a customer meeting focus on validating your assumptions and innovations while avoiding selling. We will offer more specific tactics on how to do this later.

NISI FUNDAMENTAL: FAIL FAST AND LEARN TO CHANGE

The second fundamental of the NISI method is equally hard for many entrepreneurs: change or fail fast. At heart, we like to see ourselves as optimists. That's why we suggest that entrepreneurs fail fast and learn to change. Ideas are a dime a dozen. There are literally billions of ideas out there. The real question is not whether you have an idea but whether that idea is an opportunity. Is it worth your time, effort and money to pursue? Is there a real market opportunity worth the sacrifice that entrepreneurship requires? Why waste $5M and five years or even $10K and one year on an idea that is going to fail anyway? Instead, fail in five months with $5K or in one month for $100. Then take what you have learned and change direction or move on to the next idea until you find the opportunity that has real merit—the idea that is worth your time and energy.

Of course entrepreneurship takes passion and perseverance, but often passion and perseverance lead entrepreneurs to spend years and millions of dollars on a failing idea. By remembering to fail fast, you focus on rapidly testing your assumptions, iterating swiftly, and then, because you have less attachment, you can see when you need to abandon one approach in favor of a better approach. After you've "failed," try a new angle, change direction, or pursue a new idea.

When asked what separates successful from unsuccessful new ventures, Harvard Business School professor Clayton Christensen argues simply that "successful startups are the ones who have enough money left over to try their second idea."[33] In contrast, the vast majority of startups run out of money or find it too hard to change precisely because they built their product first and then found they couldn't change in time to survive. Almost every startup we know has to change direction, or even change completely, multiple times. Even startups pursuing highly complex technology like solar cells or bio fuels, where massive investments have been made, must to learn to change direction when things don't work as planned or a competitor steps into the way.[11] Your startup is no different, and many of the most successful businesses have had to make massive changes.

As an example, although PayPal was founded to develop cryptography software for handhelds, there was little customer interest and so they moved to enterprise applications for handhelds, then moved to consumer applications for handhelds, then to a digital wallet application—but still had no success. Eventually, PayPal shifted to handheld-to-handheld payments, which at least attracted the interest of some venture capitalists, who eventually invested $5M in a famous event where the investor "beamed" the money from his Palm Pilot to the PayPal team's handheld. But although initial adoption looked hopeful, eventually users for the money transfer application topped off at around 13,000 users. During this time, almost as an afterthought to support the handheld business model, the PayPal team created a website that supported email-to-email payments. Surprisingly, the website seemed to be getting a good deal of attention, and the team almost resented the constant prodding from those "eBay" users to do something more with the product. But as the users of the PayPal website passed the 1.3 million mark, the PayPal team finally realized that their real market was in email-based payments, and so they shut down the handheld application.[34] Similarly, Microsoft started by selling compilers for five years until they discovered, serendipitously, the operating-system opportunity. Likewise, Apple Computer initially intended to sell plans to sell computers, not computers themselves. And Symantec, now one of the top five software companies and maker of anti-virus software, was founded to pursue artificial intelligence applications. The lesson is that even some of the most successful companies had big ideas that were ultimately just untested guesses about the market, which ideas had to be changed.

At the heart of it, successful entrepreneurs redefine what failure means. Pursuing a rapid experiment and finding out you were wrong and changing directions isn't failure. That is the road to success. You could have wasted years and your personal fortune. Instead, you saved yourself all that time and money and are now one step closer to finding the real opportunity! Congratulations. Thomas Edison is famous today for his response to failure: "I have not failed 10,000 times. I have not failed once. I have succeeded in proving that those 10,000 ways will not work. When I have eliminated the ways that will not work, I will find the way that will work."[35]

> *Pursuing a rapid experiment and finding out you were wrong and changing directions isn't failure. That is the road to success.*

Consider the case of a high-potential ecommerce startup we will nickname LongTail.com that tried to revolutionize the world of small businesses online. They successfully built a beautiful online markets platform, raised seed funding from a prestigious investment group, and began building the business. However, by robustly testing hypotheses in the field, they discovered that the fundamental business hypothesis was broken. The team then tried out several more alternative hypotheses in rapid succession, only to discover that they were wrong. Then came the difficult part—or so they thought. Rather self-consciously, the team returned to their investor, explained in detail how they had tested the fundamental hypothesis, then tested several alternatives, but the fundamental business model could not work. The investor's jaw dropped, and he sat in silence for a moment. Then he responded, "This is incredible. I would have given you another two or three million. You just saved me all that money." The investor was so impressed that rather than asking for the remaining capital, the investor suggested that LongTail.com shut the venture down in an ethical way, giving their employees severance and paying outstanding vendors. What's more, the investor looked them in the eye and said, "When you two have your next idea, come to me first." Was LongTail.com a failure? We would argue no. They succeeded in proving that an idea was not an opportunity and have moved on to greener pastures rather than wasting their lives on a doomed plan.

Even when a business does succeed, success often lies in the ashes of failure. Notice that PayPal "failed" at each step and adjusted until they discovered their real opportunity. Failing fast is about learning to change quickly and being dispassionate enough that you can let go and move on.

NISI FUNDAMENTAL: BRUTALLY INTELLECTUALLY HONEST LEARNING

In 1946, after almost twenty years in operation, Polaroid stood at the brink of failure: revenues had plummeted year after year as military contracts evaporated and Polaroid's line of polarized glasses and filters proved insufficient to sustain the company. As the pressure began to mount, Polaroid's founder, Edward Land, began looking for a way to save the company. Fortunately, Land was someone characterized by a desire to learn, and so he had been listening when one Christmas morning a few years earlier his daughter asked why she couldn't see their family pictures right away. Curious about the possibilities, Land launched a research project while at the same time asking customers about the potential appeal of such a product. When Polaroid later began to slide toward disaster, Land knew from experience that he already had the silver bullet to save the company. Land boldly announced the launch of the new product—the instant camera—which led to explosive revenue growth, broke Kodak's monopoly in the photography industry, and created an iconic brand name that would symbolize instant photography for decades.

Fast-forward a little over fifty years when digital photography has begun to transform the photography industry. A small team inside Polaroid, having seen the transformation coming, began to develop digital-imaging products. As one of the early movers in digital-imaging development, the team developed market-leading digital-imaging capability and the most advanced digital camera prototype of the era. But then Polaroid's top management decided to shelve the digital camera and focus on their traditional business model of selling film for cameras. When in a few years digital photography all but displaced film photography, Polaroid had fallen so far behind they couldn't catch up. Within the year, Polaroid failed, and their assets were sold in bankruptcy.

Why did Polaroid's managers make such an ill-fated decision to stick with the status quo when fifty years earlier Edward Land had not? Were the managers of Polaroid simply fools? Not necessarily. As a matter of fact, the executives at Polaroid were capable managers with impressive pedigrees and deep experience in business. Why then were the managers at Polaroid unable to recognize the coming tsunami that would wipe out the company? The real answer is that the executives weren't able to recognize the need to change—they weren't able to learn in an unbiased way about the reality they faced. But why were they unable to learn when Edward Land was able to learn? The reason the executives and so many entrepreneurs fail is that they fall into common learning traps, whereas Land was willing to engage in intellectually-honest learning that allowed him to see the need to change.

Such intellectually honest learning makes up a fundamental principle that applies throughout the NISI process. To develop this style of learning, the initial step is to understand the learning traps that blind us. In day-to-day life, such learning traps may be relatively benign, but in a business setting, such as was the case with Polaroid, they can be deadly. To save you the same fate, we are going to review the four most dangerous learning traps: the confirmation, motivation, overconfidence, and familiarity traps. Once you are aware of how these traps operate, we will then share some lessons about how to overcome these traps to develop the style of learning necessary to run the NISI process successfully.

The Confirmation Trap: The Kryptonite of Learning

Does the truth always win? Not necessarily in a legal trial. Two juries were assembled and presented with the evidence. In the first trial, jurors were given the evidence, and after deliberating, only 18% of the jurors voted for conviction. However, in a second, separate trial, the jurors were given the same evidence, but with the additional statement that an eyewitness had identified the defendant as the perpetrator of the crime. Not surprisingly, a whopping 72% of the jurors voted for conviction. Then, after having voted for conviction, emergency evidence was rushed to the jury: it turns out that the eyewitness was legally blind. Despite the obvious fact that the blind witness could not have seen the crime, most of the jurors maintained their conviction, and 68% voted that the defendant was guilty.[36] Fortunately, the trial itself was only a mock trial, but the experiment provided a frightening demonstration of the confirmation trap—that is, the tendency to see what we already believe and discard evidence to the contrary. The confirmation bias nevertheless has a powerful effect upon our ability to learn.

The confirmation trap arises from the fact that as human beings we pay attention to information that confirms our existing beliefs and ignore information that contradicts what we believe. That is why the jurors in the mock trial wouldn't change their opinion after they learned that the eye witness was blind. Not surprisingly, focusing on information that confirms your perspective while ignoring contrary evidence makes it difficult to develop an accurate view of the world. Indeed, the Achilles heel of many entrepreneurs, the fatal flaw of numerous businesses, and the kryptonite of learning, is the confirmation bias. The confirmation bias explains why the executives at Polaroid believed that selling physical film for cameras would never be supplanted by digital cameras, or why managers at the world's most successful mini-computer firm, DEC, believed that personal computers were irrelevant.[37, 38] For both Polaroid and DEC, smart managers were listening to information that confirmed their strategy, while ignoring information that suggested they might be headed for disaster.

The confirmation trap represents a particularly dangerous trap for entrepreneurs because entrepreneurs have strongly held beliefs that lead them to take action. At the same time, these strong beliefs leave them blind to contradictory evidence. Add to this that most entrepreneurs also believe they are listening to opposing views—that they are "open to feedback"—when in fact they really are caught in the confirmation bias. It isn't their fault; it is part of being an entrepreneur that makes it immensely difficult to escape the confirmation trap if you don't understand how to beat it. Many startups never change their business model and are run into the ground because entrepreneurs are unable or unwilling to see information that does not confirm their perspective. As an illustration, the CEO of a highly successful startup making "labs on a chip" lamented that in the fast-changing market, his biggest challenge was team members who didn't keep pace with the change. In part because of the confirmation bias, his managers simply couldn't see the dire need to change. As a result, the CEO had to replace some management team positions two or three times just to adapt to the rapidly evolving market. Had the CEO not been able to learn from disconfirming evidence and recognize the need to change, the startup would have died a long time ago.

The confirmation bias can be deadly to startups and blocks intellectually honest learning. The confirmation bias makes it difficult for entrepreneurs to really understand their market and their customers because they either hear what they want to hear, discount contrary feedback as irrelevant, or never look into the dark for what they may not be seeing. However, there is a solution, and entrepreneurs can reframe the learning experience in a way that produces accurate insights on which a strong business can be built. Part of the solution is to first recognize the confirmation bias and the other biases.

The Motivation Trap: The Alternative-Reality Problem

In a famous football game between Princeton and Dartmouth in 1951, scientists confirmed the existence of alternative realities. The football game itself was unusually rough, and both quarterbacks left the game early. The Princeton quarterback, who had recently been featured on the cover of *Time* magazine, left with a broken nose, while Dartmouth's quarterback was taken out of the game with a broken leg. Incensed, both teams pulled no punches, and fans were enraged by the foul play. Observing the ruckus, researchers decided to ask students at each school to report the number of infractions committed by the opposing team. An interesting phenomenon emerged. Princeton students seemed to think that the Dartmouth team was at fault, and Dartmouth students seemed to think that Princeton team was at fault. The researchers took it a step further and showed a film of the game to students who had not attended the actual football game, in hopes they could be more impartial. Surprisingly, they found the exact same effect—even students who had not been biased by attending the game saw the other team as at fault. In the end, with such dramatically different perceptions of the same event, the researchers sarcastically concluded that perhaps there had been two different football games—two alternative realities.[39]

The Dartmouth-Princeton football game highlights how powerful motivation can be in shaping how we see the world, as well as how we learn. In economics, the motivation trap is known as the problem of sunk costs and leads to irrational decision-making. To illustrate, consider the following problem: you are 90% of the way to completing a new airplane when the news breaks that a competitor has beat you to market with a faster, cheaper, better version of the same plane. What do you do? In the abstract, most people choose the economically rational choice—abandon the project. However, when motivation gets involved—when participants are told they have already invested $9M and for only $1M can finish the project—suddenly the percentage of people choosing to pursue the doomed project jumps from 17% to 85%![40] Similarly, researcher Barry Staw found in an experiment, that when managers were faced with the decision to allocate funding between divisions on a R&D project, managers actually allocated immense amounts of capital to failing divisions losing money when they felt responsible for the original investment decision. In other words, folks finding themselves "knee deep in the big muddy" committed more resources to a failing course of action, rather than pulling out.[41]

The motivation bias can be particularly dangerous for entrepreneurs and innovators because entrepreneurs and innovators often have so much skin in the game that they fall easily into the trap. When an entrepreneur stakes his or her hopes, dreams, and reputation on a startup, it can be a powerful motivating force. However, that same motivation can make it all but impossible for the entrepreneur to learn in an intellectually honest way. The motivational trap, and in particular the escalation of commitment, helps explain such massive and irrational blowups such as Webvan ,which spent over $1B in capital selling products below cost; or Pets.com, which now appears a grossly irrational venture (at the time, Pets.com sold 50-pound bags of dog food for less than the shipping to deliver it). Although these two startups represent famous flameouts, the startup landscape is littered with the corpses of companies whose leadership let the motivation trap blind them. As a result, their companies failed.

The Overconfidence Trap: Why Chernobyl Will Never Melt Down

What do experienced neurologists and their administrative assistants have in common? Not much when it comes to confidence. In a study on confidence and accuracy, Lewis Goldberg asked experienced neurologists and their administrative assistants to diagnose brain damage among patients as being organic or non-organic damage using a standard protocol in the field. What Goldberg found, not surprisingly, was that experienced neurologists were much more confident about their diagnoses than their untrained administrative assistants, who were more used to scheduling appointments. However, although the neurologists were more confident about their diagnoses, they were not more accurate. In fact, Goldberg found that the administrative assistants had just as high a rate of accurately diagnosing organic brain damage as experienced neurologists.[42] What does Goldberg's study teach us? Although we may be confident, we may not be right! And if you think this may be an isolated case, one study found that in nearly 15,000 judgments, when participants believed they were correct 98% of the time, they were wrong over 30% of the time. This kind of overconfidence can lead to disasters, such as the Chernobyl (the

Ukrainian Minister of Power stated the odds of a meltdown at 1 in 10,000 years just two months before the meltdown), the *Challenger* (NASA estimated the odds of catastrophic failure as 1 in 100,000), or Pearl Harbor (the American military believed that Pearl Harbor was virtually immune to attack).[39] It can also lead your startup to fail.

What these studies illustrate is the challenge of making difficult decisions and the tendency of experienced individuals to be overconfident about their abilities. In fact, studies have shown that our innate overconfidence goes so far that we sometimes believe we can shape purely random events, such as rolling dice or picking lottery tickets.[39] Research also shows that complex or ambiguous settings exacerbate the overconfidence bias. Unfortunately, not only do entrepreneurs face complex, ambiguous problems, they also have an above-average dose of confidence. All of this can lead entrepreneurs into the trap of not listening and believing they are right when they are wrong. In our own research we found that overconfident entrepreneurs who see themselves as "experts" are least likely to learn and change.[43] As an illustration, Mike Cassidy, the serial entrepreneur we discussed earlier who has created companies worth over a billion dollars, confessed that "the thing that scares me most is someone who is convinced they are right, because they will never change." For entrepreneurs, Mike's statement is a pertinent word of warning. By definition, entrepreneurs can only take a guess at whether they have the right product, for the right market, at the right price. Entrepreneurs act because they believe there is something there. But entrepreneurs have to discover the right combination to be successful, and the only way to do so is by learning in a truly intellectually honest manner.

Finally and equally important, don't confuse overconfidence with determination. Entrepreneurs need to be determined. We always like to say, "There are 1000 things that can kill your company, you just need to get by them one at a time." But there is a difference between determination and overconfidence. Take a closer look at our saying: what are we really saying? We are saying that entrepreneurship is hard, and you will face risks or obstacles; that you have to tackle these one at a time and take them down; but you have to stay humble along the road. The new entrepreneurship is about identifying those risks and nailing them down one at a time, creatively finding your way around obstacles, and bringing your customer-validated product to market. This is quite different from overconfidence, which is about being sure you are right to the point you don't listen and make mistakes that kill you. Determined entrepreneurs really listen and then find a way to solve the challenge.

The Familiarity Trap: Death by Sharks

Are you more likely to be killed by a shark or by a bee sting? Most people imagine the waters of the coast of Australia or San Diego and answer "shark attack." However, as strange as it may sound, the reality is that you are more likely to be killed by a bee sting or even a box jellyfish, which kills more people than sharks and crocodiles combined.[39] But why do we answer so confidently that we are more likely to be killed by a shark? The answer is that we are more familiar with shark attacks. It is this familiarity that causes the trouble in our perception of the odds and also causes trouble when we are learning.

Both individuals and organizations tend to lean on either the familiar or on their strengths—their competencies. In organization studies this has been called a *capability trap,* and many organizations have stumbled and fallen because they stuck with their strengths. Consider the case of typesetter manufacturers—the companies that make the equipment to produce books like these. In the early part of the 20th century, typesetters were based on a system of injecting hot metal into a type mold. The type would then be inked and used to print the pages of a book. Eventually, with the evolution of photography, a new method of typesetting emerged—phototypesetting. Phototypesetting could use a photographic image of fonts, rather than hot metal, to create the printing layout. Although the differences between hot-metal technology and photography seem clear to outsiders, the dominant manufacturers in hot-metal typesetting struggled for years to develop new photo typesetters. In fact, initially, they designed their new lines of photo typesetters on the old, hot-metal architecture and tried to incorporate elements of the hot-metal process into the phototypesetting. The results were ugly, and these manufacturers struggled until they eventually switched to the new architecture.[44] Similarly, the top executives at Polaroid let what was familiar overshadow a valuable new asset, killing the digital photography initiative and the company.

For entrepreneurs, the familiarity or competency traps can be a problem because entrepreneurs tend to reuse ideas they understand in settings where they may no longer be appropriate. We mentioned There.com at the beginning of the chapter. Although the company brought in a professional CEO with a background in marketing, the CEO naturally also brought his familiarities and strengths to the table. In this case, the CEO viewed the world through the lens of the "go big" marketing blitz strategy. In the case of a new technology in a new market attempting to launch in a post dot-com crash environment, this was a very poor strategy. But it was the familiar strategy. Following the familiar strategy, There.com carefully perfected its product and then launched it with a massive marketing blitz that generated a meager handful of users and a few thousand dollars in revenue. Ultimately There.com was sold for pennies on the dollar. The lesson: one of the most challenging things entrepreneurs must struggle with is discovering what they don't know or don't have. Entrepreneurs have to possess a unique brand of humility to recognize these weaknesses or blind spots and find others who can fill them in.

The Solution: Developing an Attitude of Learning

The type of learning central to the NISI process has been described in many ways by entrepreneurial veterans. John Doerr, who invested in Google, Amazon, Intuit, and Sun Microsystems, says it is about being "ruthlessly, absolutely, intellectually honest."[45] Likewise, Arthur Rock, one of the early and most successful venture capitalists, argued that the "issue I set the most store by is whether [entrepreneurs] are honest with themselves. It's essential to be totally, brutally honest."[46] Similarly, Dominic Orr, CEO of Aruba Networks (which as a pre-profit startup had an IPO valuation of $1B), argued that "brutal, intellectual honesty" lies at the heart of Aruba's success.[47] Along these lines, George Quist, founder of the well-known executive search firm insisted that the most important entrepreneurial characteristic is "intellectual honesty above all," which he defined as "a willingness to face up to facts rigorously whether they prove you right or wrong."[48]

At the core, entrepreneurs must develop an attitude of learning—brutally honest learning. By this we mean you need to learn how to seek and really receive feedback, because ultimately feedback opens the door to developing a product or solution that customers really need rather than just what the entrepreneur imagines that customers need. Furthermore, down the road, as the founder, you will set the culture of your organization, and creating a learning culture leads to a great organization rather than a one-hit wonder. But how do you develop this attitude of honest learning? The first step, which we have already described, is to recognize the learning traps discussed above. The second step is to develop an attitude of learning that has four basic components: 1) becoming an expert novice, 2) reframing the learning purpose, 3) real-time feedback, and 4) data-driven perspectives.

Moving Beyond Expertise: Becoming an Expert Novice

Most of us believe that being an expert is a good thing. But research and experience suggest that experts can be dangerous.[43, 49] When Mike Cassidy says that what scares him most is "someone who is convinced they are right," he is talking about the dangers of expertise. Experts can be dangerous because they usually are convinced they are right, and as a result they have a hard time really learning in an intellectually honest way. In contrast, Mike Cassidy argues that what made him successful was the fact that "I knew that I didn't know the right answer." Mike's observation highlights what we call *becoming an expert novice*. That is, someone who has knowledge and confidence but always maintains a seed of doubt that they may be wrong. Tom Kelley, founder of the revolutionary design firm IDEO, describes it as "a healthy balance between confidence in what you know and distrusting what you know just enough that keeps you thirsty for more knowledge."[50] When entrepreneurs have a healthy distrust in what they know, they become hungry to learn more. They also are more willing to look at evidence that may prove them wrong, or change their perspective. This willingness to look at counterfactual evidence is a central part of intellectually honest learning. Thus the first element of an attitude of learning is to move beyond being an expert to becoming an "expert novice": an individual who cultivates deep knowledge but maintains a healthy seed of doubt.

Reframe the Purpose

Another technique to develop intellectually-honest learning is to reframe the purpose of your venture to be learning itself. This may sound crazy, but Amos Tversky and Daniel Kahneman won the Nobel prize for demonstrating how framing can change our actions and decisions. Reframing the purpose of your venture to be learning what the market wants rather than proving that your idea works, is the first step to shedding the learning traps that hold you back. You will also avoid the trap of thinking the NISI process is just a shortcut to getting investment or a shortcut to success. Instead you will, like the ideal scientist, become more objective and focused on learning the truth about your idea.

Many entrepreneurs find this difficult, and so we suggest reframing around the higher purpose behind your venture. Ask yourself, what big problem am I trying to solve? Then put your heart into finding the solution regardless of who owns the idea. As an example, ClassTop had modest success building education software until they quit focusing on the software and refocused around the higher purpose of education. With this higher purpose in mind, they were able to focus on learning about the problem, and they discovered a massive opportunity they could serve: the need to educate billions of people who don't have access to university enrollments. Although the reframing around learning sounds like a "soft" concept, it is a powerful tool. By reframing, you can leave behind the persistent need to prove yourself right and instead discover the truth about a bigger, more valuable problem.

Real-time Feedback

What else can help you develop more accurate learning? First consider the following puzzle: what do professional bridge players, weather forecasters, and bookies have in common?[39] Clearly not professional training, since weather forecasters attend specialized schools, whereas bookies and bridge players don't necessarily have fancy credentials. What about process? There are some similarities, since professional bridge players, bookies, and weather forecasters all deal in calculations of probability, but this alone doesn't tell the whole story. What about accuracy? It turns out that all three are remarkably accurate (even weather forecasters, despite our complaints). The reason? Immense amounts of real-time feedback.

Significant amounts of real-time feedback help correct overconfidence, increase pattern recognition, and help us see the truth. This is one reason why an entire industry has been built up around 360-degree feedback: when executives have the opportunity to receive unfiltered, real-time feedback, it is often a powerful, career-transforming experience because they suddenly have a window into the reality of their own interactions. For entrepreneurs, unfiltered, real-time feedback is vital to an attitude of learning and becoming intellectually honest. It can also be vital to success. One of the key differentiating factors between There.com and IMVU was the contrast between There.com managers' unchallenged beliefs and IMVU's focus on gathering constant, continuous feedback. The lack of real-time feedback led There.com to build what they imagined customers wanted, whereas IMVU was able to morph an initial idea until it had the right solution for the right market to be successful.

At the same time, being open to real-time feedback can be immensely challenging. It is so difficult that Dominic Orr, who advocates brutal, intellectual honesty, actually hires therapists for his management team to help them develop the self-confidence to give and receive real-time feedback. It is easier to receive real-time feedback if entrepreneurs have already reframed the problem around a higher ideal and around learning. Whichever way an entrepreneur finds the capacity to receive honest, real-time feedback, the capacity to hear such feedback is critical to your ability to learn.

Data-Driven Learning

The final component of the attitude of learning required in the NISI process is data-driven learning. Many entrepreneurs and investors operate on beliefs and gut feelings. But as the research on overconfidence demonstrates, gut feelings and beliefs can be highly inaccurate. When engaging in the NISI process, entrepreneurs should focus on learning from the data, specifically the right data, rather than taking shortcuts and blind leaps. Good decisions require good data, and impatient entrepreneurs have discovered how expensive shortcuts can be. There are hundreds of sources of data (e.g., Gartner, Forrester, press, bloggers, random customer comments, sales meetings, celebrity investors, engineering numbers, focus groups, and so forth). The NISI process helps you cut through all the noise and places the focus on predictive data by engaging with prospective customers the right way. By following the NISI process, you will get information that Gartner and the bloggers wish they had, and you can create the context that makes sense of all the customer comments and engineering ideas. You must learn to draw your conclusions from this critical data and let the data make the decisions for you. At the same time, you don't have to wait until the data overwhelms you. As an entrepreneur you often have to make decisions from limited data (often 4 to 15 data points), but you still rely on the critical data you will discover in the NISI process.

To illustrate the power of the data, consider that few people know that Intel early in its history narrowly dodged a bullet that would have destroyed the company. In the 1980s, when Intel had established itself as a successful manufacturer of DRAM memory, top management came to believe that the company was good at designing and manufacturing memory. However, Japanese manufacturers entered and began to apply to DRAM production their expertise in large-scale, precision manufacturing. Intel's top management remained convinced that Intel was a memory company despite the slow shift of competitive advantage from Intel to their Japanese counterparts. Fortunately, at the level of semiconductor fabs, Intel had established a data-driven decision-making rule: allocate space in the fab based on profit per wafer. As a result, at the request of a customer, Intel developed and began to produce a very profitable chip—an early microprocessor prototype. These new types of chips proved very profitable, and over time, more and more of the fabrication capacity was being allocated to semiconductor production rather than memory production, despite top management's insistence that Intel was a memory company. Only after a drastic majority of Intel's production capacity had been allocated to microprocessors did top management realize that Intel was not a memory company but a microprocessor manufacturer. Once the

The most important fundamental in the entire NISI process, aside from getting into the field, is developing an attitude of learning that will enable you to successfully discover a real opportunity.

realization struck, management quickly scrambled to redefine their strategic direction around the "new" direction. Ultimately, it was the data-driven decision rule at Intel that allowed the company to change and survive.[51]

In summary, perhaps the most important fundamental in the entire NISI process, aside from getting into the field, is developing an attitude of learning that will enable you to successfully discover a real opportunity. To do so, you need to recognize the key learning traps and then apply the techniques we have described: becoming an expert novice, reframing the purpose, seeking real-time feedback, and gathering the data. If you are always intellectually honest in your learning, you will succeed at applying the NISI process in your business.

NISI FUNDAMENTAL: RAPID, INEXPENSIVE, SIMPLE EXPERIMENTS TO TEST YOUR GUESS

Another fundamental that applies throughout the NISI process is to conduct rapid, inexpensive, simple experiments in the field to test your hypotheses rather than building products. This fundamental depends on the recognition that whatever you believe about your product, customers, or market is a hypothesis that needs to be proven. In other words, whatever you believe is an educated guess and nothing more. Few entrepreneurs recognize this, and so, feeling urgent to get to market with something to sell, they start building the product. The danger is that when you build a product based on a guess about what customers want, even your best guess, you are bound to be wrong in ways you couldn't imagine. Of course a lucky few *do* get it almost right on the first try; however, probabilistically these cases are very low. Hence the high mortality rate for new ventures. Unfortunately, entrepreneurial myths are perpetuated by the few entrepreneurs who get lucky and guess right. In contrast, if you talk to a group of successful, thoughtful entrepreneurs, they will tell you how dramatically their product changed from beginning to end. A fundamental of the NISI process is to avoid building your product until you have validated your hypothesis through a succession of customer conversations using a virtual prototype, alpha, and then beta products. Turn your hypotheses into customer-validated facts. Then with the facts in hand, start building the product, all the while continuing to iteratively test your product and your hypotheses with the customer. So how do you do this?

Identify Your Assumptions

The NISI process relies on first identifying your assumptions, turning them into hypotheses, and then validating your hypotheses through rapid experimentation using "virtual prototypes" (PowerPoints, drawings, mock-ups, and so forth) during structured customer "buying panel" conversations as well as detailed information gathering by the key members of your team. But the place you need to start is to identify all your assumptions—your guesses. Often entrepreneurs overlook the very fact that they are guessing and so a very useful tool to help you in the process is to map out your business model. We recommend the work of Alex Osterwalder, who wrote *Business Model Generation* and provides his business model canvas online. In his business model canvas, Osterwalder highlights nine areas that make up a business and if you map out your assumptions on his canvas you will notice the areas you are guessing. The nine areas Osterwalder discusses are as follows:

1. Customer Segments
2. Value Propositions
3. Customer Relationships
4. Channels
5. Key Activities
6. Key Resources
7. Key Partners
8. Cost Structure
9. Revenue Streams

In this book you will notice that we don't recommend tackling all your assumptions at once. Instead we walk you through the process of focusing on the most important assumptions first and then progressively validating your assumptions. That is why we start with nailing the pain because if you aren't tackling a validated pain then everything else you do will be a waste of time. Nonetheless, we recommend that you take the time to explore your assumptions and return to them to remind yourself that you are in the business of testing your guesses, not of convincing yourself that you are right. In terms of which assumptions we tackle and when, in Nail the Pain we tackle #1(Customer Segments); in Nail the Solution we tackle #2 (Value Proposition); in Nail the Go-to-Market Strategy we tackle #3 (Customer Relationships) and #4 (Channels); and in Nail the Business Model we tackle the other assumptions.

Fast and Inexpensive Experiments

Importantly, the process of experimenting and finding the facts does take time, but it doesn't have to be expensive. It is better to keep experiments as inexpensive as possible—it helps you remember that they are in fact "experiments" and preserves your capital so you have the time to experiment. One of the challenges of heavily funded, venture-backed startups is that they burn so much money and have such high expectations that they really only have one swing at the plate. In contrast, if experiments are fast and cheap, an entrepreneur can take five, ten, maybe even fifty swings at the plate to try and hit a home run. Later we will walk you through some specific process steps to conduct your experiments but never forget the experimentation mentality: inexpensive, rapid, reliable tests that help you find out the truth and help you avoid getting into the emotional and learning traps we highlighted earlier.

Focus on Simplicity

In addition, as you conduct your rapid, inexpensive experiments, remember to keep your experiments and your eventual products simple. Simplify as much as you can throughout the entire process. There is incredible power in simplicity, and as human beings we crave the simple. A number of recent books, such as *The Paradox of Choice,* summarize decades of social psychological research showing that even though it may appear that we crave more choices, in fact, we respond to simplicity. For example, in one well-known experiment at a Bay Area grocery store, two different jam exhibits were tested. In the first exhibit, six types of jam were put on display for customers to sample, and the resulting sales were robust (30% of customers bought a jam). In a second exhibit, customers were given far more choices; twenty-four different types of premium jam were put on display in the true spirit of customer choice. Shockingly, sales dropped over seven-fold to a meager 4% sales rate.[52] In other words, despite the fact that modern capitalism has led to an explosion in choices, customers respond to simplicity more than complexity.

The observation that customers respond to simplicity has been observed in business and entrepreneurship as well. For example, examine the exhibit below (Figure 11) and consider the incredible success of the simplified iPod to that of comparable MP3 players of the time, which offered more options and buttons but were more complex both in design and use. Similarly, the hamburger chain In-N-Out® offers a very simple selection of hamburgers, French fries, and drinks but has developed a phenomenal following over the years, in contrast to the traditional, overcomplicated menu at many restaurants today. As another example, the Seattle-based coffee chain Starbucks recently simplified its menu in response to consumer confusion over its many offerings.

Figure 11: Simple versus Complex Products

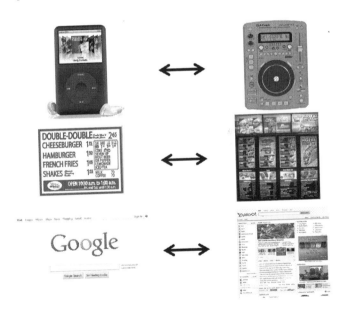

Somewhat counter-intuitively, simplifying increases customer adoption and reduces costs. Customers are attracted by simplicity and confused by complexity. Simplifying the product offering doesn't mean that you are taking away the customer's choice; rather it sends the message that you know the customers so well that you are delivering the exact solution they are looking for. Simplifying also saves the startup time and money because they can develop something simple instead of something complex. Often an engineering-driven company thinks they have to deliver every feature to every customer, whereas a market-driven company has the luxury of choosing its customer and building the right product that nails the customer's pain. However, overly complex products not only fail to satisfy, they confuse and even repel. Indeed, Mari Baker, an early senior vice president at Intuit, argued that "it's really easy to do a lot of things. It's really hard to do a few things. Focus." Instead of trying to

> *"It would have been easy to get caught up in unnecessary complexity and miss the elegance of being focused on a simple set of things that would make a difference."*
> *–Scott Kriens, CEO Juniper Networks*

satisfy every potential customer need, entrepreneurs should focus on developing the minimum feature set to close a customer purchase. Ultimately, simplicity is about what you choose *not* to do. Scott Kriens, CEO of the wildly successful startup Juniper Networks, cautions that in building the business, "It would have been easy to get caught up in unnecessary complexity and miss the elegance of being focused on a simple set of things that would make a difference."

One of the more dramatic examples we have seen of the power of simplicity and minimum feature set came from one of the startups that applied the NISI process from day one—ClassTop. As we mentioned earlier, ClassTop is an online learning company, and one of their early experiments was the development of a client-side interface for Blackboard, the dominant university online course system. In trying to understand what customers wanted, the ClassTop founders, Jayson and Jared, hired an engineer in India to build a virtual prototype using Flash, which contained the top twenty features customers mentioned, and then set up meetings with CIOs and key decision makers at several well-known U.S. universities. When they asked how much customers would pay for such a product, the answer came back a discouraging $200 per month in licensing fees—not a number on which you could build a business. But the founders continued to investigate, using a tool called the $100 game (which we describe later), in which they asked customers to allocate a dollar amount to the features that were most important to them. Surprisingly, respondents applied on average $80 to a drag-and-drop content management feature and $20 to two other features. With this insight, the team then went back to the drawing board and reduced the Flash prototype from twenty features down to four core features. With the new prototype in hand, the team went out to a new set of university customers to continue the research. The next four universities had a unanimously positive reaction to the concept, and each requested to be a beta site for the virtual product. Jayson and Jared then went back to the first group of universities to validate their reaction to the updated concept. Surprisingly, when they began to discuss the topic of price, the buying panels at each of the universities suggested a $1000 per month licensing fee for the simplified product. In essence, by simplifying the product down to the minimum relevant feature set, the ClassTop founders cut their development time and costs to one-fifth of their original estimate and multiplied the customers' willingness to pay by 500%. That is the power of keeping it simple.

Small Teams Outperform Large Teams

Finally, in the spirit of simplicity, remember to keep the team small. In any organization, teams can both accelerate and complicate your success, and the same is true of the NISI process. One of the biggest causes of premature death in a startup is premature scaling of the team—hiring good people at the wrong time: hiring the right VP of sales before the sales process is validated, hiring the right development team before the product need is established, and so forth. As the team grows, your flexibility decreases, costs increase, and communication becomes more complex, thus reducing your ability to experiment. Indeed, small teams are ideal to apply the NISI methodology. At the core you need—someone to define it, someone to build it, and eventually someone to sell it (see Figure 12).

Figure 12: The Startup Organization Chart

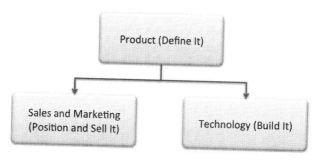

The advantage of such a small team is that communication is easy, responsibilities are clear, and expenses are low. Two to three people can investigate the solution, listen to customer conversations from different perspectives, and keep each other honest. At the same time, everyone on the team should be fully engaged in the NISI process (don't make the mistake of letting your technology team member just go start building: this person should be talking with the customers just as much as everyone else). In cases where your venture or existing business has investors, a board of directors, or a leadership team, it is absolutely critical that leadership be on board and participate. Focus on getting stakeholders from each area of your larger organization involved in the key "startup" roles. If leadership or early-stage investors observe from afar, rather than being intellectually engaged in or aligned with the process, they almost always grow impatient and cut the process short by substituting their own hypotheses for facts. We warn you now because we have seen the NISI process derail when investors or the larger leadership team aren't aligned with the process.

CONDUCTING THE NISI EXPERIMENT

As you go through the NISI process, remember the metaphor of the scientific experiment. The goal of the process is to test your guess (hypotheses) in order to discover the facts about your idea and your customer. Again, the NISI fundamentals are: 1) get into the field, 2) fail fast and change, 3) focus on intellectually honest learning, and 4) conduct rapid, inexpensive, simple experiments. With these fundamentals as a base, you are ready to go through the phases of the NISI methodology. As you progress, remember that while we have described the process in terms of "phases," the NISI process is inherently nonlinear. You may need to back up, circle back, or restart, depending on what you discover. In addition, it will help greatly if you have a coach, outside mentors, or a board of directors (even if it's just a personal board of directors) that will hold you accountable and keep you honest with yourself as you go through the process.

PHASE 1: NAILING THE CUSTOMER PAIN

In the early days of computing, a young and perhaps naïve founder, Allen Michels, showed up at the executive offices of Burroughs computers. He was trying to promote computers based on a single board—a radical idea at the time; and securing orders was proving difficult for his fledgling startup, Convergent Technologies. In previous meetings with computer resellers he had sold a handful of computers where he had hoped to sell thousands. Frustrated and confused, Michels decided to take a new approach as the meeting started. After a few minutes presenting the basic idea, Michels asked the executive team how this matched what they needed in the new product. One executive asked if the computer could come in its own case, rather than as just a motherboard. Michels quickly responded that the computer in fact did have a case. Another executive asked if it had an operating system. Michels replied that it did. To the question "does it have a word processor," Michels quickly responded in the affirmative. The conversation continued in this way, with Michels promising on a product that fit perfectly their specifications until he walked out the door with an order for 10,000 computers. The problem, or the solution, as we will argue, was that Michels hadn't actually built anything yet. Although he had a technical prototype, he didn't have a box, or operating system, or word processor, or anything else. Upon accidentally discovering his customer's real needs, he laid the seeds for a company that was successful and eventually sold for hundreds of millions a few years later. It was a lesson soon forgotten. In Michels' next company, Ardent Supercomputers, the team spent a good deal of time researching how customers used supercomputers; but they didn't spend much time exploring whether their customers had a real problem and how to best address that pain. As a result, Ardent developed an innovative but expensive supercomputer that was delivered late to market, and ultimately it didn't match the pain of any particular customers. Although the computer came close to meeting some criteria, it didn't quite match the specific needs of any one customer. The company folded a few months later.[1]

The difference between the two startups wasn't the founder or the state of the market—it was the assumptions about market "pain" that customers would pay to solve. In his first company, the founder's hunger

65

drove him to successfully discover and validate what we call a *Monetizable Pain*, whereas in the second company, flush with cash, the founder was distracted by building a better mousetrap and missed the customer pain by just a few degrees. Michels isn't alone in his mistake. Most entrepreneurs, earnestly believing that their idea solves a real customer need, start building the solution so they have something to sell. However, these entrepreneurs inevitably find out that the pain they targeted was either imagined or could not be monetized. These entrepreneurs needed to stop and assess whether there was a real monetizable pain before they started building their products, let alone raising capital. It is not hard to find out, if you know how.

The foundation of the path to success is to first identify a real, monetizable pain to solve. As Vinod Khosla, former partner at legendary venture capital firm Kleiner Perkins Caufield Byers and founder of Khosla Ventures, argues, "Any big problem is a big opportunity. No problem, no opportunity. ... No one will pay you to solve a non-problem."[53] Therefore, during the first phase of the NISI process, your objectives are to clearly understand the monetizable customer pain, determine if this pain represents an opportunity, and either discover you were wrong (and make a change) or move on to the next phase. You will also begin to formulate and test a Big Idea Hypothesis that will lead you to a virtual prototype and eventually a validated solution to the customer pain. For a visual overview of the steps in this phase, see the figure below.

Figure 13: Steps to Nail the Pain

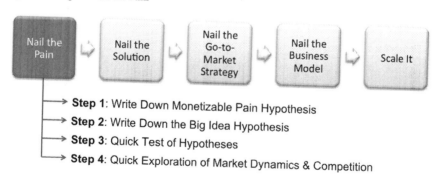

Step 1: Write Down Monetizable Pain Hypothesis
Step 2: Write Down the Big Idea Hypothesis
Step 3: Quick Test of Hypotheses
Step 4: Quick Exploration of Market Dynamics & Competition

STEP 1: WRITE DOWN THE MONETIZABLE PAIN STATEMENT: FINDING A SHARK BITE

Great businesses begin with a customer problem that an entrepreneur solves. We call this problem the *customer pain*. Your objective is to understand the "job" customers are trying to accomplish and whether the pain customers feel is worth your time to solve. There are many types of pain, some which are small and some of which are large. Recognizing this difference, investors often classify potential businesses into two groups: vitamins (which even the best of us take only on occasion), and painkillers (which most people will take universally). Underneath this simplistic categorization is the idea that for a problem to be worth your time to solve, it should be a significant pain for the customer.

As an entrepreneur, you want to focus on a big pain point, what we call a *monetizable customer pain*. Indeed, when Vinod Khosla says that "any big problem is a big opportunity," the words *big* are not accidental. In other words, if the customer pain you identify is equivalent to a mosquito bite, it may be a nuisance customers are willing to live with. However, if the customer pain feels like a shark bite, customers will be urgent to pay you to ease the pain. A monetizable customer pain represents a customer pain so significant that the customers recognize the pain, have money to pay for a solution, and will return the cold calls of an unknown startup to solve it (we have seen hit rates on returned cold calls as high as 100% for real monetizable pains). For example, to generate a monetizable pain hypothesis, startup consultant Mark Richards of Sand Hill Partners often asks startup teams to break into small groups and then "come back with a problem that is so interesting that you would return a cold call if someone left a message on your voice mail wanting to discuss this problem." Likewise, you should consider asking yourself, "What pain faced by my customers would be so significant that they would take a cold call." Who would

> *A monetizable customer pain represents a customer pain so significant that the customers will return the cold calls of an unknown startup to solve it.*

you call, and where are they in the organization? What problems do you think they are working on, and when they wake up in the middle of the night, what are they worried about and what are they trying to do? The answer to this question is the Monetizable Pain Hypothesis.

On a pain scale from one to five, a monetizable pain should be at least a four or a five to qualify as a monetizable pain. With such significant customer pain, you can attract sufficient customers to build a large and successful business. As the level of customer pain drops, you will find that customers are increasingly fickle and noncommittal. For example, Lunarr, a startup that developed visual inspiration tools such as Post-it® Notes for web pages, created interesting and unusual applications. However, the customer pain the developers were tackling was rather low on the pain scale, and as a result, adoption never took off. In contrast, when Mike Maples Jr. was looking to found his next company, Motive Communications, he describes looking for a customer pain so significant that it required a tourniquet: if the customer didn't get it, they were going to die!

Why do you need to focus on a monetizable customer pain? Because as an underfunded startup with no reputation, brand, or track record, building your business on a monetizable customer pain will exponentially increase your chances success. In contrast, the three mistakes we see entrepreneurs make are 1) guessing but not testing the pain (which is the subject of this book), 2) selecting a small customer pain (low on the pain scale), or 3) selecting a narrow customer pain (small number of customers willing to pay); and as a result, either customers aren't willing to pay or the business isn't worth the entrepreneurs' time to build. The entrepreneurs who start with the monetizable customer pain will never waste time trying to reposition their product as a "must-have" six months after launch, or writing white papers to "educate" customers, or scrambling to find a new customer with only a month left of runway, or bemoaning that they were just "before our time" or that "customers "didn't get it." Disciplining yourself now to sit down and write out the Monetizable Pain Hypothesis will help you see what you believe and then, when you test it, whether the results suggest there is a business worth your time to build.

STEP 2: WRITE DOWN THE BIG IDEA HYPOTHESIS

As kids we were always asking our parents "what if" questions. All of our "what if we could do this" questions drove them crazy. Entrepreneurs, like children, still allow themselves to dream of ideas that could change the world. George Bernard Shaw said "Some men see things as they are and say why - I dream things that never were and say why not." The entrepreneur's "what if" mindset generates the disruptive innovation that improve the world we live in. These sparks of inspiration are what keep us entrepreneurs going, but ironically most entrepreneurs fail precisely because they spontaneously act on their big idea by building a solution based on a guess about what customers actually want without having the discipline or knowledge of how to gather the facts. Entrepreneur's big ideas fall into two major categories one we call "brave new world" or breakthrough ideas that turn conventional wisdom on its head and the second category are the "better faster cheaper" ideas that provide incremental

> *"Some men see things as they are and say why - I dream things that never were and say why not."*
> *–George Bernard Shaw*

improvements on an existing theme. The challenge for you as an entrepreneur, then, is to manage your big idea at this stage of the game (and if you don't have a big idea yet, take a deep breath; this stage of the process will actually be easier for you).

One thing that makes the NISI process distinct is the focus on testing your ideas before building something. At this stage we are going to ask you to develop a B*ig Idea Hypothesis*. This Big Idea Hypothesis represents your idea about the solution to the pain you observed and is where you create the future by inventing it. The Big Idea Hypothesis can be a *breakthrough hypothesis* or a *better faster cheaper* hypothesis. Later you will transform this Big Idea Hypothesis into a solution hypothesis and an eventual solution. However, at this stage, we focus on the "big idea" because it allows you to create a conceptual straw man. Why do we ask you to develop just an idea? Because your big ideas are like uranium—they can be incredibly powerful but incredibly dangerous if mishandled. Once you let your solution take over your heart and mind, it becomes increasingly difficult to accurately listen to your customer's feedback. Because you have a hammer, every problem begins to look like a nail. Even worse, once we build something and give it a physical form, all of our defense mechanisms kick in to protect our creation. Regardless of whether your creation is a masterpiece or Frankenstein, it is difficult to be objective about your creation. That's why we agree with Kauffman Senior Fellow Paul Kedrowsky, who said, "As soon as you build something you are dead." By starting first with the customer pain and creating an abstract, big idea hypothesis, it is easier to nail the blueprint and establish the right product DNA before building anything. Eventually we will walk you through the development of a virtual prototype, then an actual prototype, and finally the solution

> *"As soon as you build something you are dead."*
> *–Paul Kedrowsky, Senior Fellow, Kauffman Foundation*

itself, so you end with a final solution that customers buy. But at this stage, the goal is to help you learn from customers and stay flexible while you nail the customer pain. Although this step may sound overly simple, we've seen entrepreneurs waste years and millions of dollars chasing an untested market pain with a "better mousetrap." Writing down and testing your Monetizable Pain Statement and Big Idea Hypothesis forces you to focus and clarify what you really believe and then gives you solid foundation to build on. Take a moment and write down your Big Idea Hypothesis:

> *For customers that have (Write "Monetizable Pain Statement") I propose (write your Big Idea Hypothesis) which is different from existing solutions because (statement of primary differentiation).*

As you develop your Monetizable Pain Statement and the Big Idea Hypothesis don't be afraid to be specific on the details of the *customers* and the *market* they represent (yet we are asking you to avoid being specific about the exact details of the *solution*, for example, don't get too deep into the features in the solution). What is the title on the business card of the person who has this pain? Define your solution and the key benefits to the customer. Get specific about the customer pain you are solving—broad, general market solutions, just like broad pains, are impossible to test. While you do this, notice the subtle difference between bringing a solution you already have or are convinced is correct and writing down a hypothesis about the solution. In this phase of the NISI process, everything is virtual: you are working with hypotheses. You don't need to build the product yet, because it can bias you, but you do need to hypothesize the solution. To help clarify how to formulate a Big Idea Hypothesis, consider an analogy to real estate. At this stage you are going to be hypothesizing about and then asking customers about which side of the city you should build on, which neighborhood, which structure, but you are not asking them what color of paint should be on the walls or trying to convince them that the apartments you have already built are the right residence for them. Another way to think about it is you are trying to find the right hill to attack before you try and optimize your position on the hill.

A good tool we have found for formulating your Big Idea Hypothesis can be found on page 161 of Geoffrey Moore's *Crossing the Chasm*. Moore calls it the *elevator message*, but we are going to turn it into our Big Idea Hypothesis. (We highly recommend *Crossing the Chasm* as a must read for every entrepreneur.) Let's fill in the blanks to get started:

1. For (target customer [remember, what is the title on the business card and which industry are they in?])

2. Who (statement of the monetizable pain)

3. The (product name) is a (product category)

4. That (statement of key benefit—that is, the compelling reason to buy)

5. Unlike (primary competitive alternative)

6. Our solution (describe the big idea and statement of primary differentiation)

Using the Geoffrey Moore's format, let's take a look at the Big Idea Hypothesis Paul Ahlstrom created in 1997 for his software company Knowlix:

(1) For the Internal IT Help Desk managers of large corporations who (2) have dissatisfied customers and are out of compliance with their Customers' Service Level Agreements (SLAs) because each front-line support rep is unable to capture and share knowledge so they can answer customers' technical questions and problems in a timely manner, (3) Knowlix is an IT Knowledge Management Solution that (4) allows the front-line IT Customer Support Reps to capture issues within their existing workflow and provide accurate answers in real-time to their corporate customers. (5) Unlike Inference, Knowlix (6) integrates large amounts of unstructured data into the existing workflow of Remedy, Bendata, Peregrine, and other leading IT Help Desk systems, thus allowing the frontline support rep to answer the question on the first call.

Now that you have a Monetizable Pain and Big Idea Hypothesis that could solve that pain, you are ready to think about how to test it and discover the facts. However, always remember that your hypothesis represents your best guess, not the facts themselves. Don't be lulled into thinking you already have it nailed until you have validated it in the market. As an example of the dangers of not writing down and testing your Monetizable Pain Statement and Solution Hypothesis, consider the case of Teqlo, a startup company developing software that allowed disparate web services to be linked together. As enthusiastic entrepreneurs, the Teqlo team believed they could solve a broad swath of customer problems (remember, overly broad problems are very hard to validate or solve). But in the process of dreaming in very general terms, Teqlo lost sight of a specific customer pain. As a result, the team developed a very general product in hopes that it would allow them to capture a massive market. The only catch was that by trying to please everyone, they didn't actually solve any specific customer's needs. Not surprisingly, without solving any particular customers' needs, no one adopted the service.

Forced to rethink their strategy, the company and its investors started by tossing out the "pretense of solving everyone's problem."[54] To rediscover the specific customer pain, Teqlo borrowed a technique from the successful online photo service Snapfish. At Snapfish, the product development team focused on a very specific customer: a mother whom they nicknamed "Emily." So Teqlo went out and defined the customer need very specifically and then, to validate that pain, went out and talked to "a small army" of those customers to rediscover the pain the team had overlooked. What happened was a complete surprise to the company—not only did the team discover an unseen customer pain, but the solution to that pain was much different from what they had envisioned. Rather than a bucket of widgets, which they had developed, their customers wanted a configurable application. Today Teqlo is restarting with this new insight. They learned the hard way that key insights about customers begin small, not broad. In the words of one of the investors, "Although you may dream of an ocean, you have to begin by understanding a puddle if you ever hope to make it to the ocean."[54] As you develop the Monetizable Pain Statement and Big Idea Hypothesis, it is fine to write down a number of different hypotheses, and later choose to focus on a few. However, each hypothesis should be specific to the needs of a particular customer group. This exercise is important to perform for every product launch, whether in brand-new startups, growing ventures, or follow-on products in established firms. Start the process from the beginning, especially if your first product has been successful. Don't get lazy!

STEP 3: TEST THE MONETIZABLE PAIN STATEMENT AND BIG IDEA HYPOTHESIS

Once you have written down the Monetizable Pain Statement and Big Idea Hypothesis, the next step is to conduct some quick tests of your hypotheses. At all phases in the NISI process, if you are going to fail, you want to fail fast and early. You don't want to waste too much time and too many resources only to discover you are wrong. The goal then is to get in the field, test your hypothesis, measure the results, and objectively determine whether you were right or whether you need to go in a new direction. Don't fall into the trap of overlooking the warning signals and convincing yourself you were right—changing course now will be easier than failing later.

To test your Monetizable Pain and Big Idea Hypotheses, you need to 1) find a sample of customers, 2) cold call or email them, and 3) capture and measure the results. To begin, identify which markets the potential customers operate in and generate lists to cold call or email them to validate that the problem you identified in fact causes significant pain for customers. We suggest you consider which customers you would like to have and then recognize that there are tiers of customers—starting at the low end will be easier, but you should still select some high-end customers in the sample. As you reach out to customers, cold calls often work well for getting the attention of businesses, whereas emails often work better when you try to initiate contact with consumers. It is also best to reach out to complete strangers because it removes any biases that might be caused by your prior relationship with people you already know. That being said, sometimes you have to start with people where you already have a relationship.

Below is a sample of the script that Classtop used in the initial customer contacts with university CIOs. This script generated a 50% response rate to emails and cold calls:

> *My name is Jared Allgood. I am currently a student, and we are developing a software application that would make it easier for teachers to manage their courses through Blackboard. As I've interviewed instructors and administrators from several schools, I hear some of the same two complaints repeatedly: 1) The first complaint from administrators is that they're paying a substantial license fee to use Blackboard, yet less than 20% of instructors actually use it. 2) Second, from instructors I'm hearing that populating Blackboard with course content is painful. Because of Bb's linear process, you can't carry out multiple functions quickly. We'd like your input and feedback on the product we're proposing to build. Do you have a few minutes to meet?*

Measuring the Monetizable Pain

Although reaching out via cold calls or emails may sound difficult, the most important initial tests of the Monetizable Pain Hypothesis is the rate at which customers return your calls. In other words, the value of the problem is the time they are willing to give you. How fast do they get back with you and the percentage response rate are important indicators of how significant the problem is for your customers. If 70% of CIOs return your cold call in twenty-four hours, you have clearly identified a monetizable pain. Although these numbers may seem high, we've had many startups achieve these kinds of response rates, and so as a general rule of thumb we use a 50% rule: if 50% of customers return your call, you have found the monetizable pain and a potential beachhead for your product. Of course the 50% rule represents more of a guideline; depending on the context or the customer segment, the cutoff may vary. Furthermore, if you get below a 50% response rate, don't be discouraged just yet: the low response rate may mean that you just haven't found the right customer niche or the right words to describe the pain to the customer. The good news is that even if the response rate to your initial request falls below the 50% cutoff, by talking to those customers who *do* respond, you can find clues about where to find the real monetizable pain. However, you will need to repeat your monetizable pain test again with a new group of customers before you move on.

> *If money is the measuring stick for how well people like your product, then time is the measuring stick for the value of the problem you are trying to solve.*

What to Say in Customer Conversations

Once you have customers on the phone, what should you say? It is important to understand that at this stage of the process you are not selling anything or even showing anything. However, the objective is to validate a pain that customers are willing to pay to solve. To do this, we have found it works best to structure your conversation around three key questions:

1. "Do you have this problem?" Describe the problem to your customer in words like, "We see this problem. Does that match your experience?"

2. "Tell me about it." Ask your customers to share their concerns, their experience, and their current solutions. Again, focus on listening, not selling.

3. "Does something like this solve the problem?" Describe the outline or framework of your problem. Again, don't get into the specific details but do give something customers something they can respond to, and ask for their feedback on whether it solves the problem.

Using these three questions, guide the conversation to test your Monetizable Pain Statement and Big Idea Hypothesis. Just as importantly if you take a close look, you will notice how these questions help you avoid the "Guardrail to Guardrail Trap" we discussed in the section on NISI fundamentals: these questions help you avoid selling and focus on listening. At the same time these questions aren't just open-ended questions where you ask your customers to innovate for you. Instead these questions establish confidence in the customers' minds that you understand their pain, help you see what you may not have been seeing, and then initiates the conversation where customers validate your innovation. In other words, used properly, these questions will help you stay balanced and avoid the extremes of the Guardrail to Guardrail Trap. Finally, as you conduct your interviews, be careful not to change your hypotheses too quickly—if you reformulate your hypotheses between every call the customer feedback will be difficult if not impossible to process, you will be like a weathervane blown every direction with the wind. Instead, test your hypotheses with a small sample of customers (three to six), reformulate, and test again. Focus is extremely important in running the NISI process. *Don't forget to focus!*

An Example of Nailing the Pain in Action

As they stood around the table for the ZipDX demo, the executives dropped their jaws when they heard the conference call. With the flip of a switch the ZipDX team transformed the grainy audio quality of an ordinary conference call into a stunning audio experience akin to a surround-sound movie theater. The response was always the same at every conference: nodding heads and big smiles, once executives heard the demo. To use the ZipDX solution, all a customer needed was a wideband audio-capable handset, easily available from Polycom resellers, and the ZipDX software took care of the rest. Nonetheless, despite a working product and an incredible demo, the ZipDX software didn't seem to be selling. Frustrated, the executive team, wondering what the problem was, and hired someone from our team to build a sales pipeline for the product with the Polycom resellers to drive sales.

Of course the instant we saw this problem we knew the problem wasn't building a pipeline—it was the Monetizable Pain and Big Idea Hypothesis. So the team helping ZipDX, led by Mark Richards, took the vague initial pain statement for the regional Polycom resellers about "growing their business" and began to study the resellers. The team found that regional Polycom resellers subdivided into segments based on the nature of their overall business. Then the team developed three hypotheses about pains that their customers might have: 1) closing VOIP customers, 2) selling high-end phones, 3) capturing conference call bridging revenue. The team then cold called nineteen of the customers, asking if they had one or more of these problems. Unfortunately, only five customers returned the call, which would be a failing grade for the 50% rule and corresponds quite accurately with the ZipDX's struggles to make progress.

However, the five customers who did respond could provide important clues, and so the NISI team called the customers. A few interesting observations emerged. First, although only five customers responded, 75% percent of the customers who also sold VOIP responded (four out of the five customers), which passes the 50% rule for a customer segment. Given the small sample size, whatever the team found would need to be tested again: nonetheless, for the VOIP segment, these interviews could provide important information. Much more interestingly, however, as the team discussed the problems the resellers faced and the ZipDX solution, the team soon found out that the fancy ZipDX capabilities didn't really matter at all for them. In fact, the fancy conference-call capabilities would be hard for the resellers to monetize. Instead, what the resellers wanted was something much simpler—they wanted reliable conference-call capabilities that worked well out of the box. That simple. Initially this proved a hard message for the ZipDX team to digest; however, with their new found knowledge of the VOIP customer segment and their monetizable pain, the CEO went and closed the largest deal in company history within a week.

The Hassle Test for the Monetizable Pain Hypothesis

In addition to finding a monetizable pain, measuring the monetizable pain is crucial because it helps you understand whether you have nailed the pain. The best test for the monetizable pain in a business-to-business application is the time it takes customers to respond and the response rate to your cold calls or emails. However, in consumer-oriented products, the response rate for some customers may provide you only weak evidence of the monetizable pain. For the business-to-consumer market, you may need to use an alternative test to understand whether customers have a pain. One test borrowed from the field is called the *smoke test*. Smoke tests are often used in engineering, software, and many other fields (including instrument making) to test whether the basics of a system work, while ignoring the details. For example, when building a prototype car, does the engine turn on and do the wheels roll? You may remember we have been emphasizing the importance of avoiding building products at this stage, and so you may wonder how a smoke test applies. One version of the smoke test for internet startups would be to spend a few dollars to post an ad for your non-existent product, and when users then arrive at your landing page, they are offered the chance to be first in line to try the beta if they provide their contact information and answer a question or two. The same idea can apply for something physical but instead would use a call-in number or other method for customers to contact you. The response rate to the smoke test and the hit rate on visitors providing you their information provide some data of interest, but those hit rates don't necessarily tell you whether you have a monetizable pain. How then could you get a proxy for the monetizable pain? Try the *hassle test*.

The hassle test takes the output of the smoke test, asks about the hypothesized problem, and asks respondents to rate the amount of hassle they face when dealing with this problem. The hassle report gives you an idea of the monetizable pain. To illustrate how this works in practice, consider the case of eKidsMovies.com, which wanted to provide movies for children in the range of five to ten years of age over the internet. How do you validate monetizable pain for the parents of children for a movie service that hasn't been built? To start, the NISI team conducted a smoke test by placing a Google ad for kids' movies online, which sent viewers to a smoke-test landing page (Figure 14 below).

Figure 14: eKids Smoke Test

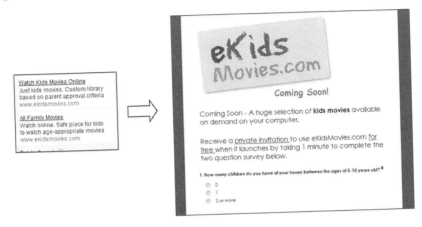

The response to the ad seemed positive: in six hours and for $30, the team received 88 respondents, of whom 36 fit the target profile. Of the customers in the target profile, 19 customers—over 50% of the target customers—offered their email. Since the response was over the 50% hurdle it passed the 50% test, right? Not just yet—receiving an email is not the same as validating the monetizable pain in an actual conversation. After receiving the emails, the NISI team tried emailing the respondents within a day of the survey, but only one person responded. Then they emailed a second time a few days later and received only two more responses. Definitely below the 50% rule of thumb.

So the team tried another tactic to see whether they had mis-phrased the pain or whether they might be barking up the wrong tree. Instead of asking for emails, the team ran the smoke test and asked those who came to rate the hassle they faced in relation to the online movies for children. The results proved insightful in several ways (Figure 15 for the results).

Figure 15: Results for the eKids Hassle Test

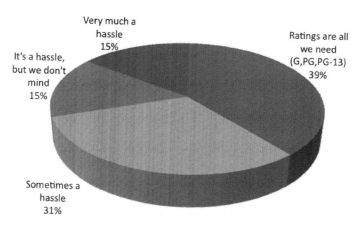

First, only 15% of customers really found the problem to be a hassle, which does not pass the test of being a monetizable pain. To move forward, a better threshold should be closer to 50%. Second, many customers reported that sometimes not having access to movies can be a hassle. These are the customers that make focus groups dangerous and have led to the saying "buyers are liars." If the eKidsMovies.com team had conducted focus groups, these customers would have been nodding their heads that finding online movies for their children was a hassle and they would pay for the service. However, only after the entrepreneurs built the site would they find out that in fact these customers wouldn't pay, because in truth, the problem did not represent a monetizable pain. Finally, the one problem with the smoke test was that the entrepreneurs didn't actually talk to customers, which means that although they found they didn't have a monetizable pain, they didn't have the clues as to how to change their hypotheses to find a real business. Clearly, online movies represent a viable business (think Netflix), but how and if that plays out for the segment of parents looking for children's movies remains to be seen.

CONDUCTING CUSTOMER RESEARCH: TURNING HYPOTHESES INTO FACTS

Getting into the field and talking to customers lets you test to see if your initial hypotheses are promising or duds. No matter what you do, remember the NISI fundamental to get into the field. While secondary research has value, most entrepreneurs fall back on this research or on the easiest forms of primary research, such as surveys. But surveys won't cut it—how do you even know what questions to ask until you have really talked with customers? You have to get into the field and actually talk to customers, which can be scary. But which would you rather do, talk to customers now and find out you were wrong, or talk to customers a year and thousands of dollars down the road and still find out you were wrong?

Three Types of Customers

As you conduct your customer research, keep in mind that there are different types of customers with whom you should talk. For many solutions to a pain, there may be up to three different customer stakeholders within the company: an end-user customer (the person who uses the product or manages people who use the product), a technical customer (the technical, often IT, person who installs or maintains the product), and an economic customer (the person who makes the ultimate purchase decision for the product). For example, for enterprise software, the end customer may be the VP of sales / sales reps, the technical customer would be the IT manager, and the economic customer may be a member of the executive team or CFO. Later in the NISI process we will have you explore more thoroughly the needs of each of these customer stakeholders, but at this point you might want to explore the different types of customers in order to validate how the customer pain you hypothesized is relevant for each customer. Even though you are conducting a quick test, it will be more accurate the more closely you target your real customers.

For example, two founders applying the NISI process targeted restaurants with a solution to communicate with customers waiting for a table. While the end users (the waiters and host) loved the solution, the economic/technical user (the restaurant owner) didn't care and saw a completely different problem (getting customers to come during down-times). Fortunately, the founders found this out early and changed to a solution that actually fit the customer pain.

Last, beware of noncustomers, for example, influential journalists, analysts or investors: while they can have wisdom, they aren't necessarily your customers. As passionate as we investors can sometimes be, it is important to remember that we are only one voice at the table and our input needs to be tempered with the real customer voices. Don't be intimidated by famously successful noncustomers—overweighting their feedback can lead you in the wrong direction. As an example, one entrepreneur we interviewed was told by Marc Andreessen, the famous serial entrepreneur, angel investor, and founder of Netscape, that his business would not work. What do you do when Marc Andreessen tells you your business won't work? If your customers are giving you indications that you have a monetizable pain, you listen to your customers and ignore the superstar. That's just what the entrepreneur did and today he is building a fabulously successful business.

Good Research Tactics

As you talk to customers, be sure to use robust research techniques so you accurately capture the conversation. You should try to record or take extensive notes on conversations so that later you and other team members can return to your notes and reflect on what you really heard. Often what you think you hear in the moment and what an audio recording reveals are much different. If you aren't able to record the conversation, one trick used by professional researchers is to sit down immediately after a conversation and take extensive notes—often notes immediately after a conversation are nearly as good as a transcript, whereas a few hours later, the details just slip from memory. This extensive record-taking should be used throughout all steps of the NISI process.

CONDUCTING SECONDARY RESEARCH: BORROWING THE FACTS

In addition to primary research with customers, you should also take a close look at secondary materials, including reports, analyses, and other published materials in an attempt to understand the customer pain. This helps you understand the competitive environment and the health of the industry you are attempting to enter. Media reports, analyst reports, or other publications may often provide clarity into a customer pain and point you to areas where you need further testing. For example, secondary research played an important role in the early evolution and founding of RecycleBank, a company that successfully tackled the problem of recycling. Co-founder Patrick Fitzgerald became curious about recycling while living in New York City during a city-wide debate about whether to continue the recycling program, given the low participation rates.[55] Fitzgerald began to do secondary research on both the economics of and barriers to recycling. His research uncovered three important facts. First, the economics of recycling are generally compelling for municipalities: cities often pay around $75 dollars a ton to dump waste, whereas recycling that same waste brings in an average $40 dollars per ton—a $115 spread per ton.[56] Second, many businesses were becoming increasingly socially conscious and looking for opportunities to be more socially responsible. Third, consumers are the major barrier to recycling because many consumers find it a hassle to recycle when they can just throw things away. In fact, despite the vigorous efforts of many states to put in place aluminum-can recycling programs, Americans still throw away enough soda cans to produce 6,000 DC aircraft per year! Fitzgerald began to wonder if he could combine the desire of businesses to be more socially responsible and municipalities' large margins to actually pay consumers to recycle.

Despite these positive signals, if Fitzgerald had stopped with his secondary research, he might have made a mistake many entrepreneurs make—taking secondary research as validation of their beliefs. The problem is that although secondary research can inform your hypothesis, it really represents borrowed facts and cannot substitute for getting out in the field to test your hypotheses. Remember, one of the fundamentals in the NISI process is to get into the field. So whatever you uncover in your secondary research, it cannot substitute for firsthand research, face-to-face with customers.

Fortunately, Fitzgerald's next step was to go out and test his hypothesis with businesses, municipalities, and consumers. The response was overwhelmingly positive—a signal that he may have hit on a customer pain and solution. Fitzgerald, and his co-founder Ron Gonen, ultimately went on to apply NISI principles in testing the market, and the business has been a dramatic success in every area it has been introduced. For example, in one Philadelphia neighborhood where the service was introduced, recycling rates shot from 7% to 90%, while landfill waste dropped dramatically.[57] In summary, use secondary research to provide insight into your Monetizable Pain Statement and Product Hypothesis; as well, it will help you identify other customer groups you may have overlooked, as was the case when RecycleBank identified three sets of customers: consumers, businesses, and municipalities.

Step 4: Quick Exploration of Market Dynamics and Competition

Finally, as you continue testing your Monetizable Pain and Solution hypotheses, don't overlook the 30,000 feet test. The 30,000-feet test simply asks you to back way off the nitty-gritty of talking to customers and ask yourself, How big is the problem I'm trying to solve, and is it worth it? While you might find a monetizable pain, you should also determine how many customers have this problem, who else is trying to solve it, and if you can assemble the right people to solve it. Many, many entrepreneurs we have talked to discover a customer pain, build a solution for the pain, and then realize only after the fact that they are actually tackling a rather small market, and the return isn't worth it or there is an 800-pound gorilla in the market that doesn't want to partner with them. Many times, customers have significant pains or desires, but because the market is small or shrinking, or because of a well-entrenched competitor, it may not be an attractive business opportunity. In the pharmaceutical industry, such small markets are recognized by the U.S. patent office as qualifying for "orphan drug status," a provision that gives a pharmaceutical company a lifetime patent, rather than the regular twenty-year patent, as an incentive to develop a drug for the market. Unfortunately, for the rest of the world, there are no "orphan" clauses that guarantee a market, and so your chances of success will be better if you try to tackle an appropriate market. The health of the market and the state of the competitive environment are two important questions to understand before your finish testing your key hypotheses.

Figure 16: Intersection of Product Strategy, Market Dynamics, and Competitive Environment

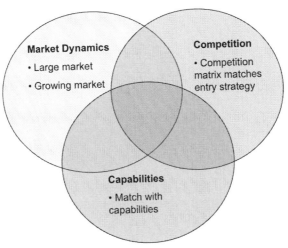

THE MARKET DYNAMICS TO TEST

The next step on drilling down on the market dynamics is understanding if the market you have chosen is big enough to care about and is growing or declining. If you succeed in this market, will the size of your success pass the "who cares?" test to make it worth your time. By using secondary research, you can determine if your market is growing, stagnant, or shrinking.

Sufficiently Large Market

Building a business in a tiny market can be challenging because there may be little room to grow, whereas in large markets there may be greater rewards to scaling the business. If you would like to build a business that is a candidate for venture capital financing or an initial public offering, you should probably only consider markets that are over $1B in addressable sales and where your company has the potential to achieve $100 million in sales. If you want to bootstrap or go a different route, a much smaller market can still be attractive. Regardless, the spirit of your answer should be whether the total addressable market (TAM) is large enough for you to spend your time on it. And although bigger could be better, there are several important caveats as you think about the initial attraction of big markets. First, large markets often have large competitors. If that is the case, the actual addressable market may be smaller, and you may have to tackle the edges of the market first or pursue a cooperative strategy to succeed in that market. Second, large markets are often composed of smaller vertical niches, and you should consider tackling a smaller niche first, knowing that you can tackle the larger market when you are successful. Third, disruptive products often attack new markets from the low-end and then work their way up to the high end of the market. In such cases low-end may mean initially smaller markets, lower-tier products, or addressing underserved customers.[38]

Rapidly Growing Market

You should also examine whether the market is growing. It is much easier to compete and succeed in growing markets. The old adage that a rising tide lifts all ships is particularly true in entrepreneurship. As Tom Siebel observed of early days in the information-technology industry, the market was growing so quickly, "all you had to do was show up and not screw up and you made money."[58] Although Siebel's comment has an air of sarcasm, researchers who examined the semiconductor industry found that firms in growing markets were much more successful than firms in mature or emerging markets.[59] In contrast, contracting markets may be the most difficult markets to tackle because customers are no longer investing, and existing competitors are desperately fighting for business.

Competition

Finally, when it comes to competition, the worst thing an entrepreneur can say is (and as it turns out a frequent thing they say) "We don't have any competitors." The truth is that you have competitors. Every good idea is probably being considered by someone else. Don't ignore them, but don't get too worried about them either. Some competition can be a good sign. The first company entering a market often faces significant challenges because they have to both educate customers about the product and learn each lesson by costly trial and error. Such challenges are called *pioneering costs,* and they are one reason why it can be beneficial to tackle a market where you can learn from the experience of competitors. In fact, Costas Markides and Paul Geroski, professors at London Business School, observed that for a large number of radical innovations—from tires, to cars, to plastics, to internet search—later entrants to a market often dominate the early pioneers to a market.[60] In the end, your application of the NISI process will differentiate you and put you ahead of competitors.

Of course, the second worst thing an entrepreneur can say is "There is an 800-pound gorilla in our space, and we are going to kill it because we have a better mousetrap." Such a statement is naïve and shows a lack of sophistication and appreciation for the battle you are about to undertake. Whether you have one large competitor or many small competitors, successful entrepreneurs create a competitive matrix to better understand their competitive landscape. With a competitive map in hand, you can create a battle plan for how you will attack this market. There has been a great deal written about strategy and attacking competitors, from Sun Tzu's *The Art of War* to the entire field of competitive strategy. Many lessons from this field may help you. For example, an 800-pound gorilla cannot be ignored. You will have to be careful not to attack the behemoths head-on; either tackle the edges of the market they can't serve or work cooperatively with them. Still, contrary to what you might think, markets with no competitors at all are not necessarily attractive either. In closing, let us remind you, when we talk about competition we aren't asking you to write a business plan—that will most likely trap you. Instead we are asking you to be aware of your competitive environment so you don't try to nail a pain that others have already definitively nailed.

CAN YOU RENT A HARLEY?: RULES, PATTERNS, AND CYCLES OF THE MARKET

Have you ever wanted to ride a Harley down the California coastline? Regardless of your preferences, if you tried to rent a Harley from one of the many dealers advertising rentals you might be in for a nasty surprise—they won't actually rent you a gleaming Hog with custom handlebars. At least they won't rent you a Hog if you are a novice, because you need experience riding motorcycles, particularly smaller bikes, before you have the skills to handle large Harley bikes. What the experience of trying to rent a Harley teaches us is that although the markets you are looking at may be attractive, you cannot overlook the rules, patterns, and cycles of the market. In particular, pay attention to government or industry rules and regulations. Often, simple regulations can block or enable a particular market solution.

In addition, be sure to look closely at the length of sales cycles (and always double your estimate of the sales cycle) and the entry point to those sales cycles. One startup had developed an incredibly disruptive technology for military applications. The founders leveraged their personal networks to contact the right customers in the military, and both the commanding officers and the purchasing agents were genuinely excited and ready to buy. The only problem was that in order for the military customers to buy the product, the military had to plan for the purchase in the next year's budgeting cycle, which meant actually planning to purchase the product in the prior year—a minimum two-year sales cycle! Although the founders were able to bootstrap for the next two years until the orders closed, it was an unpleasant experience to wait through a long sales cycle they had failed to foresee.

Finally, take a close look at the overall technology cycle of the industry. Although your customers may have a significant pain, is the market lifecycle ready to adopt your technology? Markets often progress through stages, and at one point in the cycle a product may fall flat, whereas at other points the product may succeed. Consider the Apple Newton, one of the first handheld devices. Although the Newton addressed what is clearly a customer pain today, the market wasn't ready yet, and the Newton failed miserably. Similarly, consider the case of YouTube: although there were many video-sharing sites before them, YouTube brought the right solution to the market at the right time.

OPTIMIZING YOUR OUTCOME FOR SUCCESS OR FOR EGO?

Last, consider how your capabilities fit or don't fit the ability to solve the customer pain. Lacking the capabilities to deliver a solution is fine if you can find people who can fill in those gaps for you. In fact, knowing your weaknesses and hiring or co-opting complementary talent is a critical entrepreneurial skill. On the flip side, be careful of situations where you have capabilities but are tempted to force fit them to the situation. Are you trying to create the best outcome for your company, or are you trying to optimize your company around a weaker market solution that you happen to have access to? Ask yourself if you could add other technologies or partnerships to create a better path to success. Take a moment now to allow yourself to be intellectually honest and consider if there is a better approach you could embrace. Are there other technologies I should partner with or additional patents I should license to increase the strength of my position? For example, successful venture capital firm ARCH Venture Partners has built a successful investment franchise by working with many competing universities to tie up all of the important IP before launching a new company. Therefore, don't let your current capabilities misshape your choice of the best opportunity. Many technologists get into trouble because they can't let go of their mousetrap in order to pursue a great opportunity, or they waste their time going after a weaker opportunity that happens to fit the mousetrap they designed. The famous organizational thinker Jim March called this the *garbage can model* of organization: rather than looking for a real problem to solve, sometimes organizations have solutions and spend their time fishing for problems that fit their solution.[61] This is one reason why Phase 1 of the NISI process focuses on the customer pain, not the solution. Find a real pain, and you find a real opportunity.

A REMINDER ON INNOVATING

We said it before, but it is so important we will say it again: entrepreneurs innovate, customers validate. As the entrepreneur, you should formulate the hypothesis about the customer pain; customers will validate whether you accurately understand the customer pain. However, customers won't usually tell you the customer pain. Simply asking customers what they want, or how they would solve the problem, usually produces answers that lead to bland "me-to" products because customers have a hard time imagining something that doesn't exist. But if you closely observe the jobs they are trying to get done and the obstacles they face, and truly understand the pain they are feeling, you are now well positioned to create an innovative hypothesis to solve that pain.[22]

Another way of thinking about the "job" your customer is trying to get done is to think about the outcomes customers would like to achieve.[62] To do this, try to leave behind traditional product categories and think instead about what your customers would really like to accomplish or how they might ideally solve their pain. As an example, Michael Ahearn, former CEO and Chairman of First Solar, the world's largest thin-film photovoltaic manufacturer, said that in the early days, the company

89

wouldn't even use the word *solar* in sales and product-development meetings. People didn't have a "solar problem," they had an energy problem. The goal of focusing on the pain, or what job customers are trying to do, is to allow you to think broadly about potential solutions. Anthony Ulwick provides an excellent example of this process in his discussion of Cordis, a medical-device company suffering from less than 1% market share for angioplasty balloons used to open blocked arteries. Although Cordis had come up with many new products, such as a balloon that increased blood flow while the surgery was being performed, the developers continued to struggle. When the Cordis team actually started talking to customers, they discovered that their product-development approach was completely off target. To reinvent their process, they instead focused on the outcomes customers were trying to achieve (the job) and asked surgeons what outcomes they were trying to realize. When surgeons tried to suggest solutions, they just dug deeper to discover the real job that surgeons were trying to accomplish. When surgeons said they wanted the device to be easy to maneuver, Cordis asked why, and found that surgeons wanted a way to navigate winding blood vessels. When cardiologists said they wanted the balloon to be smooth, the investigators asked why and learned that the desired outcome was to avoid accidentally slicing a vessel. Using these insights about the job their customers were trying to complete, Cordis completely reinvented its product line. The result was a tenfold increase in market share and a fivefold increase in revenue.

For you, the key at this stage is to do the hard work of understanding your customers' pain in terms of the job they are trying to do so that as an entrepreneur you can innovate a solution to that pain. Once you develop a solution, customers can play the role of validating your solution but they can't create it. In the next phase, you will develop and test a solution to the customer pain you have just validated. Not surprisingly, in the next phase the same logic applies—customers don't innovate, entrepreneurs do. And when you come up with a solution, customers will validate whether what you propose solves their pain. As you go through the process, you may find it helpful to review the brief NISI "checklist" at the end of the book where we summarize the steps in each phase of the process.

A Note on Monetizable Pain

We emphasized that if you identify a Monetizable Pain and solve it, you will be successful. However, we want to highlight that the "pain" that entrepreneurs encounter in the B2B market is significantly different from the type of pain entrepreneurs encounter in B2C businesses. For consumer-focused businesses, the "consumer pain" is often focused on solving their unmet needs. As consumers work to meet their needs of love, friendship, and diversity in their lives, they turn to social networking sites like Facebook or activities like the movies. According to Maslow, individual needs fall into three basic categories: 1) the basic needs of food, shelter, clothing and security; 2) the psychological needs of love, friendship, and the need to feel important; 3) self-fulfillment needs, like the need to create and experience diversity. If you can satisfy a core need, you will discover a business that has significant potential. But you have to ask yourself whether your solution is a vitamin or a pain killer? While it is true that some businesses are more "vitamins," in these cases the question should be, Is the vitamin sufficient to drive a customer purchase, or is there a hidden pain? For example, in our view, movie theaters and Facebook actually solve important pains: movie theaters fill a crucial need for entertainment, and Facebook fulfills the innate desire for social connection—services that people are willing to pay for with their money or their time. However, if you are tackling a "vitamin" business, you need to think carefully about how the principle of monetizable pain applies to your business. Will customers still pay for the vitamin? You will need to take extra caution, because while you can build a business on a lower pain scale than a shark-bite size monetizable pain, it will be more difficult. Also think carefully about businesses that draw their value from a massive user base, like eBay or Facebook. For businesses that benefit from network effects, you can still apply the principles discussed in this book, but the question of willingness to pay may need to be deferred in order to build a massive user base. In these cases, you want to proxy the Monetizable Pain with measures such as engagement and retention. Ultimately, often the best way to test a vitamin or pain killer is to follow our advice and as quickly and cheaply as possible test whether customers actually care or not.

PHASE 2: NAIL THE SOLUTION

In the early part of the 21st century, Intuit was already a multi-billion company with a bevy of blockbuster titles such as Quicken, QuickBooks, and TurboTax under its belt. It would be hard to argue that Intuit's products hadn't effectively "nailed" the solution to the customer pain they had observed long ago. But then managers at Intuit conducted some research that revealed a disturbing fact: although QuickBooks was number one in market share and name recognition for small-business accounting software, over 50% of American businesses didn't use accounting software. Instead, these entrepreneurs still kept their books with spreadsheets or even paper and pencil! Realizing that they may not have nailed the solution as well as they thought, a research team set out in 2004 to try and understand the problem. The team, led by Terry Hicks, visited over forty homes and offices, only to be quickly rebuffed. Not only did small businesses feel that traditional accounting had little to do with good small-business management, most business owners were actively hostile towards accounting software, as evidenced in the words of one business owner, "I don't need no stinkin' accounting!"[63]

Despite the outward hostility toward accounting software, the Intuit team did see a customer pain within that same market that was being poorly solved, even if it was their own product that had overshot the mark. Because the reaction from small business owners was so hostile, the team decided to build a series of rapid, inexpensive prototypes rather than following the traditional model of defining product specifications and building a new product. In the first prototype, Hicks and the team stripped down the existing QuickBooks software to make it simpler and then took it out to test with another round of customers in their homes and businesses. Once again, the reaction was negative, but the experience provided a catalyzing experience that helped the team see what had been blinding them. For one, the team realized that their definition of *simple* was much different than that of their customers—even the stripped-down prototype had 125 screens to set up the program. Moreover, the prototype still used standard accounting language, which was off-putting to the customers and piqued their distrust. According to Hicks, "It wasn't until we tried and failed with a prototype that the entire team was like 'Okay, now I get it.'"

In response, the team made a series of dramatic revisions to the prototype and through a number of iterations removed the accounting language and reduced the startup process from 125 to 3 screens. After a few final cycles of iteration, the product was named QuickBooks: Simple Start Edition and launched in September 2004.

The process the team used to define this new solution produced dramatic results—in the first year the Simple Start edition outsold all other accounting software in the United States with the exception of QuickBooks itself! By the end of 2005, revenue at the multi-billion dollar company rose 20%, and the stock price rose over 30%, most of which was due to the success of Simple Start. Although Intuit had long been a proponent of listening to customers, what the Simple Start team rediscovered was the power in nailing the solution for a specific customer pain.

In this phase of the NISI process you will develop and test your hypothesis about the solution. Another way of saying "the solution" is to say the "product or service," but rather than the traditional model of building a product, we will show you that you can move from the Big Idea Hypothesis in the previous phase, to a virtual prototype, and then an actual prototype, creating the solution in iterations, so that by the end you create a solution so perfectly matched to customer needs that your customers are the ones asking *you* for it. The process begins with you turning your Big Idea Hypothesis into a hypothesis about the minimum feature set based on the validated Monetizable Pain. Then you will conduct three sequential "tests" of your hypothesized minimum-feature-set solution. The tests progress from a virtual prototype test, to a prototype test, and finally to validation of the solution. Depending on what you find, it may be necessary to repeat a test, but by the end you will develop a product that fits the customer's need perfectly. Customers and outsiders will say, "Wow, they really nailed it!" To hit this goal, we will discuss three successive tests, or steps, you should apply.

Figure 17: Steps to Nail the Solution

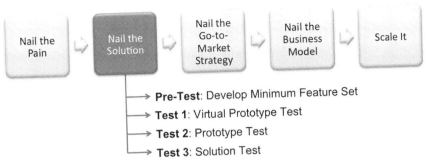

Pre-Test: Develop Minimum Feature Set

Test 1: Virtual Prototype Test

Test 2: Prototype Test

Test 3: Solution Test

In each test you will focus on the minimum feature set necessary for a customer to purchase.

PRE-TEST: DEVELOP A MINIMUM FEATURE SET (MFS) HYPOTHESIS

After completing the first phase of the NISI process (Nail the Pain), you should have some facts about the monetizable pain and a Big Idea Hypothesis about the product. The next step is to get more detailed about the solution by creating a hypothesis about the minimum feature set (MFS) that will solve the customer pain. Many people today have discussed the idea of a minimum viable product, defined as the smallest amount of product that will allow entrepreneurs to learn about their customers. This idea represents a powerful advance in the way we think about building companies and decreasing the cycle time to market. One challenge with the minimum viable product approach is that entrepreneurs can sometimes get lost in developing features customers like, but which ultimately do not drive the purchase. In contrast, the minimum feature set represents the smallest, most focused set of features that will *drive a customer purchase*. Think of the minimum feature set as the bull's-eye in a target—each concentric ring represents the features customers would like to have, but the bull's-eye represents the must-have features that drive the product purchase.

> *The minimum feature set represents the smallest, most focused set of features that will drive a customer purchase*

Discovering the minimum feature set has incredible power—it increases your flexibility dramatically because there are fewer features to change, it appeals to customers' desire for simplicity, and most important, it helps you discover the real core of what customers desire. Indeed, discovering the core features that drive purchase provides immense clarity about what to build and surprising power to attract customers. We have seen entrepreneurs strip down their well-featured product to the very core-purchasable product, only to find that the much more rudimentary product outsells their full-featured product by orders of magnitude. The reason has to do with what Malcolm Gladwell called *thin-slicing* in his book *Blink*. Gladwell argues that many experts are able to make accurate snap-judgments because subconsciously they have developed the ability to sort out the two or three core features of a problem that really matter from a sea of irrelevant features. In an entrepreneurial context, when you focus on the MFS, you help customers go through this same process by stripping out all the noise created by extra features and help them recognize the real value in your solution.

In addition to helping customers recognize your core-value proposition, focusing on a minimum feature set can be a powerful development tool. If a startup focuses on developing fewer features, they can move much more quickly for much less money. Playcafe was an innovative, participatory broadcasting network that failed in part because they forgot about the minimum feature set. When reminiscing on his experience, one of the founders lamented the fact that they hadn't kept it simple. By keeping it simple, they could have

> *By keeping it simple, they could have moved more quickly and tried more things before the money ran out ... "A chess novice can defeat a master if moving twice each round."*

moved more quickly and tried more things before the money ran out. In his words, "A chess novice can defeat a master if moving twice each round."[64] The speed of a minimum feature set also allows you to get to the market faster to get feedback on your product. That rapid feedback in turn gives you both the information and the time to make changes. Because you haven't invested deeply in the product, it is easy and relatively painless to make changes that really do respond to the feedback you have received.

So how do you know if you have the minimum feature set? This can be challenging, because your customers will ask for dozens if not hundreds of features. There are three general rules of thumb to follow. First, look for the key themes in the conversations you have had so far. Focus on the areas that customers repeatedly discuss and try to avoid the temptation to develop something cool but tangential. Second, ask your customers! You can assess or even rate the degree to which a feature is central to solving the core customer pain, but you can also ask customers which one feature matters the most to them. (We will provide you some specific tools to do this later in the chapter.) Third, simplify, simplify, simplify. Despite your desire to add features, strip out these features and focus on the absolutely core features. There is elegance in simplicity. French author Antoine de Saint-Exupéry said, "In anything at all, perfection is finally attained not when there is no longer anything to add, but when there is no longer anything to take away."[65] If a feature isn't absolutely critical, or if you have to debate it, leave it out. The features you view as necessary are almost always more, by an order of magnitude, than what is required for the minimum feature set. Although you might feel the product is terrible, it is better to create a prototype based on these features than one that takes you a great deal of time. If you are having a hard time keeping it simple, use this simple trick to convince yourself and your customers: simply assign those extra features to the next release, and you will be mentally freed up to focus.

The Minimum Feature Set Fallacy

Many entrepreneurs naturally resist our advice because it cuts against everything they know about building products. We've all heard the statistics about the danger of word of mouth: every unsatisfied customer tells ten other customers. So how could we tell you to risk negative word of mouth? The reason has to do with not understanding the technology-adoption life cycle we described earlier. If we take a closer look at the technology-adoption life cycle, you will see that your intuition is right—customers can be put off by an imperfect product and spread negative word of mouth; but this only matters when a product reaches the early majority *after* crossing the chasm (Figure 18). For this reason Moore argued that to cross the chasm, startups need a Whole Product Solution—the complete solution to a customer need. But the truth is that most new ventures never get close to the chasm, and the reason is that they think they can build the Whole Product Solution on day one by planning and then executing their way to success. Once entrepreneurs start building their product, they almost inevitably develop *Feature Creep Syndrome*. Over and over, we've observed that once entrepreneurs start building a product but then struggle to sell the product, their knee-jerk reaction is to add another feature in the hopes that the one missing feature will open the magical door to more sales. Entrepreneurs react so predictably by adding features we call it Feature Creep Syndrome. But Feature Creep Syndrome covers up the core of what your solution does that drives customer value and purchase.

Figure 18: Minimum Feature Set versus Whole Product

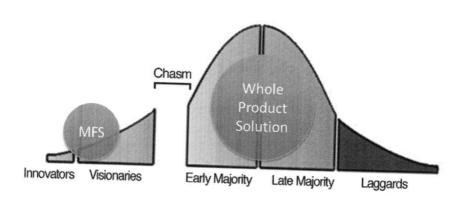

The path to success begins with a minimum feature set that strips the product down to the absolute core value exchange that drives purchase. By simplifying the product, you can uncover this core exchange and features, and once these features are discovered, the product can be perfected through a series of iterations in partnership with customers until you reach the whole-product solution. But if you start trying to build the whole-product solution first, you will waste time, money, and resources, and fight your way uphill to a downward failure without ever seeing clearly what makes your product successful.

Develop the Minimum Feature Set Hypothesis

To develop a minimum feature set, rely on your observations of customer pain and hypothesize a solution. Once you observe a customer pain, it is your job to come up with a solution to that problem. If you make the mistake of relying entirely on your customers to create a solution for you, you will likely find unsurprising and unimaginative responses that don't actually solve the pain. Steve Jobs said, "You can't just ask customers what they want and then try to give that to them. By the time you get it built, they'll want something new." As an example, several years ago Kawasaki was the leading producer of jet skis. Kawasaki observed that customers felt a very literal pain from having to ride their jet skis standing up. Wanting to respond to the customer pain, the designers at Kawasaki asked customers how to solve the problem, and customers suggested thicker padding to protect their legs. Like good listeners, Kawasaki did just as customers asked and added more padding. However, more innovative competitors realized something customers hadn't suggested: a seat is more comfortable than standing, no matter how much padding you have. When Kawasaki's competitors came out with the new, seated jet skis they stole so much market share from Kawasaki that Kawasaki lost their market lead forever to innovative new market entrants such as SeaDoo and Wave Runner by Yamaha.[62]

> *"You can't just ask customers what they want and then try to give that to them. By the time you get it built, they'll want something new."*
> *–Steve Jobs*

As the entrepreneur, you are responsible for defining a solution to the problem. You might begin by brainstorming, sketching, or writing down potential solutions. At this stage, you should be focused on getting your best guess written down on paper—*paper* being the key word. You don't want to build anything yet. The reason is that if you earnestly start to build the product, you will more likely get locked in to the solution you are developing. The goal is to have something you can discuss with customers but which won't commit you to a particular path. The rest of this phase of the NISI process will focus on validating and developing your solution hypothesis so that when you begin to build your product or service, you make what customers really want. If you are applying the NISI process midstream and already have a product or technology, then test your existing solution but take extra care to allow yourself to really listen to customers.

So how should you interact with customers? Although customers typically won't innovate, they can give you crucial information, including validation of your hypotheses. Before you can appropriately listen to customers, you will first need to remove your own personal bias, which we discussed in the fundamentals section as "developing intellectually honest learning." In addition, throughout this phase and the other phases, you should focus on deep observation of the job your customers are trying to get done. Don't ask your customers "what" they want, try to understand the job they are trying to do, the problems they have and the "why" behind them. More specifically, try to understand the root "why," not just the surface "why." To do this, you can apply the Toyota *5-why* approach, where you keep asking "why" to get to the root cause. The 5-why approach is simple: each time you come to an answer, you ask another why, until you discover the base driver of a problem.

As an example of this approach, consider the example of Motive Communications, which tried to increase the efficiency of IT help desk. At first, customers responded that the problem was the growing time it took to handle IT support calls. When the Motive team asked "Why?" they found that IT support professionals complained that their callers' computer systems were more complex than they once used to be. When the team asked why it took more time to handle these problems, the customers told them that they had to spend more time diagnosing a caller's system than it took to even begin managing the problem. By continuing to ask "Why?" eventually the team discovered that the real problem was the time it took the IT support professional and the user to establish the specifications of the users' support plan, their computer, and their software configuration. Motive's big idea was that they could save IT support operations time by automating the communication between a user's computer and the IT support database. By creating software that allowed computers to communicate directly, Motive could entirely eliminate this time-consuming process in IT support operations. If Motive had only focused on the surface problem—an increase in call time and volume—they might have missed the deeper root problem and developed a product that only partially fit the real pain.

To really understand the pain and solution to that pain, you have to get deep into customer thinking. Focus groups won't do the trick, in part because focus groups are so easily manipulated and biased by the abstract nature of the situation. Surveys are also tempting, but they only provide you the illusion of genuinely understanding customers. Before you get out and talk to customers, you won't really know what questions to ask in a survey anyway. Sometimes startups, especially web startups, confuse online surveys and A/B testing with having gathered adequate information. For example, one company we will nickname WebBusiness argued that they had tried to gather the data from customers using online surveys, but customers just wouldn't respond, and so they couldn't get the facts. A closer look suggested that not only had the founders of WebBusiness failed to actually talk to customers, they had created a gargantuan survey that even their most fanatical customers wouldn't sit through. Please do recognize that surveys, A/B testing, and other quantitative metrics have their place, but only when you understand what questions to ask.

Instead, if you talk to actual customers and get deep into the customers' pain and the work they are trying to accomplish, you will find valuable insights. Trader Joe's is an extremely successful gourmet grocery chain that began as a small shack and today has spread throughout most of the United States due to their understanding of their customers. In fact, Trader Joe's has doubled the industry average in sales per square foot, and their interaction with customers is masterful. Rather than tracking how much customers buy, Trader Joe's tries to understand their customers deeply—who they are, what they like, what their habits are, even what they read. Outside observers have noted that their approach "goes beyond the superficial findings of focus groups into

> *"We feel really close to our customers. When we want to know what's on their minds, we don't need to put them in a sterile room with a swinging bulb."*
> *—Audrey Dumper, VP Trader Joe's*

the realm of retail anthropology and social science to observe consumer behavior and root out unfulfilled needs."[66] In fact, Trader Joe's popular tropical theme was developed by the founder, Joe Coulombe, who observed that his customers loved to travel and were enticed to try new things in foreign locations. Today, Trader Joe's not only asks and listens to what customers want, they anticipate what customers want by understanding their needs deeply. According to Audrey Dumper, VP of marketing, "We feel really close to our customers. When we want to know what's on their minds, we don't need to put them in a sterile room with a swinging bulb."[67] The approach of listening deeply to customers is central to the success of the second phase. Spend your time listening to customers and try to understand their work from their perspective.

TEST 1: THE VIRTUAL PROTOTYPE TEST

The focus of the first test is to discover whether your minimum feature-set hypothesis is anywhere near the mark of solving the customer pain. The results of the test should provide you some deeper validation of the customer pain, some initial validation of the solution, and plenty of insights and surprises about the actual solution to the customer pain. In fact, most startups that carefully go through this process are shocked at what they find, so be prepared for surprises. The objectives of the first test are to develop a profile of relevant customers, refine your initial hypotheses about the minimum-feature-set solution, outline a customer-defined solution that adds value to all the relevant stakeholders, and determine which is the best market to attack first. And of course, as we've already emphasized, you should always be willing to change direction if needed.

DEVELOP A CUSTOMER PROFILE

Based on your work in nailing the pain, you should have a sense of the markets and applications where your customers have a problem that you can solve. The first step in the solution-hypothesis test is to conduct a more scientific analysis of the relevant customers you need to address. You will create a Customer Profile that will be useful as you conduct research on your customers in all the remaining steps.

The Customer Profile begins with the recognition that there are multiple types of customers. In particular there are three especially relevant customers to understand: the economic, the technical, and the end users. Economic users are the ones who hold the purse strings and buy the product. Technical users are the ones responsible for implementing, integrating, or maintaining the product. End users are the individuals who actually use the product in their day-to-day lives. Sometimes these users are all the same person, but if the users are different people and you fail to address each of them, it can mean losing the sale and failing. For example, although an end user may rave about your product, if the technical user refuses to implement the product because it is built on the wrong operating system or doesn't have the right open architecture ... then the sale is dead. The way out of this dilemma is to add value to all the relevant users, and to do that, you first need to analyze and understand these different users.

Another way to think about this problem is to consider the customer *buying panel*. In other words, who are all the customer stakeholders that will be involved or have influence in buying this product or service, and what are their opinions? Ford discovered this lesson the hard way in 1958 on the back of their terrible failure in developing the Ford Edsel. Ford spent over $400 million developing the Edsel in secret, promising American consumers an innovative line of cars that fit their needs. But when the cover was finally taken off the Edsel in a promotional television spotlight, people were disappointed—the styling didn't click, and the fundamental design didn't seem to break new ground.

Figure 19: The Ford Edsel

Not only did Ford forget the relevant customer buying panel, they hid from the customer panel altogether. Stinging from this major loss, Ford took a different approach in developing the next line of cars. This time, Ford designers, led by Lee Iacocca, brought customers into the design process as well as into prototype showrooms and asked for feedback. And not only did they bring the customer, they brought the entire buying panel together at the same time, which in this case was usually husband and wife. Six years after the failed Edsel launch, on April 17, 1964, Ford released the Mustang and sold 22,000 Mustangs on the first day of sales. After the first year, Ford sold 418,812 units, making it the most successful launch in Ford history.

The Customer Profile Matrix

To develop a profile of your customers, create a matrix of target markets and organizations within those markets. Then do some searching to see if you can find some of the relevant buyers in each organization within each market. Table 1 is an abbreviated example of the kind of matrix you might develop.

Table 1: Customer Profile Matrix

Market A	Market B
Organization 1 Economic buyer = V.P. Marketing - John Cheap, jcheap@organization1.com 800.555.1212 Technical user = System Administrator - Matt Tech, mtech@organization1.com 800.555.1212 End User = Marketing Manager - Mary Friend, mfriend@organization1.com 800.555.1212	**Organization 1** Economic buyer = V.P. Marketing - Jeff Cheap, jcheap@organization1.com 800.555.1212 Technical user = System Administrator - Mac Tech, mtech@organization1.com 800.555.1212 End User = Marketing Manager - Missy Friend, mfriend@organization1.com 800.555.1212
Organization 2 Economic buyer = V.P. Marketing - Jerry Cheap, jcheap@organization2.com 800.555.1212 Technical user = System Administrator - Mike Tech, mtech@organization2.com 800.555.1212 End User = Marketing Manager - Mandy Friend, friend@organization2.com 800.555.1212	**Organization 2** Economic buyer = V.P. Marketing - Jason Cheap, jcheap@organization2.com 800.555.1212 Technical user = System Administrator - Marty Tech, mtech@organization2.com 800.555.1212 End User = Marketing Manager - Macy Friend, mfriend@organization2.com 800.555.1212

Although it might seem difficult to fill the matrix in, through a combination of online networking and social-media tools (such as LinkedIn, ZoomInfo, and Facebook), as well as asking around, making some phone calls, and leveraging your network, you should be able to begin to fill in at least part of the matrix. Once you identify a key influencer within an organization, task that person to help you organize a meeting with other key decision makers within that organization. If the pain is significant enough, they will be glad to bring together their internal buying panel to discuss with you potential solutions to the pain they are feeling. In fact, with your help, this may be the first time they have been able to pull together a cross-functional team to discuss this important issue.

Another important question to consider is which customers would you like to have? Customers often fall into different groups or segments. How do your customers differ in terms of their needs, their willingness to pay, and their openness to working with a new venture? For example, even among similar types of customers, some customers will be at the lower end and others at the higher end. Would you like to work with Microsoft, or a smaller software company? As you build customer profiles, keep two things in mind. If you have really hit on a monetizable pain, even large customers, like a Microsoft, might be willing to work with you. On the other hand, because these large customers are often early-majority customers (rather than innovators or early adopters), they will most likely be reticent to work with you. Nonetheless, that shouldn't prohibit you from understanding your customers at that tier, and if you find an innovator, that company may work with you. One startup that was developing media-rich online channel software approached the Kansas City Chiefs and the Cincinnati Bengals while applying the NISI process and received an enthusiastic open door. However, most likely you will need to focus on innovators or the lower tiers of the market who will be more open to working with a new venture. You will find you are able to get your foot in the door with the innovators, and then over time you can work your way up to the top-tier players.

CHOOSE A RAPID PROTOTYPING TECHNOLOGY AND DEVELOP A VIRTUAL PROTOTYPE

During the first test, your objective is to develop a virtual prototype to test the minimum feature set with as little cash as possible. To do this, begin by developing a prototype of your eventual product solution. Prototypes are an inexpensive way to quickly test to what degree an idea will work or a product will solve a customer's problem. Rapid prototyping is a tool employed by the most prolific innovators, from IDEO to Google. For example, IDEO, an innovative product-design firm famous for coming up with unusual new ideas, always uses inexpensive, rapid prototypes to quickly discover whether a product fits the needs of the user. In one case where an IDEO team was designing a medical device on paper, a team member made a prototype with modeling clay, put it in the hands of a physician, and the physician immediately reacted that the placement of the handle was awkward and needed to be moved. Similarly, Google has a rule of thumb that any new ideas should be prototyped quickly and cheaply in a day, or at most a week. Google has found that prototyping quickly and inexpensively is a key part of rapidly developing the solution. In the words of Marissa Mayer, VP at Google, "By limiting how long we work on something or how many people work on it, we limit our investment. In the case of the Toolbar beta, several key features (custom buttons, shared bookmarks) were tried out in under a week. In fact, during the brainstorming phase, we came up with about five times as many 'key features.' Most were discarded after a week of prototyping. Since only one in every five to ten ideas works out, the strategy of limiting the time we have to prove that an idea works allows us to try out more ideas, increasing our odds of success. Speed also lets you fail faster."[8]

For the first test, we encourage you to develop a virtual prototype, rather than an actual prototype, because it will allow you to test your solution hypothesis immediately and then rapidly change course if needed. A virtual prototype allows you to get out in the field rather than wait to build a physical actual prototype; and a virtual prototype represents the ultimate tool in keeping your mental flexibility high and your commitment to sunk costs low. To do this you should choose a prototyping technology or approach that costs a fraction of what the actual development technology costs. You might consider using PowerPoint/Keynote, Flash, HTML, Visio, Creately or any number of other technologies, including pen and paper, to create a prototype. The key is that your prototype or "virtual prototype" should be inexpensive and quick to develop relative to the traditional approach. Examples include creating a Flash-based mock-up for software, an HTML model of a solution, or a PowerPoint presentation. If you are building physical products, try a drawing, but if you must have a physical prototype, be creative, use standard components (parts you can purchase from a hardware store), or find a partner.

Phone Calls and Visits to Understand How the Solution Solves the Pain

Next you should engage your customers in a dialogue about the potential solution to the problem you observed. To do this effectively you need to focus on detaching yourself from your biases, get on the customers' side of the table, look at the problem from their perspective, and make them feel that you truly want to learn how they feel about this problem and potential solutions. Remember the "Guardrail to Guardrail Trap": Avoid selling, because that will distort your ability to hear what your customers are saying. If your potential customers feel that you are not selling but earnestly want to learn about their problem and get their feedback, they will respond to you in surprising ways, even if you haven't correctly identified the pain. They will provide open and candid feedback. If you use the interview as a ploy to sell your product, they will either reject you outright, or you will fail to hear what customers are really saying and build a product that fails to meet their needs. On the other hand, use the questions we highlighted earlier to create confidence in your customer and make sure you are using your conversations to validate your innovation instead of making the mistake of asking customers to innovate for you.

Develop an Interview Guide

To begin the process, you should develop a list of questions you would like to ask your customers. The interview guide shouldn't be too long, not more than a few questions. The interview questions should focus on trying to understand the pain, how they solve that pain, and their reaction to your solution. The three questions you used earlier can be modified to test the solution hypothesis:

1) Seek to understand. We believe you have this problem. Is this accurate? (Create confidence that you understand the problem but listen to understand their problem. Ask them to describe it and how they solve it.)

2) Show solution. Does this solution solve your problem? (Share your virtual prototype and ask them for advice on the solution. The more specific your prototype, the better your feedback.)

3) Test customer demand. What would this solution need to have, for you to purchase it? (Push your customer as to whether they would actually purchase. However, as you do so, remember the purpose of this question is not to sell but to observe the customer's reaction. If you close a sale, you have validated the demand for your solution! But, if the customer hesitates, use this question to explore their concerns and understand the hurdles that stand between you and a future sale.)

In the first question, you are creating confidence in your customers that you are legitimate, while at the same time trying to understand their pain. Specifically, you want to describe yourself as a company working in the area or developing a product, describe the pain, and then search for a customer reaction to tell you whether you are on the right track. You should take some time to ask further details about the problem they face and how they deal with it. Your goal is to understand what they are doing and why.

For the second question you want to show the customer your virtual prototype and react to it. Specifically, you want to tell customers you are developing the solution and would like their advice about whether it solves their pain. Take care: if you are too general in seeking advice, you will get general, rather worthless feedback. That is the point of the virtual prototype—if you give customers something specific to react to, they will give you specific feedback. Ask follow-on questions, such as what would it need to have to solve the problem?

Finally, for the third question, ask the tough question whether customers would purchase the product and what they would expect to pay. Don't dodge this question because you are afraid to sell. At this point you aren't selling. If the willingness of customers to give you their time was the measure of nailing the customer pain, the willingness of customers to pay is the measure of nailing the solution. At this stage it is highly unlikely that you have nailed the solution and that customers will sign-up to pay you (if they are interested, add them to the beta). Instead, think of the payment question as an indicator of how close you are to nailing the product. In other words, if your customer isn't interested in purchasing, politely drill down as to why he or she doesn't want to purchase. The answer will tell you what to do in order to nail the solution.

For an extended suggested set of interview questions and guidelines, see the appendix. Remember that in general, avoid questions that will produce a yes or no answer (you get no information), and steer clear of questions that are too complex or require the customer to fully "solve" the problem.

Develop a Credible Company Image

Last, as you prepare to take your virtual prototype out on the road, take a moment to develop a credible company image. For just a few dollars you can use Logoworks.com or 99designs to create a logo and professional business cards; and put up a website that will make you look like a legitimate and credible business. Again, you can spend a modest amount. You don't need to hire a custom website developer at this stage or a graphic designer to create a $10,000 logo and letterhead. Instead use the many free tools and templates available to create a quick and credible image. Businesses such as Weebly or Wordpress can give you configurable templates, tools, and applications that allow you to develop and host a website for free or an extremely modest sum. Ultimately, create a credible image, but don't let it slow you down or spend much of your resources.

Craft an Introductory Email and Contact Relevant Stakeholders

Next you should craft text for an email/call to set up an initial phone conversation or an onsite customer visit, much as you did in the previous phase. You might include language such as "We have observed that this market issue is a challenge and are very interested in your feedback on a potential solution," or "We are creating the next version of our software, and while we are formulating our ideas we are looking to get customer feedback before we lock in the features." If you have an introduction to a customer at this stage, feel free to use it, but cold calls or emails are an important test of the customer pain, as discussed earlier. If you can make cold calls, they are preferable, because they are much more likely to catch the attention of your customer (we all receive many emails, and they are easy to ignore). Remember that the "hit rate" on your cold calls or emails is a strong indicator whether you have correctly identified and verbalized the customer pain. For B2B cold calls, the threshold should be 50%, and for cold emails the threshold can be a bit less. As specific evidence, one new venture applying the NISI process with a web-content monitoring solution approached retailers such as REI, Barnes and Noble, Under Armor, and Skechers, as well as smaller brands such as Skis.com and Evogear. In framing the message they tried to get into their customer's shoes and think about what keeps the executives up at night. Then they made cold calls with a message about this pain and achieved an over 70% hit rate. Another startup sent out emails to CIOs in large organizations and had an over 50% hit rate. These rates of response are very strong validation that they were tackling the right pain with the right message.

In contrast, as MyFamily.com was working to develop a new genealogy product, they had the right general idea—they talked with customers—but they completely forgot about the need to focus on the customer's pain. The first mistake the team made was that when initial appointments with customers were hard to make, the executives passed off the task to administrative assistants. For one, failing the cold call test means you may have missed the pain, you are not communicating the pain in your customer's language, or you may simply be speaking to the wrong customer. For another, by passing off the task of making calls or emails to an administrative assistant, the team also lost the opportunity to observe how customers reacted—specifically the valuable lesson that can be learned from an awkward silence or an enthusiastic reception. Yet another mistake was that the phone caller asked simply to come and observe customers doing genealogy in their home—the assistants didn't mention the customer pain or a potential new solution for it. If you don't mention the pain point, you won't be able to connect to the customer's pain. Instead the calls to customers had a very low hit rate, and after making hundreds of calls, the administrative assistants were only able to scare up a few customers willing to talk. Ultimately, these customers weren't really people who personified the customer pain; rather they were just polite people who conceded. So remember, contact customers yourselves, talk to them about the pain, avoid selling, and be prepared to listen.

Conduct Detailed Phone Interviews or Visits

Once customers agree to talk—and ideally you should aim for 30- to 60-minute interviews—key representative members of your team should listen to the phone call as you tease out the issues with the customer. It would be ideal if your key team members were present, for two important reasons: first, different people often "hear" different things, and combining these multiple perspectives after the fact will help keep you honest; second, it is important that everyone on your team understand the pain and get aligned with the solution early on. Remember, when Intuit developed QuickBooks Simple Start, only after the entire team had feedback from relevant customers did it really begin to click. While it may seem that bringing your team together may be inefficient and take too much time away from work, in the words of Stephen R. Covey, author of *The Seven Habits of Highly Effective People*, "When it comes to people, slow is fast and fast is slow."[68] The quickest path to achieving team, customer, and product-market alignment is to involve your team in the process.

In addition, you should record and then transcribe the meeting. Again, the reason is that in the heat of the interview, the engineer and the product manager will hear different things. You will miss certain nuances in what your customers tell you which a transcript will help you see. As a side note, you should always ask for permission to record a conversation, and you might consider offering to keep the contents of the interview confidential. If your customer doesn't want to be recorded, here is a trick that researchers use—take copious notes during the interview and then immediately thereafter find a quiet place and create your own pseudo-transcription. You will capture a surprising amount of content if you do it immediately. But if you wait a few hours, or worse, an entire day, you will forget most of the subtleties of the interview.

During the interviews, pay attention to how your customers describe their pain and respond to your proposed solution. You should focus on listening to your customers' responses as evidence for *or* against your hypothesis. Remember, the purpose isn't to prove you are right by selectively listening; the purpose is to find out the facts, even if they prove you wrong. With the facts, you can either move forward or return to the drawing board.

Analyze then Revise Your Minimum Feature Set Hypotheses

Once you have had four to six phone calls or meetings with potential customers, analyze the transcribed interviews for common themes that can be used to revise your solution hypotheses. Something you may notice as you start interviewing customers is that the first few interviews may not yield any coherent insights. However, after you have a handful of interviews, themes and trends will suddenly begin to emerge. These themes are the key to understanding what your customers are really telling you. Once you have these facts in hand from the customers, you may need to revise and adapt your solution hypotheses and take your revised ideas to a second or third round. Once again, take the attitude of the scientist—be passionate about solving the problem, not proving your solution. Remove your own personal bias and be willing to abandon what you thought was a great idea if the market tells you otherwise. All great artists, inventors, scientists, and entrepreneurs are willing to abandon an idea in favor of a better one. The same applies as you revise your minimum-feature-set solution hypotheses: you may need to let go of your solution in order to come up with the right solution. If you have identified a real pain point and a solution to that pain, you will know it by your customers' enthusiastic response. But again, don't fall into the common entrepreneurial learning traps—don't move forward if you don't have any supporting facts. Either revise and retest or move on to the next idea.

An In-depth Example: Motive Communications

Motive Communications is another company that applied these ideas and one we will reference as a case study throughout the following chapters. Motive Communications, which was founded in the late 1990's, tried to tackle the burgeoning problem of offering tech support. At the time, tech support was a $69 billion market (big market), expanding rapidly (growing market), and with some vendors in the call tracking space, but few in the tech-support automation space (moderate competition). More important, tech support was becoming radically inefficient (big problem). Indeed, tech support was being solved largely by a rapidly growing and expensive cadre of support personnel who would get on the phone, spend a good deal of time interrogating customers about their system, and then try to solve their problem by trial-and-error based on their own exposure to similar problems. As computers became more complex and the knowledge-base expanded, tech support was becoming a massive headache for many organizations.

Prior to founding Motive Communications, the founders, including Mike Maples Jr., did an extensive search to identify and test customer pain. This included identifying twenty different customer pains, which they tested with experts and customers in the industry before finally settling on the problem of tech support. In reflecting on this time period and the search for a problem to solve, Maples recalled that they weren't just looking for a pain, they were looking for a tourniquet—something so painful that the company needed a solution immediately.[69] However, when it came time to test their solution, Mike and his team applied three progressive tests. In the first test, Mike and his team didn't build the product yet. In fact, one of the founders, Scott Harmon, recognizing the importance of understanding the danger of building a product, first mandated that "no product shall be developed prior to customer input."[70] Instead the Motive team focused on testing their hypothesis about the solution. To do this, the Motive Communications team decided that both phone calls and on-site observations of how their customers currently solve the problem currently were going to be necessary. As you may remember, at this stage in the process you should be focused on listening, and that is precisely what the Motive founding team did. In particular, during the on-site visit, the founding team spent most of their time watching support engineers do their job. Several important insights emerged; most important, they found that support engineers spent up to 75% of their time figuring out the level of service a customer was entitled to and the details of the customer's computer system. Although Mike and his team had hypothesized that they could apply software solutions to improve the IT support process, not until they began to test their solution hypothesis did they see the problem and solution clearly. Suddenly the team realized that the root problem was one of communication, and if Motive could automate the communication process around identifying the service level and the system specifications, they could cut out a massive portion of the time and cost of the process. The insight was staggering. In a $69 billion industry that was growing rapidly, they were just beginning to discover a solution worth close to $50 billion in savings to the industry!

BAD NEWS, GOOD NEWS, AND LEARNING TO ADJUST

During this phase you will get both bad news and good news from customers. Take the facts as they come and either adjust or realize that another idea might work better. Entrepreneurship is a roller coaster with extreme highs and extreme lows—elated on Monday and dejected by Thursday—but before you give up, be sure to consider how you might tweak or change your model. Each time we encounter a serious challenge in one of our startups, we say, "Between launch and the finish line, there will be one thousand near-death experiences that could kill my startup. I just need to move past them...one at a time." Successful entrepreneurs have an optimistic mindset (almost a survival instinct) that requires them to constantly adjust to negative feedback and optimize a new path forward based on the new hand they are dealt each day. Given our earlier warnings about the dangers of passion leading to blindness, notice the subtle distinction: the willingness to change in response to feedback, and the optimism to innovate a new path versus persistence in your own isolated beliefs. For example, consider the company E.piphany, a customer-relationship management system that went on to become one of the biggest IPOs of its time. When Steve Blank, one of the founders of E.piphany, went out to test the team's hypothesis with customers, the feedback was often positive. In one meeting with Silicon Graphics, a $2B company at the time, the VP of Marketing validated everything Steve suggested in the product, but when Steve asked whether Silicon Graphics would work with E.piphany as a pilot customer, the VP of marketing blurted out, "No, of course not." The VP went on to say that Silicon Graphics had already recognized the problem and built its own software to solve it. Steve's heart sank. As he described it,

Talk about feeling your bubble deflate fast. I went from feeling the high of believing that I might have an early customer in an innovative company to the low in realizing that they'd never buy anything from us. And worse, what we had envisioned as a product so unique that no one had thought of it, someone had already built. We wouldn't be the first. We were doomed. I left Silicon Graphics feelings discouraged. But on the drive back to E.piphany a few things hit me: A credible customer told me that we had hit on a high-value problem, they couldn't find commercial software to solve this problem, it was an important enough problem that they invested effort to write their own software, it had been deployed inside their company and there were real-world users, I could now point potential investors and visionary customers to the widespread use of the product inside SGI as a proxy for our product. The more I thought about it, the better I felt. This was a validation of our ideas not a negation.[71]

After this experience, Steve went on to recruit the fellow who wrote the software and for a dollar licensed the code to Silicon Graphics software. At one point, E.piphany's market cap exceeded Silicon Graphics' value! Don't lose heart. Listen honestly and adjust or restart if necessary.

TEST 2: THE PROTOTYPE TEST

At the startup incubator Y Combinator, entrepreneurs get a t-shirt that says, "Build Something Customers Want." If they eventually build a successful company, they get another t-shirt that says, "I Built Something Customers Wanted." That message is the goal of what you are trying to accomplish in this phase of the NISI process. Paradoxically, the way to get there is not to start building something right away, but to build it iteratively and incrementally with your customers. In the second test, you finally start to build something, but not all at once. Instead, you will transform your virtual prototype into an inexpensive physical prototype that you can use to test your solution face-to-face with customers.

DEVELOP AN INEXPENSIVE, RAPID PROTOTYPE

At this point in the process you want to find an inexpensive way to turn your insights from the virtual prototype test into a prototype that includes only the core minimum feature set. Avoid building out the full product and instead employ rapid prototyping technology, such as is available at justinmind.com or jmockups.com, to create something your customers can use. Alternatively, hire offshore developers at Elance or oDesk to build out a bare minimum product. If you need to develop a physical product, again find a creative, fast way to get the physical product. For example, if you are going to source physical products from a supplier, ask the supplier for a sample first. Or if you need to build something, find a way to create a prototype quickly. Many services are now available that can manufacture rapid prototypes inexpensively and quickly. Or as a final alternative, see if a partner could help carry some of the weight for you. As an example, RecycleBank—the company we described earlier that pays consumers to recycle—did extensive work to validate the pain and the solution before building anything. But at the end of the day, they still needed to try out the solution to see if it worked. To test the idea, RecycleBank needed a few thousand recycling trash cans with embedded RFID tags. In addition, they needed to provide the recycling truck driver with a laptop that could read the RFID tags and record the data. A traditional approach would be to raise a few hundred thousand dollars, buy all the equipment necessary, and conduct a test. Instead, RecycleBank found an engineering firm with a vested interest in making the recycling cans for future operations. Because RecycleBank had so carefully validated the problem, the engineering firm also became believers and agreed to provide the first few thousand cans at cost. Then all that was needed was an inexpensive device to capture the data, some light software development, and the team was able to test what would otherwise have been a very expensive prototype.

At the end of the day, your prototype should be inexpensive while giving customers a picture of the solution you are proposing. You can use the opportunity to test your most critical features—the minimum feature set. But don't get caught in the trap of slowing down or trying to develop a "better" prototype. The point of the prototype is that it is a quick and minimal representation of what you plan to do. If customers are interested in the bare version, you are on to something.

PROTOTYPE ROAD SHOW

Now that you have a prototype in hand, the next step is to go out on the road and test that prototype in front of the full buying panel of customers. The prototype road show is a secret tool used by many of the most successful companies, including Intuit, Cisco, and others who in the early days used this technique to validate their solution. In fact, Intuit was famous for going out, showing early versions of Quicken to customers, and using their feedback to adjust the product. Not surprisingly, the prototype road show is one of the most important steps in the entire NISI process; nothing can substitute for the firsthand experience of having customers yawn in boredom or sit on the edge of their seat in excitement when you show them your prototype. To illustrate the power of the prototype road show, consider the case of ManyWheels, a startup that developed automated routing for auto shipping. ManyWheels began the process by validating the customer pain and the hypothesis about the solution. However, the prototype road show took their learning to an entirely new level. In the words of founder, Kevin Dewalt:

When we first began engaging the market on our ideas for ManyWheels we started with meetings and phone calls. We listened. We asked people about their problems. We sat next to the people doing the work and asked them about their frustrations. We tried to get a sense for the market dynamics and what type of solutions might work. And we learned a ton about the solution we thought we needed to build. Or so we thought. Once we started creating mockups and showing them to prospective customers, the conversations took on laser-like focus. People instantly rejected many of our core ideas and offered alternatives. Some customers wanted to see high-level data flows to understand how ManyWheels would work in their business. It took us several iterations like this to get to the point where the conversations moved from "interesting" to "When can I get it?"[72]

On-Site Meetings with Customers: Maximize Listening

Begin by arranging on-site meetings with the full customer buying panel. Ideally, you should try to arrange a new sample of customers (who will have a fresh perspective on the solution) and at the same time try to have meetings with the end, technical, and economic users for a particular organization. The customer-buying panel represents all the influencers in the purchase decision—your jury, in a sense—and bringing them together at the same time can create powerful buy-in. As before, you should prepare an interview guide and be ready to record and transcribe the conversation. When requesting a meeting, you should highlight the pain you are addressing, emphasize that you are not selling, and explain that you would like feedback as you create the solution. As before, your hit rate will give you some insight into whether you have correctly identified or verbalized the pain. You might consider using language such as this to request a meeting:

We are going to be in your area. We are talking to so and so (one of your competitors, partners or another individual at the organization). We would like to talk to one of your team members about this big problem (talk about the pain). We are developing this next-generation product that solves this pain. We aren't selling anything, but are in the development stage, and before we lock this product down, we'd like to get your feedback, because you are a thought leader in the space. Can we come and talk with you and your team next Thursday?

Whatever language you use, the key communication strategies are to 1) communicate the pain, 2) highlight you are not selling, 3) reinforce that they are an important voice and thought leader 4) identify the members of the peer group or competitors you will also be talking to and 5) solicit feedback.

When arranging meetings, try to get as many of the relevant customer stakeholders (from a single organization) as possible into one room at the same time. When you have the full buying panel in one room you will get richer comments and feedback, because the comments of one type of stakeholder will elicit a reaction from other team members. You should bring your entire team and then spend as much time as possible listening. When you have both your team and the customer-buying panel in the room, each member of your team contributes a different listening perspective which, when combined, will help keep your team honest about what was said, and the customers hear each other talk about the problem and get aligned behind a solution. To this end, let your customers talk and use the prototype as a prompt to elicit their feedback. Again, there is a fine line between just asking if customers "like it" (which is fairly useless in the end) and using the prototype to really understand if it solves the problem. The purpose of the prototype is to get specific and focused about whether this particular prototype solves the problem or not.

As an example of this process in action, remember the company we described at the beginning of the book—CrimeReports.com? CrimeReports was developing an advertising-supported website that allowed users to see statistics and a map of crime in their area (Figure 20 for a screenshot of an early version of CrimeReports.com).

Figure 20: Crime Reports 1.0

After many years working on the offering as a hobby, the founder, Greg Whisenant, decided to turn his good idea into a business that would improve the quality of life for millions of people around the world. Greg raised a seed round from vSpring Capital and launched his business. After the first year and half a million dollars in investment capital, CrimeReports still only had one customer—the Metro DC police, with whom Greg had a personal connection. After he'd spent many years of his life and hundreds of thousands of dollars of investors' money, it still wasn't clear if CrimeReports.com was a hobby or a business. When I requested that the next tranche of financing be contingent on the company running the NISI process, it created a crisis that drove Greg to stop selling and start listening to the customer and understand what was missing in order to break through the barrier of customer adoption. He created a road show to take his product prototype and business model hypothesis out to the market and really listen—and what he learned shocked him. Greg and his team set up meetings with the full buying panel at four different police agencies to get feedback on their "prototype" and business model. For police departments, the buying panel meant the police chief, the IT director, the crime analyst, and the police officer. Once Greg had his team and the entire buying panel in the same room, a rich discussion ensued in which a few key insights emerged. First, the founders were on to something—police departments were feeling increasing pressure to share information with the public about crime and to increase transparency and their accountability. Second, the police departments felt that the website was ugly and needed to be improved. Fair enough. Third, although the founders believed that the business model depended on hosting advertisements, police departments absolutely refused to have advertising hosted on the site.

At this point, the founders began to despair, but as they continued to listen (rather than sell), they found out some crucial pieces of information. For one, police officers were actually fascinated by the data possibilities of the website and were truly excitied about the possibility of leveraging the internet to increase the quality of their communication with the citizens of their town. The chiefs of police were interested in sharing data with the citizens and leveraging that data to increase the quality of their policing efforts. Many police chiefs were familiar with how New York City had used the "Comp Stat" model to decrease crime by identifying patterns and targeting "hot spots"; but for most departments, "hot spots" were tracked with a spreadsheet, cork board, and colored pins. If the data was hosted online, police chiefs could use a data "dashboard" to track trends and daily activity. For the first time, police officers could see what had happened on their beat the night before. As it turned out, this was surprisingly difficult for existing departments to do. As one police chief stated, sometimes it took up to six months to see what happened the day before. As the enthusiasm built in each conversation, the CrimeReports founders learned that police would actually pay them to post their data—advertising wasn't necessary. But they also learned, from the IT directors, that they needed to significantly improve their security protocols in order to allow CrimeReports to host the data. Last, the founders discovered that a touch-and-feel approach was the best approach to selling the new product. At the end of the day, by showing a "prototype" to customers and then listening rather than selling, the CrimeReports team learned crucial facts that had been hidden from view for years.

You already know the end of the story from the first chapter, but to provide more detail, Greg Whisenant took all the feedback, refined his prototype, and then took it out on the road for another test (test 3 in this phase of the process). The new website was greatly improved in look and feel and had no advertising (Figure 21).

Figure 21: Crime Reports 2.0

In addition, the team added the concept of a dashboard for the police departments (see Figure 22).

Figure 22: Crime Reports Prototype Police Dashboard

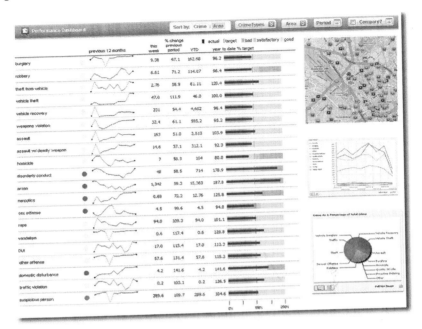

When the Public Engines team took the new version back to the potential customers, the feedback was astonishing. Their customers said things like:

"This blows other choices out of the water."

"This is a great idea. You guys have really hit on something here."

"We've been trying to do this for years."

"It used to take us six months to get this kind of data. Now we can get it the next day."

Not only did their customers clamor to sign up, but every day citizens (whom they also tested in the process) began to respond. Within six months of launch, the website went from being the 10-millionth most popular site to the 10-thousandth most popular website. The number of police departments purchasing the product went from one customer to over 2,000 paying customers in the first three years. Applying the process was nothing short of transformational.

Refine the Minimum Feature Set

There is a saying among sales reps that "buyers are liars." This saying comes from sales reps who have been burned by jumping through hoops for customers, adding this feature, or responding to that customer request in order to make the sale, only to find that customers didn't buy. Customers don't mean to lie; in fact, they feel they are telling you what they honestly believe. The problem is that customers are good at describing features they want, but they are lousy product managers and have a poor track record in nailing the solution. The second reason "buyers are liars" is that a single voice within a company does not speak for the needs of the entire organization. Many startups have failed by building exactly what a customer told them to build, but the product manager failed to fully validate the solution with a "buying panel" that included all the key stakeholders. Wearing your product-manager hat, you need to arm yourself with tools that will allow you to accurately listen to the right customer, cutting to the core issues of the customer buying panel, and capturing a true picture of what addresses the real customer pain. During this step, your goal is to listen as much as possible to customers, and you may want to employ several techniques to make sure you listen accurately. The most important tactic is a face-to-face meeting. This includes a full-team meeting between your team and the customer's buying panel, in which you keep your mouth shut, let the customer talk, and record everything. Remember that almost nothing can substitute for the nuances of an in-person meeting with your customer-buying panel.

Sometimes customers may not give you much information, or they may give you so much information you don't know how to prioritize that information. Three tools we have used to find out what customers really want are the $100 game, feature testing, and rating systems.

$100 Game: If you show a prototype to customers and their response seems inconclusive, or they give you a laundry list of features they want, try the $100 game, originally developed by Frank Robinson, to focus the conversation. To do this, ask your customer, "If you had $100 to invest in any features of this product, what features would you invest your money in?" Customers will often vote for the features they most care about. This type of information is invaluable because you can use it to see patterns across your customers and focus your efforts on the minimum feature set that your customers really care about. For example, when ClassTop first took their prototype out to customers, they had about 20 key features which they believed customers would value. The initial customer reaction to their prototype was moderately positive but not stellar. In one meeting with an official at the University of Southern California, the ClassTop founders asked how much the official might expect to pay for the product. The answer was only about $200 a month—not a great margin to build a business on. However, as ClassTop continued their road show they used the $100 game and discovered something staggering. On average, customers allocated about $80 on a drag-and-drop file-transfer feature and $20 on two other features. ClassTop soon realized they could shed the other seventeen features and drop the development costs and time for the minimum feature set to 1/5 of what they had it anticipated. More important, customer interest in this simpler product skyrocketed. In fact, when the team returned to the very same official at University of Southern California with the simplified product, the official was not only more enthusiastic than before, but when asked how much he might pay for such a product, he responded that he would easily pay $1000 or more a month— a 5x increase!

Feature Testing: Another way to determine where to focus when showing a prototype to customers is through feature testing. This approach includes tactics such as A/B testing, surveys, and feature tracking. The use of these metrics can help you identify the features customers really care about. For example, Google constantly uses A/B testing, where they show one version of a product to one set of customers and another version of the product to a second set of customers, then determine which version customers prefer. As an example of another tactic, the startup Knowlix used feature tracking to help create a solid win in the IT management industry. Knowlix was one of the early innovators in the IT knowledge-management field—or the process of cataloging, indexing, and recalling information about IT solutions to IT professionals. Knowlix's predecessor had taken an unfocused approach and floundered for years in the market. Knowlix, tackling the same market niche, created detailed tracking tools, such as customer surveys and keystroke tracking, in their beta product to identify precisely which features customers used in order to focus on those features alone. Through relentless focus and simplification, Knowlix went on to become a success, winning multiple awards and receiving three competing acquisition offers within two years of company launch.

Rating System: Another method to help focus the conversation is to use a rating system. You may consider asking your customers to rate which features are of most value; but more important, as a team you should rate which features connect most with the pain point so that you can focus your efforts on the minimum feature set. When having customers rate features and products, it is important to keep focused on a single market and keep customer comments within the context of 1) the market they are in and 2) the problem they are trying to solve within that market. I learned this lesson the hard way while leading product management at Folio Corporation in the early 1990's. I was in charge of the new Windows release of Folio VIEWS electronic publishing software. The product was a year late and over budget because company management was torn between building a product for both its publishing customers and its various corporate customers. The product was "designed by committee." Because the team attempted to satisfy all of the various customer needs across multiple market segments, they ended up prioritizing feature requests for reference publishers, IT support organizations, and ISVs all within the same product. When the product was finally launched, it won a PC Computing Award. The confused editor was wowed by the gadget geek factor and called Folio VIEWS the "mix master, slicer dicer, Ginsu knife of software products." Folio VIEWS won the award, but lost the customer battle by building a product that almost met several customers' needs but actually met the needs of no specific customer group.

In closing, as you decide on the minimum feature set, you might also consider two additional tactics. First, depending on your context, you may need to weight the responses of one particular customer type (economic, technical, or end users) more heavily than others—in most cases the end user. Additionally, if you look at your customer's responses and they don't seem to group in any reasonable way, see if you can subdivide your customers into segments. You will notice that different segments have different requirements, and so you may need to pick which segment you will focus on.

CHECK THE CRUCIAL TESTS OF YOUR HYPOTHESES
Hypotheses Tests, Price Points, and Breakthrough Questions

Last, always remember that your objective is to find out the facts with legitimate tests of your hypotheses. At the end of the day, no matter how much positive feedback you receive, if customers won't buy your product, then you have nothing but an expensive hobby. Entrepreneurs often delay these real tests by avoiding asking about price, or giving away the product for free. This is a huge mistake. The price your customers are willing to pay is the measure of the degree to which you have nailed the solution. If your product truly must be given away free because there is value in the driving scale and going viral (think Facebook), then you need to develop an alternative measure, such as engagement or the degree to which customers evangelize your product (for more on this topic see what has been written on Net Promoter Score). By the end of the second test, customers should be prepared to pay for your product; and by the third test your customers should be willing to pay for the product, or something is dreadfully wrong: either the pain is too small or the solution isn't correct. We'll repeat this advice a few times, but for now, you need to be sure to address two key questions in this stage and the next stage: price points and breakthrough questions.

Price points: Although you aren't trying to sell explicitly (because you are focused on learning), you should take the opportunity to begin to learn about price points while you prepare your initial customers. Without selling anything, you can ask questions that will identify price points, such as "How much would you expect to pay for a solution like this?" or "If someone came up with this solution, how much do you think your firm would pay for it?" Whatever you do, be sure to find out whether your customers will pay and how much—it is a crucial indicator of the pain point. One startup we worked with went through the entire NISI process, but they were too nervous to ask about price points. Although they had validation of the solution, they didn't have the most critical piece of validation—that customers would pay for the solution!

Breakthrough Questions: Asking about price points is the soft-touch approach to solution validation. When the rubber meets the road, we call them *breakthrough questions*—the tough questions that determine whether you have a solution that will lead to a high-value venture or just smoke and mirrors. Breakthrough questions are inquiries such as "Would you be willing to prepay for this product?" or "If I gave this to you for free, would you install it today system-wide," or "Would you be willing to purchase this today?" Breakthrough questions are the measure of whether you have nailed the solution, and the most reliable answer is cash from customers. Depending on the context, your breakthrough question will differ, but finding out the answer can be absolutely critical.

As an example, consider ManyWheels, which we introduced earlier. ManyWheels, which was developing a routing application for shipping cars, followed many of the principles we have been discussing. The founders spent significant time interviewing car dealerships, auction houses, and rental agencies to understand the pain. When it came time to propose a solution, rather than following traditional logic of building a product, the founders instead used an inexpensive, Flash-based prototype to show to customers. This proved a critical stage in the process because customers rejected the first few prototypes but eventually began to ask when they could get the product. With the prototype road show validation in hand, the team started to build the software solution, but as they took the solution out on the road to customers, they discovered that they had forgotten two crucial breakthrough questions. The first question goes back to the first phase of the NISI process in which you not only validated the customer pain, but you also conducted an analysis of the target market characteristics, such as size of the market, competition, sales cycles, and so forth. The breakthrough question the founders missed related to the market-opportunity question: is the pain also a market opportunity? As it turned out, although customers had a pain point, it was small (not a mosquito bite but much, much smaller than a shark bite), and the sales cycle would require far more than they imagined. The team had discovered a pain, but they had not discovered an opportunity. The second breakthrough question related to the willingness of customers to pay. The founders admitted

> *The test of nailing the pain is whether customers return your cold calls; the test of nailing the solution is whether customers purchase.*

that they were reluctant to ask about price points because such responses can be all over the map, but they were equally reluctant to ask for commitments from customers. As a result, customers kept playing along, but when the founders finally faced the question "Will customers commit to a pilot?" they found that in fact the pain wasn't sufficient to commit. Although the founders eventually shut down the project, the story has a happy ending—they learned to fail fast. Because the founders followed the principles discussed here, they learned all of these lessons "in months rather than years" and came away financially intact and ready for the next startup.[73]

What If You Get It Wrong? Learn to Change

Despite your best efforts to validate the customer pain and the solution, you may find that when you take your prototype out on the road, your solution is wrong. This is actually a fabulous outcome! Finding out you are wrong can save you years and thousands of dollars or more. Remember, one of the fundamentals of the NISI lab is to fail fast, and you may discover at this stage that your solution doesn't solve your customers' pain. At this point you need to assess the data and the alternatives to determine whether you need to change or abandon ship. The ability to change is a crucial entrepreneurial skill, and most successful entrepreneurs make such changes on their road to success.[11] How do you know when you should change? You have to frame your hypothesis, look at the data, and be willing to let go. As you go through the prototype-testing process, you may have to repeat it several times. For most startups, the second test may have to be repeated several times before you get it right, each time with a different sample of customers.

A Note on Testing Your Hypothesis versus Changing

Changing can be critical when you hit a roadblock or find out you were wrong, but you should be careful not to change too fast when you are testing your hypothesis. Specifically, when you are showing customers your prototype, for each sample or set of customers you test, be scientific and don't change the product too fast. When a pharmaceutical company tests a product, it tests it on a sample of patients, and if it doesn't work, the company reformulates or abandons the drug. However, the pharmaceutical company doesn't reformulate the drug between each patient. When you test your prototype, avoid the temptation to change your message between each customer. If you are altering your message or product concept between conversations, there is no baseline to test against, and the customer feedback will be very difficult to interpret. Try getting through at least three or four customer conversations with the same message and product concept before adjusting.

IN-DEPTH EXAMPLE: MOTIVE COMMUNICATIONS

For its first test, Motive Communications performed both phone and on-site interviews. The second test consisted of the development of a prototype and a series of iterations that refined it. Motive Communications called this the *non-disclosure phase* (because they didn't want competitors to find out what they were doing), and they selected about 25 companies (which is a high number) to test and refine the prototype. By taking prototypes to the customers and showing them their solution, Maples and his team discovered many important pieces of information. For one, even though customers claimed they wanted an entire host of features, the team narrowed down the minimum feature set by rating whether a feature solved a specific critical problem or whether it was just "nice to have." Nice-to-have features were delayed until the second release of the product. Another important observation the team discovered through their prototyping was the need for them to have "content" or a knowledge-base of common solutions that support engineers could use. In addition, they discovered that their prototype needed to "tie into" existing help-desk solutions that were used to track call resolution. By the end of the process, Maples and his team discovered several critical aspects of the product that they might have missed had they not taken their prototype on the road. Had they skipped this step they would have built a product, tried to sell it, and found that customers had very little interest in the product because it didn't actually solve their problem in an acceptable way. Even with this deep validation, in the third test, Motive Communications faced a real challenge to their confidence.

THE THIRD TEST: THE SOLUTION TEST

The third test is simple but challenging. In the third test, you partner with your customers to develop a solution, usually through a pilot program, to take your solution through a final round of iteration to refine it into the solution customers want. On the one hand, the test is simple because it resembles the second test, but with an actual product that becomes saleable. On the other hand, the test is challenging because at this point, if you have correctly validated the pain and the solution hypotheses and your customers should be willing to begin paying for the product. It is where the rubber meets the road, and you should begin closing paid pilots or be selling your product. In a traditional product-development model, new ventures don't face this kind of pressure. Instead, the product is still in what is often called "beta" stage, and most of the time engineers are quietly pounding away on the product without showing anyone. If the product is being shown to customers at all, it is often to assess problems with the technology or marketing strategy, not with whether the product actually solves the pain. By the end of this phase and the next phase (which runs parallel with this phase), you should have nailed your product solution and be ready to begin turning the crank on selling your product.

The objectives of the third test are to refine your product to an exact match with customer needs. At this stage the validation of your product, or definition of success, is paid pilots, validation on the price point, and breakthrough questions.

VALIDATE THE SOLUTION

In the final phase of nailing the solution, you will return to your customers while actually building the solution to validate that you were listening correctly and have solved their problem. Rather than repeat what we discussed in the second test, it is easier to say that the tactical steps resemble test two: contact your customers, get the buying panel around the table, show them the solution, record the conversation, and spend your time listening. If you have nailed the solution, your customers should be excited and willing to pay if they haven't already. They will be asking you when they can get the product, or how they can be in a pilot. If you are already in a pilot, these customers should be helping you make the final refinements to commit over the long-term. Their excitement should be visible and tangible. If not, you need to change the solution based on their feedback. To do this you will need to keep listening honestly to your customers.

Three Important Things to Remember: Price Points, Breakthrough Questions, and Minimum Feature Set

During the third test, remember the critical importance of price points, breakthrough questions, and minimum feature set. As we will discuss in the next chapter, during the third test you should be closing paid pilot customers if you are developing a B2B solution. If your customers are unwilling to pay or the price point is too low to build a business, you haven't identified a big pain point or a big opportunity. Similarly, be honest with yourself about the breakthrough questions. Identify them and get answers now. Hiding from the answer will only make the eventual truth more painful. Last, keep the minimum feature set sharply in focus. You can avoid feature creep by deferring all the extra features to the next version.

IF YOU GET IT WRONG, ADJUST OR MOVE ON

Even at this stage of the process, it is possible to discover you were wrong. In such cases it is better to adjust or move on. For ManyWheels, the answer was to move on. For many entrepreneurs, the answer is to adjust. Consider the startup Riya, which was founded by experienced Web entrepreneur Munjal Shah, to develop face-recognition technology. Shah's vision was that users could use the software to search and organize their photos. In many ways, Shah was right, and customers expressed not only enthusiasm but over 94% satisfaction with the product when surveyed. The only problem was that customers never returned to use the service again. The reasons for this were confusing to Shah, and it took him some time to come to grips with the need to change his vision: "Changing ... means acknowledging that your initial vision wasn't right," he explained, "and that can be very difficult."[74] However, Shah noticed that users seemed to be using the service to do visual searches on the web, like searching for a shoe or other product based on an image. Shah changed the company name and website to Like.com and slowly began iterating on the features. Less than two years after making the change, customers were making more than $100M in purchases a year on the site.

IN-DEPTH EXAMPLE: MOTIVE COMMUNICATIONS

In the third test, Motive Communications focused on validating the final solution with a group they called *lighthouse customers*. The goal of the final test was to perfect the solution in partnership with the lighthouse customers and then, when the product was nailed, scale it. However, Mike Maples Jr. and his team wanted to be sure their customers were committed, and so they established three criteria for the lighthouse customers. First, the selected companies would have to pay $50,000 for the beta; second, the customers had to deploy the solution; and third, the customers had to be willing to be references for future customers. To conduct the test, Motive selected twelve potential customers who were interested and from this group extended offers to five of the customers.

Without explicitly recognizing it, Maples and his team were testing several crucial breakthrough questions at once, including would the customers pay and would they install the software system broadly. Despite the initial positive feedback, as the deadline for payment drew nearer, none of the pilot customers had sent in their payment. This was troubling to the Motive team, particularly in light of the prevalence of free-ware and free beta tests being conducted by other companies. The team tried everything to close the deal, including follow-up visits and exploding offers for discounts on the full product. But none of it seemed to work. Mike and his team began to wonder if perhaps they should offer the beta test for free.

If you are operating on traditional product development logic, then a "beta" product is one that has been built according to specifications by engineers, tested for technical flaws, and been shown to a handful of customers in large focus groups. According to this traditional logic, customers should not be charged for the product, because the product has not been completed. However, if you have followed the NISI process, then at this stage the "beta" has had deep validation with customers. If customers won't pay now, then they probably won't pay later, and avoiding that confrontation is just delaying the pain.

So what did Maples and his team do? They believed in the process and held out. If customers didn't pay, that would be an important signal that they had not yet nailed the solution. If customers did pay, that was also an important signal. In Motive's case, the five customers did pay the $50,000 to be part of the beta. Not only did the five selected customers pay, but all twelve of the potential customers they selected paid for the beta. These customers went on to spend millions with Motive Communications, and the company eventually went public, in part because they validated the solution and answered the breakthrough question.

PHASE 3: NAIL THE GO-TO-MARKET STRATEGY

At the time of their initial public offering in 1987, Cisco—a company making routers that allowed different networks to communicate—was already worth several hundred million dollars. At one time the company's market capitalization reached a height of nearly $500 billion. However, even by the time they had a public stock offering, Cisco had no professional sales staff, no standard marketing campaign, and didn't even purchase advertising until 1992, eight years after launching the company. Cisco's lack of marketing runs counter to the traditional wisdom that a large marketing budget is requisite for success. The reason Cisco succeeded was that they nailed both their product and their go-to-market strategy. Cisco nailed the product by applying the principles underlying the NISI process. The early Cisco made their customers into partners, even to the point of allowing them to modify the router source code. In fact, the multiprotocol router, which came to dominate the market today, emerged because customers felt the pain Cisco was trying to address so much that they modified the router source code themselves (Chuck Hendrick at Rutgers University added DECnet routing, and Greg Satz added XNS routing). But Cisco also succeeded because they intimately understood the go-to-market strategy that was relevant to reach their customers. If Cisco's founders, Len Bosack and Sandy Lerner, had followed conventional Silicon Valley wisdom, they might have spent hundreds of thousands on advertising and marketing that would have been wasted. However, because they had come to understand their customers intimately, they also understood their customers' buying process and the market infrastructure needed to reach those customers. In this case, the best way to reach customers was through referrals over the emerging ARPAnet/Internet. Through what might today be called a rudimentary social-media campaign, the founders reached out by spreading the word about Cisco systems for almost nothing, and were soon turning an average profit of $300K per month!

Cisco's success illustrates the power of nailing the go-to-market strategy before spending money on marketing and sales. The purpose of the "nailing the go-to-market strategy" phase is to develop a deep understanding of the process by which your customers find out about and decide to purchase your product or solution. This involves understanding the job your customers are trying to get done, ascertaining their buying process (the information chain from the moment they find out about your product, through the purchase, to when they dispose of it), mapping the market infrastructure, and closing paid pilot customers. Really understanding this information provides you a heat map of how to target your customers and the facts on which you can build a sales and marketing strategy unique to your business. It requires more than just understanding the "what" of your customers; more important is the "why."

The nail the go-to-market phase actually runs in parallel to the preceding phase: nail the solution. The reason for discussing these two phases (nail the solution and nail the go-to-market strategy) in separate chapters is to emphasize how these ideas are distinctly different from each other. However, nailing the solution and nailing the go-to-market strategy are actually done at the same time. In fact, this chapter is organized around the three key tests we discussed in the prior chapter (virtual prototype test, prototype test, and solution test). The intention is that during each of the tests from the prior chapter related to the solution, you will also engage in specific activities to discover and validate your go-to-market strategy.

Figure 23: Steps to Nail the Go-to-Market Strategy

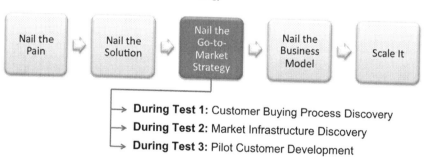

These activities include understanding the customer-buying process, discovering the market communication and distribution infrastructure, and pilot customer development. They correlate with the three tests in Phase 2 as follows:

Figure 24: How Go-to-Market Phase Steps Correlate with Nail the Solution Steps

Nail the Solution Steps		Nail the Go-to-Market Strategy Steps
Virtual Prototype Test	➡	Customer-Buying Process & Sales Model Discovery
Prototype Test	➡	Communication & Distribution Infrastructure Discovery
Solution Test	➡	Pilot Partnerships

DURING THE FIRST TEST (THE VIRTUAL PROTOTYPE TEST): CUSTOMER-BUYING PROCESS AND SALES MODEL DISCOVERY

CUSTOMER BUYING PROCESS DISCOVERY

Apple didn't revolutionize the sale of MP3 players just by making a better MP3 player. Of course, part of the iPod's success was due to its being a great product—simpler and easier to use than prior MP3 players. But another important reason for the iPod's success is that Apple looked beyond the product to the entire buying process for customers. When they looked at how customers used digital music from beginning to end, they discovered that for most people, the challenge of acquiring, transferring, and managing digital music was not just difficult, it was overwhelming. Recognizing this critical flaw in the buying process, Apple developed the iTunes music store and software, which made it easier by an order of magnitude to purchase, organize, and transfer music to an MP3 player. By carefully understanding their customers' buying process and taking ownership for their customer's success, not only did Apple position the iPod for success, they opened up an entirely new segment of customers who previously had shied away from purchasing digital music and MP3 players. Apple's success is a powerful example of the importance of understanding your customer's buying process.

Having a great solution alone is not enough for a startup to succeed—new ventures also need to understand the customer-buying process. The customer-buying process is more than just a sales process; it is the map of your customers' activities from the moment they find out about your product through the purchase and use to the ultimate disposal of your product. Even for the most well-trod markets, understanding the customer-buying process can be powerful. When one of the major pharmaceutical firms was launching an antidepressant in the SSRI class of drugs, they were going up against well-established products, such as Prozac. Although the firm's new drug was effectively the same class of drugs and so roughly similar in effect, rather than launch a "me-too" drug that might have fared poorly against such entrenched competitors, the company launched into an extensive analysis of the customer-buying process. What they discovered was that in prescribing drugs, physicians often associated certain descriptive labels with a particular product. For example, physicians seemed to associate Prozac with depression, and when a patient came in complaining of "depression," a very high percentage of new prescriptions were written for Prozac. An analysis of the competing drugs and their "labels" revealed that no drug was clearly associated with anxiety. So when the company launched their new drug, they emphasized "anxiety," and although the drug had roughly the same chemical effect, the differentiated labeling (which the firm discovered by exploring the buying process) led the "me-too" drug to become a multibillion-dollar blockbuster.

The customer-buying process is defined by the job your customer is trying to get done and all the relevant activities that surround that job. To discover the buying process, you need to specifically ask customers about how they accomplish or try to complete that "job" with any relevant solutions, from beginning to end. For example, key points in the process include how your customers become aware of the product, where they gather information, how they use that information to make purchases, and so forth. The figure below provides a typical map of the customer-buying process, or *consumption chain*, as it has been called by other authors.[75]

Figure 25: Generic Customer-Buying Process

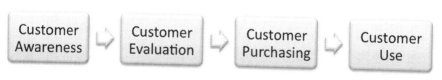

A simple way to start would be to ask your customers questions about each of these steps, such as how they solve the problem currently, how they decide which solution to purchase, and so forth. Simply take a stage and phrase a question around it. For example, you might ask questions such as "How do you find out about new products?" If your customers respond that they read magazines, you'll want to drill deeper. Perhaps ask, "Which magazines do you like to read?" and "What part of the magazine do you find most informative?" When we work with new ventures, we literally ask customers these four categories of questions and drill down until we feel comfortable. Although we have described this briefly, it represents a major step in nailing the go-to-market strategy. Don't overlook it.

Last, as you do this exploratory work, you may want to take note of how the buying process may differ when customers are buying from a big company versus from a startup. Also, as we emphasized earlier, begin to explore price points. Remember that you aren't trying to sell the product. You are focused on listening. Customer willingness to pay is a validation of your solution, and you will fine-tune this issue of prices during the prototype test so that by the time you get to the third test—the solution test—you should be closing paid pilot customers.

DISCOVER A SALES MODEL BASED ON THE BUYING PROCESS

At this stage, you shouldn't expect to fully master the buying process—you are making preliminary observations that you will want to reinforce with more data. Throughout the rest of the process, you should continue refining your understanding of the buying process. However, as you make observations, begin to think about how to turn the buying process into a repeatable sales process. It may be helpful to draw out your target customer's buying process and try to identify leverage points at which you can influence purchase decisions. Leverage points are all the points in the buying process that could influence your customers to make a purchase decision.

As an example of the power in understanding the customer-buying process, consider the case of SuperMac. Early in its history, SuperMac was an innovative Apple computer peripherals company that sold one of the first external disk drives, the first color paint programs, the first color graphics boards, and the first color monitors for the Macintosh computer. Despite SuperMac's many inventions, the company still went out of business and into Chapter 11 bankruptcy. But before selling off the assets, two venture firms invested $8M on the gamble that SuperMac could be revived. At the time, SuperMac's competitors had over 90% market share, and the company had been operating at a significant loss. The team believed they could be successful if they could just out-market or out-innovate their competitors. But when the new VP of marketing, Steve Blank, arrived and asked who the customers were, the SuperMac team's response matched the official segmentation chart—SuperMac customers were "professionals and computer users." Blank recognized that the SuperMac team, like most entrepreneurs, seemed to be acting on unexamined assumptions about their customers. For example, when he asked whether anyone had examined all the product registration cards that customers filled out when they purchased the product, there was only a stony silence. So Blank pulled 10,000 unexamined product registration cards and started personally calling customers to understand who they were, what their pain was, and the buying process by which they purchased products. Remember, this was the vice president of marketing, not an undergraduate summer intern or even the director of marketing, making the calls.

At the end of three months, Blank emerged with facts that completely shattered the company's prior assumptions and changed the course of the company. First, he discovered that the customers weren't "professionals" but desktop-publishing professionals. Second, these professionals purchased graphics cards solely for the purpose of running four desktop publishing applications: Quark, Adobe, and their competitors. Finally, desktop publishing professionals cared much more about performance than price. These simple facts shed new light on the "solution" that SuperMac should focus on developing. In addition to this radical information, Blank's customer interviews revealed a great deal about the customer-buying process. Previously, SuperMac had spent a great deal of money advertising in various magazines, attending conferences, and paying an award-winning graphics company to design the SuperMac box (which had a nondescript picture of a light beam on the front of the box). He found out that the target customers didn't pay much attention to advertising but instead relied on product reviews to guide their purchases. Furthermore, although SuperMac tried to exhibit at many different conferences, customers cared only about the MacWorld conference. Last, when customers made an in-store purchase decision, they were looking for specific data to guide purchase decisions, not fancy graphics. After a few months of work, SuperMac discovered they didn't understand their customer and that they were wasting their marketing budget.

With a deeper understanding of the customer-buying process, SuperMac set about creating a repeatable sales model. One problem for SuperMac was that the company's products generally performed poorly in product reviews. However, with a deeper understanding of the "job" the customer was trying to accomplish, the team noticed something interesting: most product reviews were based on highly technical details, such as bit-rate, which desktop publishing professionals didn't care about. So the team set about creating a set of objective benchmarks that measured how a graphics card performed on the four publishing applications that the customers did care about. To give the benchmarks an added air of objectivity, they called them the *Portrero benchmarks* (after the street address for SuperMac in San Francisco). To be fair, the benchmarks were objective in relation to the core software applications customers cared about, and at first, SuperMac products performed well on only a few dimensions. But with measurable benchmarks, the engineers found it easy to tweak and optimize their graphics cards so they performed well on all dimensions.

Next, Blank approached the different magazine editors one-by-one and in a friendly conversation pointed out that most of their reviews were based on technical dimensions that were irrelevant to desktop-publishing professionals. Not only did the editors agree, but they asked if SuperMac had discovered a better solution. Enter the Portrero benchmarks! Soon SuperMac was being reviewed in the magazines their customers read, citing the benchmarks SuperMac had designed and for which their products had been optimized. In addition, the SuperMac team quit attending other conferences and focused all their efforts on MacWorld.

Last, SuperMac redesigned their box with a sticker that emphasized the competitive advantage over competitors on desktop publishing software. SuperMac nailed their customer pain and the solution, and then, by discovering the customer-buying process, created a powerful sales model. The results speak for themselves: with a marketing budget a tenth the size of that of their competitors, SuperMac turned the company around on a dime and in three and a half years catapulted from 11% market share to 68% market share, and from bankruptcy to $150M in sales.

DURING THE SECOND TEST (THE PROTOTYPE TEST): MARKET INFRASTRUCTURE DISCOVERY

Selling to customers is rarely a direct communication channel from your company to your customers. Instead there are many intervening participants in the communication and distribution infrastructure who can affect your success. Marketing guru Regis McKenna calls these relationships the *market infrastructure*, which have some overlap with the distribution infrastructure (or value chain). To be successful you must understand the organization, links, and motives at each level of the market infrastructure. During the second test, you should continue to validate the customer-buying process, but you should also begin mapping both the market communication and the distribution infrastructures. With these maps in hand, you can then develop a strategy to leverage these infrastructures to your benefit. The objectives of market communication and distribution infrastructure discovery are to map the market infrastructure and develop a strategy to influence key leverage points, with the goal of making early customers comfortable with their purchase decision.

MAP AND UNDERSTAND THE MARKET COMMUNICATION AND DISTRIBUTION INFRASTRUCTURE

The market infrastructure consists of all the players between you and your customer who ultimately influence the customer's purchasing decision. Therefore, at its heart, the process of understanding the market infrastructure is closely linked to your eventual sales, branding, and business-development efforts. One useful way to describe the market infrastructure was developed years ago by Regis McKenna,[76] who characterized the market-communication infrastructure with an inverted-pyramid model that we still find useful today. After years of trial and error, we have modified Regis McKenna's basic market-infrastructure pyramid to emphasize the "types" of players in the market infrastructure, which customers looking to make a purchase will rely on, or "check," when making a purchase. This market infrastructure can be prioritized into five key business development activities. Starting at the bottom at level one and moving up, each level influences the level above it. (Figure 26). Each group in the pyramid represents a set of stakeholders whom customers directly or indirectly reference when making a purchase decision. Furthermore, not only is each group of stakeholders in the market-communication infrastructure important, but there is an order in which to work with each group, progressing from the bottom of the pyramid up to the top.

Figure 26: Market Communication Infrastructure

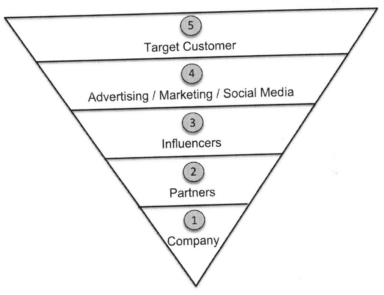

Level 1 - Company: Starting first with the company, level one represents all of the things you can do within the four walls of your company to influence the purchase decision of the customer. Starting first with nailing the product, but also when nailing the go-to-market strategy, the team has influence over brochures, marketing materials, website, pricing, and dozens of creative decisions that build credibility and help position and influence the sale of the product to the customer.

Level 2 - Partners: The next level in the market communication infrastructure is your partners. A partner could be defined as anyone who sits on the same side of the table as you and wants to sell to the same customer at the top of the pyramid. Partners could be resellers, content providers, ISVs, other companies with a related economic interest, and early-reference customers (early-reference customers are eager for others to follow and validate their pioneering efforts). When you develop a communication strategy based on the market infrastructure, most of the time your partners are the first group of stakeholders you work with and target.

Level 3 - Influencers: The next level of the market infrastructure is the industry influencers. This influential group of stakeholders is the boundary spanners that influence both sides of the equation—they sell to both you and your customers. These industry influencers are groups like the press, media, industry analysts, trade associations, user groups, thought leaders, and others who influence the industry. Depending on the nature of your solution, there may be other important influencers for your solution than might not be identified in traditional marketing. Social media influences a great deal of customer opinion and thought. Whereas in the past, customers might have relied exclusively on reviews in a magazine, today your customers may supplement or even substitute those reviews for the opinion of the crowd or of key influencers. Key influencers for some customers may more likely be an influential blogger, an online review aggregation site, or some other resource. Keep your eyes and ears open for these influencers.

To effectively mobilize influencers you will need to understand what matters to them and communicate that. Some influencers, such as gurus or thought leaders, can be co-opted by bringing them in as board members or advisors. Social media influencers may care more about the angle on your product (is it cool, disruptive, etc.?) or about your motives (are you focused on making money for yourself or changing the world?). Still other influencers, such as in the open-source domain, may care about your engagement with the community. Finally, for more traditional influencers, like industry analysts, most likely they will care about customer/market traction and may only interact with you once you have a few customers under your belt. For example, when I was trying to get favorable coverage from analysts for my startup Knowlix, I went in to Patrick McBride, an analyst at the Meta Group. I was told that if you want to gain mindshare with the analysts, "Never come and ask me my opinion. Come and tell me what the market and customers are saying." The good news for you is that if you are following the NISI process, you should be developing the exact customer feedback that analysts care about.

Last, the press and media are important influencers but ones that should be used with caution. Many experienced entrepreneurs argue that you only get one chance at a big media launch, and so you should save it until you really nail the product. In fact, early-stage investor Tech Stars explicitly avoids investing in companies that have received lots of media attention, partly because they have used up their big launch and partly because media exposure can go to entrepreneurs' heads, and they become hard to work with. So you don't want to seek too much press coverage too early in your development. Wait until you have nailed the solution and the go-to-market strategy and are beginning to make sales. Then you can leverage the media.

Level 4 - Advertising/Marketing/Social Media: This is the last level before your target customer, and represents the various advertising, marketing, and social-media outlets or vehicles that will get you in front of targeted customers in a credible way. As your company and product begin to establish momentum within the market, this is where you can lean in to a model that is working. As you interacted with your customers, you should have picked up clues along the way about your customers' advertising and marketing preferences. Which magazines, websites, tradeshows, conferences, or other vehicles, such as blogs, newsletters, webcasts, or white papers, do your customers care about? Whichever medium you choose, you should be very selective in picking the most targeted and relevant channels to your customer and then focusing all your resources to go big or go home. Whether you are looking for a targeted lead generation or a general brand building, keep your efforts focused and consistent. Just as important, measure the results. Last, targeted repetition increases your customers' comfort with your company and solution.

Your social-media strategy deserves some special attention. Social-media interactions, depending on whether you are influencing or broadcasting, can span categories 3 and 4, but to keep things simple we will focus the discussion here. Social media can be a powerful tool when applied effectively and virtually worthless when done poorly. Simply creating a Facebook page and a Twitter account for your new business won't have much effect. Furthermore, launching a blog and posting every day feels more productive, but blogs take time to gather viewers, and so it may be a year or two before anyone really listens to what you are writing. Therefore, as you think about social media, you should think about two things: structure and timing.

Although the structure of a social interaction may seem obvious once we point it out, few people think about it (which is why they launch rather useless Facebook pages or fire off useless blog postings and tweets). Structure refers explicitly to the "structure" of the social network. In the terms of researchers who study these things, networks are composed of two things: nodes and connections. In any network, some nodes lie at the center of a network, with many connections coming into them, while other nodes are quite tangential with few connections. As an example, if we mapped the network of news websites about entrepreneurship, TechCrunch and VentureBeat would be very central; many other websites refer and point to them, whereas the website your friend started six months ago has few if any connections. The same applies to blogs, tweeting, and any other form of social media. Being at the center matters, but it takes a great deal of time and work to get to the center. That is the why if you launch a random Facebook page or Twitter account, you will most likely get very limited leverage if you are in a crowded network (you should still launch them, because you can start building momentum). That means you have two options: either find a new/less crowded network or study the network structure and find a way to leverage the players at the center.

If you are in a new market, you may be able to essentially create a new network around you by creating an exciting or innovative message around yourself. For example, companies from Apple, to Redhat, to Google have built up messages around Microsoft as the Evil Empire and put themselves at the center of the discussion. Similarly, if your solution creates a new market or can redefine an old market, you may be able to create new conversation and be at the center of it.

Most likely you cannot create a new market, so the key will be to identify the "central" players in the social graph and then find ways to both influence and monitor them. You may need to work your way into the conversation, establish credibility as a key player, or find another way to be featured or broadcast in a social-media channel. You may also want to monitor the social-media conversation to find points where you can insert yourself or leverage an event to your benefit. If you don't believe this is possible, consider the example of Banyan Branch, a startup paid millions of dollars by a global portfolio of firms to monitor social-media conversation and then insert a positive message or do damage control when something bad occurs. For example, when Banyan Branch hears something negative about their clients in the blogosphere or Twitterverse, they often reached out to the key influencer and offer to take them to lunch or have a conversation with a high-profile executive at the client to see if the client can "help clarify" or answer questions. Sometimes a little love can go a long way. Although we cannot cover all the tactics here, you can study examples of others to learn how to influence the key players in the industry.

In terms of timing, once you recognize the structure of a social network, the insight follows rather quickly that it takes time to build up a conversation and become a central player. That doesn't mean you don't try, but it does mean start now if you want to have a broadcast platform in the future. You may also want to think carefully about the timing of messages in terms of the larger conversation of which you want to be a part.

Finally, don't forget that since the social media are less constrained by traditional distribution channels, you can be creative. Take for example the tactics of Grasshopper, a phone system for entrepreneurs. They created an inexpensive (but professional looking) video as a pun on the popular video *Empire State of Mind* (about New York) by Alicia Keys and Jay Z.

Grasshopper called their video *New Dork* and featured an entrepreneur in San Francisco who rises from obscurity to prominence through his web and SEO skills. This funny video received over a half million views in two weeks—very effective.

The Value Chain Wrapped Inside the Market Infrastructure

As you try to map and understand the market communication infrastructure, also pay close attention to the distribution infrastructure or value chain. The value chain maps the flow of inputs and outputs until they reach the final customer (for an example, see Figure 27).

Figure 27: Sample Value Chain

The value chain helps describe the distribution infrastructure of the industry, and while it may differ in some respects from the communication infrastructure, the two structures often overlap significantly. It can be useful to analyze the distribution infrastructure simply for the fact that the experience may help you recognize players in the market infrastructure that you may have missed. In particular, be sure not to miss distributors. They are partners in the process, and although they also want to sell to the customer, as we described above, they may have unique requirements of which you need to be aware.

In-depth Example of the Market Communication Infrastructure

Earlier we discussed Knowlix as an example of a company that applied the NISI process from end to end. Knowlix launched after I did a market and product analysis for Folio Corporation, where I ran product management and then business development. Folio, a search-engine pioneer, received many awards for their PC- and CD ROM-based products. Folio had established a market leadership position in the legal and professional publishing industry but was having difficulty translating their early success into other markets. Folio started out as a technology-driven company, then transitioned to a sales-driven company. In an attempt to transform the company into a market-driven company, I did an analysis of all the industries and applications into which Folio sold products over its eight-year history. The result was a 22 by 84 matrix of industries across the top and applications on the vertical axis which identified 1,848 different solutions. I then totaled all the historical revenue generated by each application in each market and ranked all the opportunities. The biggest number was the intersection of reference publishing and Folio's electronic publishing solution. The surprising discovery was that the second biggest revenue spike was the intersection of the IT industry and a problem-resolution-solution application. Folio was a major player in an industry it had not even been targeting. After delivering the analysis, the question was then asked, "What would happen if we focused?" Not surprisingly, the advice to the Folio management team was to focus on dominating a few key verticals that had a natural affinity for the Folio technology. Unfortunately, the company was considering an acquisition, and management decided that this new idea seemed like a distraction.

Since the company was unwilling to pursue this opportunity, I secured permission to spin out the software and focus on one tiny market niche: IT problem resolution. To the management at Folio, the niche seemed so small that it was barely worth the time. Many in the company wished me "good luck doing anything good with a niche that small." License agreement in hand, I quit Folio and founded Knowlix in late 1997, applying the NISI principles of validating the pain and the solution, keeping it simple, and relying on customer feedback to iterate on the solution. Starting with a prototype, our team gathered early feedback on what customers were looking for to solve their pain. In later versions of the prototype we took this as far as developing feedback-monitoring tools for the alpha and beta versions of the software, which allowed us to see which features customers cared about and how they were being used. We also worked very closely with customers to understand their workflow, iterating hundreds of times to simplify the product before launch.

As the development team was refining the right feature set and nailing the product, we focused on understanding the market-communication infrastructure and creating a go-to-market strategy that would get the product accepted in the marketplace. From potential customers I learned who mattered in the ecosystem and what they needed

149

to do to convince their customers to purchase. As an example of how this process works, examine the conversation between an IT director of John Deere and myself:

Ahlstrom: "I am following up from meeting you at the HDI trade show and wanted to see if you are still in the market for a knowledge-management solution for your support operations."

John Deere IT Director: "What do you mean knowledge management?"

Ahlstrom: "It's like problem resolution but adds in a knowledge database so you can find answers easier."

John Deere IT Director: "We've been looking for a problem resolutions solution like this. Does what you are doing integrate with Remedy?" (Note the key insight into important partners)

Ahlstrom: "Yes, we are integrating with Remedy."

John Deere IT Director: "Are you a certified Remedy partner?"

Ahlstrom: "No. We're working with them but are not a certified partner yet. What else would be useful?"

John Deere IT Director: "Do you have content?"

Ahlstrom: "Yes, we can index any content."

John Deere IT Director: "No, I don't want just any content, I want Microsoft and Novell content in the box."

John Deere IT Director: "Who are some of your customers?"

Ahlstrom: "We spun out of Folio and are just launching this new product. While Folio has many customers, we don't have any customers for this new product yet."

John Deere IT Director: "I'm not going to be a guinea pig and probably wouldn't be interested in purchasing your product." (This provides insight that this is a mainstream customer, not an early adopter.)

Ahlstrom: I understand that this may not be a good fit for you now, but would you help me understand what would we would have to look like to make you comfortable buying our product?

John Deere IT Director: Which analysts track you?"

Ahlstrom: "Which analysts do you care about?"

John Deere IT Director: "The Gartner Group."

Ahlstrom: "Anyone in particular there that you follow?"

John Deere IT Director: "Bill Keyworth. We can't make a purchase decision unless Gartner group buys off on it."

Ahlstrom: "What else would you need to know?"

John Deere IT Director: "Have there been any press stories written about you?"

The conversation continued like this, asking which magazines the IT director read, how he bought software, and what he wanted in a complete solution. We then took these responses and tested them by asking other potential customers. We even created an online survey and trade-show survey to gather more quantitative data about what mattered to customers. Meanwhile, we continued to perfect the solution, and at the same time, began to develop and shape the market infrastructure. This included developing deep partnerships with key providers such as Peregrine Systems, HP, Remedy, and Bendata and then taking customer evidence to influencers, such as Bill Keyworth at the Gartner Group and key industry consultants such Ivy Meadors, and Char LaBounty. By the end of the process, we had not only nailed the solution, we also nailed the go-to-market strategy, in particular the market communication infrastructure. Leveraging this information, within 18 months from product launch, in our little niche, Knowlix became #1 in product sales, #1 in aided and unaided name recognition, and received three acquisition offers resulting in a successful exit to Peregrine Systems in summer 1999. Furthermore, the Knowlix exit generated more shareholder value in less than two years than the parent company Folio generated in ten years.

Whereas in the rest of the NISI process we generally focus on talking to customers (and being wary of noncustomers), as you explore the market infrastructure, it may be helpful to think broadly in terms of who you talk to. Because the market infrastructure is bigger than your customers alone, conversations with others in the infrastructure may be helpful as long as you structure the conversation such that you won't damage the chance to make a good impression in the future. For example, one startup team we worked with was focused on developing next-generation waterproofing technology. While they were busy trying to understand the market infrastructure, they had a conversation with the CEO of an industry leading firm, and while the CEO wasn't interested in their product, the CEO went on to open door after door for the founders. This experience with someone who "wasn't interested" led the founders to the insight that when trying to discover the market infrastructure, "talk to everyone."

DEFINE A MARKET INFRASTRUCTURE STRATEGY FOR YOUR STARTUP

Once you understand the market infrastructure and the motivations for each group of stakeholders, you can begin to shape a strategy to leverage the infrastructure to your benefit. Your strategy, and the resulting tactical plan, should include both the activities you will undertake and the order in which you will tackle the stakeholders. For example, we emphasized that startups often need to prepare evidence of customer interest and performance before successfully capturing the attention of certain influencers, such as analysts. The actual tactics you use will vary by market, but the guiding principles are 1) map the key categories of the market infrastructure, 2) identify the top three partnerships in each category 3) understand the motivations and needs of each player, 4) create measurable and time-bound objectives for each potential partner and a strategy to leverage the infrastructure based on your interactions with customers, and 5) assign an owner to each partner. (At Knowlix we made this process very visual by drawing a large inverted pyramid on our war room wall and pinning 3x5 cards for each partner with objectives and the owner's name on the card for the different levels of the pyramid.)

The Market Infrastructure Will Be Different for Startups Versus Established Firms

On the surface, the market infrastructure may seem obvious, but the ways in which a startup can leverage the infrastructure may differ dramatically from how a big company (with an established reputation, market power, and deep pockets) can leverage the infrastructure. Thus you need to recognize that how your startup tackles the market infrastructure may be very different from how another company, particularly a big company, does so. If you just assume that because you can map the infrastructure, you have mastered it, you may be in for a big surprise.

Although Intuit did a great job of nailing the solution when they developed their first product, Quicken, they overlooked the importance of the market infrastructure, assuming they could use the same sales model that larger software companies used. At the time Scott Cook and Tom LeFevre were developing Quicken, the predominant model was to sell software through large retail outlets. Assuming they could leverage the existing sales model used by large companies, Cook went out to retail outlets to start selling Quicken. At one software store, Cook encountered a massive bin full of software titles, discounted by 90%. When Cook asked why these titles were on sale, the manager replied, simply, "These were the titles I decided to sell."[77] Consistent with the manager's statement, as Cook traveled from outlet to outlet, he discovered that large software outlets generally had a hard time selling software they selected on their own, and so they refused to carry software unless large numbers of customers were requesting the product. Typically, big companies spent millions of dollars advertising their software to create just the kind of demand the vendors needed to feel comfortable carrying their software. Cook discovered that one of the rules of the channel is that the channel doesn't create demand, it fulfills demand. The problem for Cook was that he didn't have that kind of money to create demand, and when he tried to raise it from venture capitalists, they turned him down flat. As a second approach, Cook tried to stir up good press in PC magazines to jumpstart demand. But even though Quicken received positive press in PC magazines, it didn't seem to create a significant increase in sales.

By this point Intuit was down to their last few hundred dollars, and in a moment of desperation, Cook tried selling Quicken at retail bank branches. Although a few bank branches agreed, sales trickled in at a meager pace. While Cook desperately and unsuccessfully tried to close more bank branches, Tom LeFevre finished an Apple version of Quicken, hoping to generate a few more sales. However, when the Apple version began selling in bank branches, a surprising thing happened. Not only did the software sell more quickly, but Apple software magazines began to cover Quicken. Suddenly customers began to call Intuit directly, asking for the product.

What changed? It was the buying process that the Intuit team had failed to understand but had accidentally stumbled on. As it turned out, PCs tended to be used primarily by businesses, which had little interest in personal-finance software. As a result, the PC version not only had limited appeal, good press in PC magazines also had a limited effect on sales. In contrast, most people interested in personal-finance software used Apple computers and read Apple software magazines to discover new products. When Quicken began to be featured in these magazines, customers were willing to try it, and sales began to grow. Finally recognizing the real customer-buying process for Quicken, Cook and LeFevre scraped together the rest of their money and borrowed a little extra to launch a $125K advertising campaign in the magazines their customers read. The result was a phenomenal spike in sales, and it was all due to understanding how the buying process differed for them, as a startup, as opposed to a larger company.

Changing Customers Means a New Market Infrastructure

One reason we emphasize testing your assumptions early, using tools such as virtual prototypes, is because it is so much easier to change course when you aren't emotionally and psychologically committed to a particular product or solution. Another reason we emphasize early testing relates to the market infrastructure: changing customers means that you will face a new market infrastructure. Why waste money and time to influence the wrong market infrastructure? In the case of Quicken, the founders wasted a great deal of time pursuing coverage in PC-related magazines, which might have been the correct market infrastructure for PC-users, but PC-users were the wrong customers. Although we emphasize the costs of changing market infrastructure, we do so not to prevent you from changing when needed—be willing to change directions; we do so in order to remind you of the dangers of locking in to a particular approach too early.

PLANT SEEDS FOR EARLY CUSTOMERS AND PILOT DEALS

Your goal has been to learn, not sell, because when entrepreneurs go into selling mode, it becomes hard to listen deeply to customers. However, paying customers are also the ultimate validation that you have nailed the solution. In the words of one serial innovator, "The only valid market survey is a signed purchase order. A signed purchase order was worth a whole hell of a lot more than any ten market surveys you could name."[78] We agree with the spirit of the comment: as you continue to nail the solution, your customers should begin to ask when they can get it, without your having to sell them on it. Furthermore, in the next test, unless customers are willing to pay to be pilot customers (or some comparable metric of engagement), something isn't right. At this stage, you don't have to close deals, but you should be planting the seeds of early customers by understanding their needs to the point that they want your solution soon … and they would even pay for it.

DURING THE THIRD TEST (THE SOLUTION TEST): PILOT-CUSTOMER DEVELOPMENT

As you prepare for the final test of your solution, on the marketing side you should be closing pilot-customer relationships to refine both your solution and go-to-market strategy in partnership with your lead customers. The objective at this stage is to validate your go-to-market strategy assumptions by closing paid (or other relevant proxy of commitment) pilot-customer relationships and then using these relationships to finish the solution with your customers.

CLOSE PILOT-CUSTOMER RELATIONSHIPS AND DEVELOP REFERENCE CUSTOMERS

When Motive Communications tried to close pilot customers at $50,000 a seat, nothing seemed to happen at first. Initially. Motive had offered the opportunity to be a pilot customer to five of twelve firms that could become great reference customers, and these pilot customers seemed willing to pay the hefty price. However, as the payment deadline drew near and no checks arrived, the Motive team began to question their strategy. Perhaps in the era of free-ware, charging customers to use your beta-product was out of line. After all, why would customers pay Motive Communications to be a guinea pig and to help Motive build the product? If you are following traditional product-development model, where the beta-product is a buggy solution that has been hidden from the view of customers, this logic makes sense. But if you are following the NISI process, if your pilot customers aren't willing to pay, you haven't solved their pain (or solved a big enough pain). Although $50k was a lot of money, it was a drop in the bucket compared to the millions that the eventual full product would cost. Fortunately, the Motive team knew they had done their homework and held their ground. In the end, not only did they close five deals, they closed all twelve!

During the third test, you should close and launch pilot-customer relationships, preferably paid pilot-customer relationships. The pilot customers are the sandbox in which you can put the final touches on the solution and refine your go-to-market strategy. In a pilot project you can get deep into your customers' workflow and optimize the solution to meet their pains. You can also get a deeper understanding of their buying process and how they interact with and gather information from the market infrastructure. Most important, pilot customers can become reference customers.

What are reference customers? Reference customers are customers who will speak in glowing terms about your product to other potential customers. These reference customers can be absolutely crucial in closing future deals because they may act as explicit references when you try to close a future sale, or they may be implicit references as they spread the news about your company via word of mouth. But reference customers don't just happen; they are chosen and nurtured. To begin the process, you should actually select reference customers who would be good partners and strong references. It is crucial that your reference customers be credible, committed, and good to work with. Once you have selected potential good-reference customers and have them committed to work with your company, in the words of Donna Novitsky, founder of Clarify (a public company that sold to Nortel in 1999 for $2 billion in stock), "You do absolutely everything you can to make those reference customers happy."[79] If you properly nurture these reference customers, at the end of the pilot you will have a robust solution, a deep understanding of your go-to-market strategy, and a reference customer for future sales.

REVISIT PRICE POINTS AND BREAKTHROUGH QUESTIONS

In the prior phase we addressed the importance of understanding price points and breakthrough questions. They are so critical that we'll remind you again. At this point, you should understand what your customers are willing to pay, or at least a range of what they might be willing to pay. You should also answer the crucial breakthrough questions that are relevant to your business. Breakthrough questions are the "big" questions on which everything hangs. For example, will customers replace their existing database with your database? Will they sign up for an account today? Will they pay for the account? Remember, the ultimate measure of nailing the solution and go-to-market strategy is whether your customers will pay you. If you don't ask or push for the answer, you will be avoiding a key point of validation. Find out these crucial answers and the earlier the better.

> *The ultimate measure of nailing the solution and go-to-market strategy is whether your customers will pay you. If you don't ask or push for the answer, you will be avoiding a key point of validation.*

PHASE 4: NAIL THE BUSINESS MODEL

The dot-com bubble is filled with famous stories of companies that failed to nail their business model and instead rode the wave of optimism to their demise. Pets.com represents one of the most famous burnouts. Founded in February 1999, Pets.com raised over $300 million, went public and failed, all by November 2000. Many pundits have questioned whether a market niche existed for Pets.com or whether it made sense to ship heavy bags of cat litter for free. Probably not, but a closer look at the Pets.com business model highlights how crazy the startup really was. Not only was shipping free, but during the first six months of business, Pets.com was selling merchandise at one-third the price they paid, shipping it for free, and spending millions on advertising (including a $1.2M Super Bowl ad).

It would seem that after the massive failure of Pets.com, future ventures that sold pet products online would be scarce or even non-existent. However only a few years later, Ted Rheingold and his partner launched Dogster, a site aimed at selling pet accessories online. Based on the Pets.com failure a few years earlier, most observers predicted that Dogster would fail too, and they were right. Dogster's plan to sell pet accessories online stumbled, but because the founders had taken great care in nailing the business model, including keeping the burn rate very low, they were able to change the business based on what they learned. And what was their next crazy idea? A social network for pet owners. Despite the droves of skeptics, Rheingold and his partner actually nailed the solution and the business model. One reason for their success was the willingness to fail by releasing product features early, getting customer feedback, and then adapting. The other reason for their success is that they nailed their business model. As a result, within a year they were profitable, and with almost no promotion the unlikely business has secured big-name advertising clients such as Target, Disney, and Holiday Inn.[74]

The contrasting cases of Pets.com and Dogster.com illustrate the importance of nailing the business model before scaling the business. However, nailing the business model is where most entrepreneurs excel, right? Not exactly; and here is why. In the traditional startup, an entrepreneur has an idea, writes a business plan, and then tries to execute on that business plan. The problem with this approach is that although the numbers, milestones, and strategy that went into the business plan were the product of thoughtful effort, they were still best guesses at the time. But as soon as these guesses got written down, rather quickly they get turned into "facts." This process has a fancy name—*institutionalization*—and dozens of professors have made careers of talking about it in the abstract. But for entrepreneurs on the ground it means that entire businesses and millions of dollars get invested on the basis of guesses and unexamined assumptions. If you don't believe us, sit in on the board meeting of a startup that has started to "miss" the numbers in the business plan. Founders and even whole sales teams will begin to make excuses. If there are professional investors, they will start to question the executive team, pointing to the missed numbers, asking what might be wrong. Soon the team is finger-pointing, and thoughts of firing the head of sales or marketing, or even the founder, begin to float around. Of course, the problem with this is that the "revenue plan" was made up to begin with, and not hitting those numbers really doesn't mean a great deal. But unfortunately, founders, employees, and investors can be slowly convinced that what was in the business plan is the truth and that the remaining challenge is to execute on that plan. Eric Ries observed this critical mistake when thinking back on his experience at the failed startup There.com:

> *We didn't fail to execute the plan. That was not our issue. We had a flawless execution. ... We were very rigorous about making sure that we hit deadlines and we did what we said we were going to do and we made the plan. And there's a reason why we were able to execute that good plan. We held everybody accountable for doing really good work. The only problem is we didn't have a mechanism for asking ourselves, is this plan any good? Is it worthwhile to advance it?*[29]

For that reason, although we have encouraged you to do your homework about the market opportunity, we haven't really emphasized anything related to a business model or even the business plan. In fact, while we believe the business plan can be a useful tool for raising money and communicating to outsiders, we focus instead on the business model. The business model differs from a plan in that the model is the map of how you create value and deliver it to customers, but with a twist. We use the business model to uncover and identify all the assumptions about how you might create and deliver that value and then use the NISI process to test those assumptions. At this stage, you have already done a great deal to uncover and test many of your assumptions, including nailing the pain, solution, and go-to-market strategy. If you have followed the process to this point you have actually done an exceptional job of uncovering your assumptions and turning them into facts. You are no longer acting on just guesses—you have data. So now it is time to fill out the remaining assumptions in your business model in a robust way and launch the product. Specifically, in this phase you will round out your financial model to validate feasibility, launch your product and go-to-market strategy, and then develop a continuous-flow data dashboard to monitor your progress forward. By the end of this phase, you have nailed it, are beginning to grow, and are on your way to scaling it!

Figure 28: Steps to Nail the Business Model

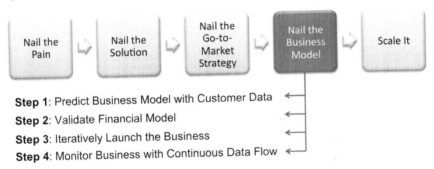

Step 1: Predict Business Model with Customer Data
Step 2: Validate Financial Model
Step 3: Iteratively Launch the Business
Step 4: Monitor Business with Continuous Data Flow

LEVERAGE CUSTOMER CONVERSATIONS TO PREDICT THE BUSINESS MODEL

The first step in nailing your business model is to think carefully about the different components, or assumptions, that underlie your business model. There are many resources available to map the components of your business model, although Alex Osterwalder and Yves Pigneur wrote one of our favorites, *Business Model Generation*. Their business model canvas, which is available broadly online and even has a very cool iPad version, can help you think about the different categories in your business model. So can some similar models which are derivative or similar to Osterwalder's. The question then becomes, how do you decide which business model components to choose, and which work the best for your business? By this point you will likely have had many customer conversations in which you tested the customer pain, solution, and go-to-market strategy. Not surprisingly, one of the best resources in nailing the rest of your business model is these conversations.

You can leverage your customer conversations to predict and then validate your business model. For example, when you think about the distribution channels, revenue streams, or the relationship with the customer, you have likely already asked, or should have asked, the customers what they expect. For example, in trying to decipher the right distribution channel, you might ask customers questions such as "how would you want to buy something like this?" Drill down on their answer to define your business model: would they buy it directly from you, from a distributor, from a partner, or from a large company? What would they need to feel comfortable making the purchase? What would a potential deal look like (specifically, what sort of terms or follow-on service would they expect, such as hosting or service calls)? When you are on the customers' side of the table in exploratory mode, they will literally give you incredible information for your business model. You can even explore, in a round-about way, questions such as customer acquisition costs or lifetime customer value. When you asked earlier about how customers evaluate a purchase decision, what did they say? Who was involved in the decision-making process? What will be the cost of reaching those individuals and convincing them of your product (for example, the cost of advertising in the magazines they read or hiring a direct sales person)?

VALIDATE THE FINANCIAL MODEL

After racking up losses of over a billion dollars, Webvan is another poster child for the dot com fallout. Of course, hindsight is 20-20—in the rear view mirror it is easy to point out the online grocer's many flaws. Nonetheless, the reasons for Webvan's failure are clearly related to two fundamental flaws: Webvan didn't nail the solution or the business model. In terms of solution, it wasn't clear that Webvan ever tried to nail the solution. In the words of consultant Phil Terry, "One of the fundamental mistakes everybody made is the assumption that because there are some problems with the offline experience, everyone would flock to online."[80] Rather than testing that assumption as cheaply as possible, Webvan spent a billion dollars to find out they were wrong.

Essentially, Webvan gambled on their business model. Although the team had no experience in the grocery industry, they surmised that by replacing nasty brick-and-mortar stores with highly efficient distribution centers, they could revolutionize the business. But a closer look at the numbers raises some questions. To begin, the grocery business is a low-margin business with return on sales of 1 to 3%. This means that a successful grocer needs high volume to be profitable, and that there isn't a great deal of room for extras. Webvan assumed that by taking out retail stores and replacing them with delivery from distribution centers, they could cut costs. However, retail stores were big, cheap boxes, whereas Webvan distribution centers cost in the hundreds of millions of dollars. Digging even deeper reveals more critical flaws. For example, without solid evidence that customers would adopt, Webvan predicated their financial model on being able to utilize their massive distribution centers at full capacity within three quarters after opening. As it turned out, no Webvan distribution center reached full capacity—ever. Another critical assumption revolved around the costs of servicing customers. As it turned out Webvan spent on average $210 to acquire customers. Then, although they had anticipated customers would make an average order of $103 on a regular basis, actual orders were both less frequent and lower in dollar value ($81 average) than anticipated. But the real killer came in forgetting that although the plain vanilla grocery store bears the costs of a brick-and-mortar establishment, customers carry their own groceries home. As it turned out, the average cost to deliver an order using Webvan's complex delivery network was $27. The numbers just didn't work in a business with 1 to 3% margins when it costs $210 to acquire a customer and then $27 to deliver an $81 order. Not surprisingly, Webvan folded.[81]

At this stage, with so many facts about your customers in hand and a deep understanding of the market infrastructure, you are now ready to validate your financial assumptions by building a robust financial model. The financial model will be one of your final hypothesis-testing activities before you launch your business in full force and is an important step. In this forum, we won't go deep on how to build pro-forma financial statements or the nitty-gritty of building forecast models. Many excellent resources on the finances of new businesses provide excellent advice and go into more detail (see, for example, *The New Business Road Test* by John Mullins). Instead we will emphasize that you need to take the time to sit down and model all your assumptions, putting numbers on each of them, and determine if the business still makes sense. It's that simple. When all the data goes into the spreadsheet, does it still make sense to build the business, or should you shut it down? You can put many metrics into your spreadsheet, many of which are important. However, here we emphasize just a few that are particularly important: fixed versus variable costs, margins, customer acquisition costs, and break-even.

Fixed Costs and Variable Costs: First, as a rule of thumb, maintain your flexibility by keeping your costs as low as possible. Keeping your burn rate low will preserve your options and allow you to abort, adjust, or restart before you actually get to the end of the runway. Second, when building out your model, take a close look at fixed costs and variable costs and try to "variabilize" any fixed costs that you can. For large businesses it makes sense to invest in lowering fixed costs—such as factories, equipment, cars, or leases—because total costs are lowered by lowering variable costs and spreading out fixed costs over a large volume of products. But a small company isn't a big company, and it is far better to save the cash outlay and preserve your flexibility. If you variabilize your costs (by which we mean turn fixed costs into variable costs), not only do you have more cash up-front, but you have the flexibility to scale up if needed. You also preserve a vital flexibility that many people forget about: the ability to scale down! Examples include using Google documents, Skype or Grasshopper, crowdsourcing answers via Quora, and literally hundreds of other resources. Regardless, the last thing you should do is invest lots of money in cars, equipment, leases, or anything else that chains you down and makes it difficult to change directions. Borrow office space, avoid equipment purchases, keep it cheap, and keep it variable!

Margins: Pay attention to your gross margin (product revenue minus product cost) as well as your net margin (gross margin—the cost of everything else). Generally you want your gross margins to be high (hopefully around 50% or more) because everything will cost more and take more time than you originally thought. In contrast to Webvan's attempts to enter the grocery business, with average net margins of 1 to 3%, having a large margin gives you leeway to make mistakes and recover. Take the example of Google search. Their margin is so high it almost feels like printing money. As a result, they can afford to spend a billion dollars "experimenting" on an ultrahigh-speed-fiber network and have it fail, because their margins are so high that even this radical expense represents only a little more than 10% of Goggle's yearly free cash flow!

Customer-Acquisition Costs: One of the most overlooked metrics is the cost of acquiring a new customer. Customer-acquisition costs refer to all the advertising, marketing, and promotion costs of acquiring a new customer to use your solution. Some entrepreneurs we've met have no idea what these costs are, but failing to understand them can absolutely kill your business. As we highlighted, Webvan paid $210 to acquire each customer. With an average order size of $81 and an average delivery cost of $27, in a low-margin business, the amount of volume needed to recover these costs was incredibly high.

By contrast, most successful entrepreneurs with whom we have worked are very conscious of their customer-acquisition costs, always modeling them in advance and then managing them as they acquire customers. For example, Erik Allebest built the web's leading retailer of chess equipment (wholesalechess.com) as well as the leading social network for chess players (chess.com) primarily by carefully managing customer-acquisition costs. In contrast, the founders of failed startup PlayCafe, which tried to create interactive online entertainment, pointed to customer-acquisition costs as one reason why the company failed. One of the founders, Mark Goldenson, recounted how he and his partner imagined they could keep customer-acquisition costs low simply by being creative (creating viral videos, pounding the pavement themselves, developing unique campaigns). After the music stopped and PlayCafe shut its doors, Goldenson realized that "the best marketing is controlled and calculated. If you know exactly how much it costs to acquire a user and you control the entire process, you then know how much capital and revenue you need.

Thus you reduce your marketing plan from fuzzy guesswork to a clean formula."[64]

Break-Even: Break-even, or the point at which your revenue matches and then exceeds your expenses, is a central metric in your business. The sooner you can break even, the greater your freedom. Profitable companies not only survive, they command respect. If they need to raise money, they have a lot easier time doing it. Be sure to look at all your costs and determine the time to break even. If you need to raise money to get to break-even, we suggest you give yourself plenty of extra time (at least double what you expect). We have described the NISI process in a linear fashion, but in application you will have to circle back when you make a mistake. It's important to have the financial leeway to do so. That's one reason why Dogster remains a viable company today—the company reached break-even early and continues to grow to this day.

THE IMPORTANCE OF BEING SENSITIVE

One thing that Webvan didn't do well was look at their financial modeling using sensitivity analysis. Sensitivity analysis is a fancy way of asking, "What does the world look like if things don't go the way we expect them to?" When you build your financial model, it is important to look at how your model holds up when things go well, as expected, poorly, or terribly. Is your model robust in some rough water? If so, you should move ahead, but if not, you may want to rethink the viability of your business. Although Webvan could make their business model work on paper, it wasn't very robust to things not going well (such as an $81 average order). But as we have pointed out, things always end up differently than you planned in a new venture, so be sure your financial model can handle less than optimum conditions.

ITERATIVELY LAUNCH THE PRODUCT AND GO-TO-MARKET STRATEGY

Now that you are comfortable that you can make money with your business model, you should be moving full scale into launching and growing your business. During the third test of nailing the solution, you should have developed and refined your initial product; and with the lessons learned from pilot customers, you should take all you have learned and focus on selling your product. Yes, that's right, now go into full sales mode. If you have nailed the solution, some of the customers you have been working with are eagerly demanding your product, and you need to capture the value in your waiting audience. But you also need to begin to turn the crank on your go-to-market strategy to create new customers.

As you launch the product, your goal is to develop a *repeatable business model.* Such a model means quite simply that you put money or effort in, you get money out—predictably. As you settle on this repeatable model, you should continue to iterate with your customers, evolving the product to fit their needs. Do *not* stop talking to customers. At the same time, you should also slowly be transitioning to the point where your product is becoming a complete solution; and as sales continue, you change it less and less until the sales and business models become truly scalable. Rather than repeat what we have discussed in earlier chapters, it may be simpler to say—just go do it. Act on the facts you have. But as a word of caution, stay focused on your core-value proposition. In the early days of Yahoo! the company was so busy pursuing interesting avenues, such as Yahoo! Finance, Yahoo! Sports, and the vision of being a media channel that they overlooked the importance of search. Because they couldn't make money on search, Yahoo! largely ignored it and eventually plugged the hole in their offering with an outside vendor—Google. One senior executive admitted in confidence that Yahoo! had overlooked the importance of search by a factor of at least 100, largely because they became so distracted by the other obvious opportunities. Contrast Yahoo!'s example with that of Google, where the founders and team stayed clearly focused on search until long after they had turned it into a multibillion dollar business.

The key to your continued success as a business depends on two things: continuous data flow and measuring the right things. By continuous data flow we mean continued interaction with your customers.

As you begin to scale the business model, remember to stay focused on the core opportunity and remind yourself that after you conquer one kingdom, you can go on to conquer the next. But you can't conquer the world all at once. The successful companies we have worked with have stayed focused on the solution they have discovered, executing patiently and iteratively. From Knowlix, to RecycleBank, to Intuit, and Cisco, each company grew steadily with a focus, and as they nailed their core market, then they could branch out and seize other opportunities. In contrast, companies that moved too fast (the classic "get big fast" strategy) or got too distracted tended to stagnate or fail.

THE KEY TO YOUR CONTINUED SUCCESS: KEEP TALKING TO CUSTOMERS

At this point you may feel you have nailed it—and you may be right—but that doesn't mean you have a guarantee for success in perpetuity. To stay successful you cannot turn off the interaction with customers and go into blind-execution mode. The key to your continued success as a business depends on two things: continuous data flow and measuring the right things. By continuous data flow we mean continued interaction with your customers. That may sound strange, given all the work you will have gone through to nail your business, but we aren't asking you to endlessly hold back from building your business. We are asking you to keep your pulse on the customer pain, on how your solution matches that pain, on your go-to-marketing strategy, and on the business model. To keep your knowledge fresh you will need to maintain intimate involvement with your customers. You will also need to measure other variables that represent critical success factors.

Depending on the type of business, the data you track might be customer-acquisition costs, customer-retention rates, sales per customer, net promoter score, or whatever metric gives you insight into how the business is going and where problems might be slowing your growth. As you begin to grow the business, the key is to identify the metrics that are most relevant to the growth of your business and keep a close eye on the data. Don't get sucked into gut feelings or metrics that look good but miss the point. Gut feelings can only take you so far, whereas data gives you facts, which lead to real insights. Some metrics, such as number of new users, can make you feel like the business is succeeding, but they may be covering a fatal flaw. For example, recall the startup we mentioned earlier, nicknamed Longtail.com, with the vision of creating attractive online marketplaces for small business owners. At first everything seemed to be going well, and the rates of new user signups increased. The two founders began to get excited about the possibilities of their new business. The team successfully raised venture financing and began expanding until one of the founders began to dig into the data a little. What that founder discovered was that while the number of new markets continued to grow, costs were actually increasing with each new user and the amount of web traffic was decreasing. Recognizing that the real measure of success was being able to decrease costs with scale while also increasing overall web traffic to the markets, the duo frantically set about testing different ways to fix the broken business model. Ultimately the team was able to develop a steady cash-flowing business but decided that the small amount of income missed their business aspirations by a long-shot, and they shut down the business. In the end, the duo felt happy that they had discovered the fatal flaw in their business before going any further, but they also lamented that they hadn't recognized the flaw earlier.

One tool you may consider using to maintain a continuous data flow on the right measurements is a business dashboard, which represents a single place where you capture a set of metrics that provides insight into the operations of a business on a regular basis. These metrics can be incredibly powerful tools to help you recognize when something might be awry. There are several excellent perspectives on business dashboards. For example, John Mullins and Randy Komisar, in their book *Getting to Plan B,* offer excellent advice on establishing a dashboard of key metrics. In closing, as you begin to make sales, keep gathering real data from customers, as well as other important business metrics that can help you monitor your business and recognize whether the business is on track as sales start to grow.

PHASE 5: SCALE IT

Now that you've discovered a repeatable business model—one that predictably generates revenue—you can scale your business. Interestingly, once you have nailed your business, the Get-Big-Fast strategy that led so many dotcom startups to their death actually works well. It killed the dotcoms because they hadn't nailed their business, but once you have a validated, repeatable business model, you can get big fast. Now is the time to scale and grow! Sounds simple, right? On the one hand, turn the crank on your model. On the other hand, there are some bumps on the road and some tools you can use to manage the scaling process. Very few people have discussed the scaling process in detail—one factor that sets this book apart. As an example of the potential challenges, consider the following all too common story:

As software applications have increased in complexity, the challenge of integrating all the disparate software modules and diagnosing flaws, and then repairing those flaws, has become increasingly complex as well. One day, as Lew Cirne drove the windy Highway 17 between Silicon Valley and Santa Cruz, it dawned on him that he could use an emerging software language, Java, to create a self-diagnosing system that would solve many of these problems. He was so excited he nearly drove off the road, and by the time he reached the coast-side town of Santa Cruz, he knew he needed to build a company. Not only did Cirne found a company, Wily Technology, but he developed the initial product vision, raised money, built a robust team, completed the product development, and even closed the first few customers. By every measure, Cirne had been phenomenally successful as a first-time founder and CEO. Imagine his shock when his investors—well-respected venture capitalists—asked him to step aside and find a new CEO to replace himself. Although Cirne had his weaknesses, one of them being that he had never scaled a startup into a large company, the affront was tangible. In big companies, when a CEO brings a product to market, grows the company, or meets milestones, he or she is rewarded. Why was Cirne being fired?

As it turns out, Cirne isn't alone. In many cases, founders who successfully bring a product to market, raise the next round of funding, and/or meet a major milestone find themselves out of a job and being replaced.[82] This may seem counter-intuitive and as paradoxical for you as it did for Cirne, and the common response is to blame the investors, or "vulture" capitalists, as being greedy barbarians. But the truth is that the investors may be recognizing something the founder-CEO may not have— that as the company grows, it is changing.

NO STRAIGHT LINES TO A BILLION DOLLARS

Few things in life resemble a straight line. Although we describe the NISI process as a chronological process, the truth is that the process of "nailing it" is recursive, meaning that you often have to circle back to get things right. But once you have nailed the product, shouldn't growth to a billion dollar company be a straight line? After all, you've spent so much time discovering the product that fits your customer and a repeatable sales process, can't you just turn the crank forever on what you have discovered? While it's true that following the NISI process will get you past the crucial early stages of growth, it is equally true that the very process of growing will change your company in fundamental ways that will make what you did in the early days obsolete in the later days.

> *The very process of growing will change your company in fundamental ways that will make what you did in the early days obsolete in the later days.*

The reason is that as startups grow, the nature of how they operate begins to change. In the early days, startups focus on innovation— discovering unknown opportunities by matching market problems with solutions in a highly unknown and uncertain context. At the core, startups are engaged in a creative act of discovery, and the early phases of the NISI process help you to validate the discovery. But as startups nail the product and begin to grow, what was once unknown becomes known, and a new set of problems begins to emerge. As more and more customers come on board, the company has to change to be able to serve the customers well. For example, in the early days, a low-tech spreadsheet could be used to track customer bills and relationships; now the sheer volume of a growing customer base requires the installation of automated billing as well as a customer-relationship management system. Support calls used to be handled on a one-off basis by the founders; now the volume of calls requires the creation of a support group with a support database containing the answers to frequently asked questions. The sales team used to be one charismatic rock star; suddenly the needs of a growing market require a team of salespeople, and they need standardized sales documentation and procedures to be effective. Benefits used to be pay plus a bare-bones health plan; now as the employee base grows, the founders need to implement an HR policy, expand benefits, and offer tiered compensation plans. Partnerships used to be formed by the founders one-by-one; but now as the web of distributor and strategic partner relationships grows, robust documentation and relationship management are suddenly required. And on and on.

As a company grows, a shift occurs from facing an unknown problem/solution at the outset, which required radical exploration, to facing a known problem/solution that requires execution. As a result, new ventures actually go through one or more phase changes on the way to becoming a big company, and during these transitions the way they operate has to fundamentally change to reach the next level. As the company gets bigger, the nature of what it has to do to be successful changes. A good analogy is the transition from being a child, to a teenager, and then an adult. Although in the Middle Ages people believed that children were just "little adults," we've discovered that what children need in order to grow and be happy is much different from what a teenager or adult needs in order to grow and be happy. Similarly, while the early-stage market discovery and validation tactics we have discussed here are absolutely vital to success in the early stages of discovery, as more and more customers come through the door, what changes will make the company need to make to stay successful?

Although many aspects of the company will change as you grow, we will focus on the transition of three key areas from startup to the next phase. These areas include 1) market, 2) process, and 3) team transitions. We hope to provide advice about when these transitions should occur and how to manage them—advice we have used in helping companies scale.

MARKET-SCALING ACTIVITIES

As startups begin to scale, they often have early success, followed by a period of stagnant growth that confuses and perplexes the founders. Geoffrey Moore nicknamed this period the chasm, based on his analysis, and highlighted where it fits in the overall *technology-adoption life cycle* (TALC).[83] According to the TALC, most innovations follow a pattern in which a group of early adopters are willing to use the new product or service because they are especially open to trying new innovations, but the majority of the market (consisting of an early and late majority) wait to adopt new innovations until they feel comfortable that a full product solution has been delivered which is reliable and safe to use (Figure 29).

Figure 29: Technology-Adoption Life Cycle

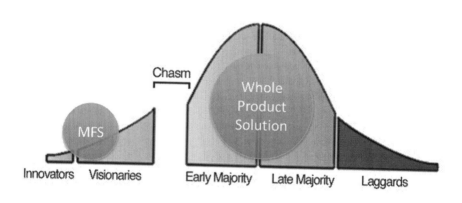

The problem is that for founders, when early adopters begin to purchase their product, it looks like the beginning of a hockey-stick sales curve, and so they rapidly scale up their sales team to meet demand, only to find that sales mysteriously drop off. Founders then scramble because they are burning cash on an expensive team that isn't producing the expected results. Usually the sales, marketing, or engineering team get blamed for not executing, but the real reason for the drop in success is that they are in the chasm—the company has failed to establish repeatable sales systems and a trusted brand with the mainstream customer.

REACHING AND THEN CROSSING THE CHASM

In truth, startups that reach the chasm are lucky. Most startups never even make it to the chasm. Most startups fail because they are able to attract only a handful of customers, if any. The purpose of this book, and the "nailing it" part of the process, is to give startups the tools to actually reach the chasm, as well as the fundamentals to cross it. However, once a startup reaches the chasm, it will likely need to adjust its tactics in order to cross.

So how do startups cross the chasm? The answer to this question is part of what drove the years of thought and effort that went into this book. Over the years we have read hundreds of business and marketing books, consulted with the McKenna Group, Geoffrey Moore and dozens of other marketing gurus and industry thought leaders who have put their ideas into practice in real startups. After reading Geoffrey Moore's books *Crossing the Chasm* and *Inside the Tornado*, we even asked Geoffrey Moore himself in the board room of Folio Corporation, "Step by step, how do you cross the chasm?" His honest answer, "I don't know," has led to more than a decade of research and trial and error to find the answer to this question.

Although Geoffrey Moore became one of our marketing heroes, and his valuable insights have been foundational in solving this puzzle, let's take a close look at what Moore suggests and discuss how these insights integrate into what we have learned in helping companies cross the chasm. At the heart of crossing the chasm is the need to deliver a full-product solution to customers which they feel safe buying. Notice that this represents a significant shift from the advice we gave you earlier to develop a minimum-feature-set solution. As you begin to cross the chasm, you have to shift from the minimum features to the whole product. Then you have to leverage your resources to cross the chasm. To do this, Moore suggests that startups begin by 1) focusing all resources on a specific market niche, 2) identifying the target customers, 3) finding their compelling reason to buy, 4) building the whole product, and 5) understanding the competitive and market landscape. The good news is that by following the NISI process, you have already done all of these things—you have the understanding and validated product that will succeed once you cross the chasm. However, once your crop of early-adopter customers has begun to run dry, to actually convince the early-majority customer to purchase, you need to make the early majority feel comfortable. At the core, early-majority customers are conservative pragmatists and want to feel they are buying from a legitimate market leader; and that by spending money on your product, they won't lose time, money, prestige, or whatever else they value—they want to make a solid, branded choice. To convince them, Moore uses the analogy of the D-Day invasion during World War II when allied forces concentrated all their military power (160,000 troops landed in one day) to establish a single beachhead, to emphasize the need to focus your resources on helping to convince early adopters. Specifically, Moore suggests that one way to do this is to define the market such that you are the market leader, shape all your communications to clearly emphasize your competitive leadership/-differentiation, and then focus all your efforts on the sales process and satisfying those early customers. The good news is that once you land a few of the early-majority customers, they can become amazing word-of-mouth advocates and reference customers that will help you win the rest of the early majority quickly and with less effort.

But what does this process look like in the real life of an early-stage startup that has gone through the NISI process and is starting to scale? Perhaps we can provide some insight through an example. In a previous chapter we discussed Knowlix, an early-stage company selling knowledge management software to the IT support industry which I founded. Knowlix followed the NISI process, validating the customer pain, iterating to develop a solution, and discovering the right go-to-market strategy, which included the customer-buying process and market infrastructure. If our Knowlix team had skipped these steps and followed the traditional startup model, we likely would have spent a few million dollars developing a product that sold to one or two customers and then floundered, leaving the investors and ourselves with a product that was halfway to nowhere. Instead, by following the NISI process, Knowlix had a great deal of early success as innovators and early adopters purchased the product. As the company started to scale, we were fortunate enough to bump up against the chasm but then of course immediately faced the challenge of crossing the divide. As you may remember, at the core, crossing the chasm is about focusing all your resources to make the early majority comfortable that you have a reliable, whole-product solution to their problem. Because the early majority prefers to avoid risk, they are often suspicious of products with limited momentum and wait for external evidence of broader market adoption that you are legitimate and safe to purchase.

For Knowlix, convincing the early majority involved leveraging what the company learned in the first phases of the NISI process: gathering more information where necessary, using all their resources to convince a few early majority customers, and then taking care of those few customers so they remain extremely happy. During our effort to understand the customers' buying process and the market infrastructure, our Knowlix team learned which magazines our customers read, which conferences they attended, and what they viewed as important in making a purchase decision. To convince the early majority to adopt, one of the things we did was to redefine the market category so that Knowlix was positioned as the market leader. Previously, the market had been defined as problem resolution—a broad field encapsulating technical support. Knowlix was focused on managing an organization's answers to common problems in context of their workflow, which we recognized as a problem of managing a firm's knowledge. So at Knowlix we renamed the niche *knowledge management* and then focused resources on defining ourselves as the leaders in the space. As wild as this may sound, it's a common tactic. Companies from Amazon.com to small startups have tried to redefine markets around themselves.[84] The key to successfully redefining a market around yourself is to choose a space that is unoccupied in which there is a legitimate need—you can't simply redefine an existing well-defined space. For example, Rhomobile, one startup applying the NISI process to develop cross-platform, smart-phone-application development tools (the Ruby on Rails for smart-phone applications) would be foolish to try to redefine the mobile application space with themselves as the leader. They chose instead to carve off a smaller piece of that space by creating the label, "smart phone application frameworks," and then defining themselves at the center of that "emerging" space.

Furthermore, it is important to note that when we discuss how Knowlix or Amazon renamed a category, it was only after they nailed the business and were in the process of scaling that they did so. In the words of Mark Richards of Sand Hill Partners, who applies the NISI process in his consulting:

So many startups think the first step of their business is to create a new category name for what they do and then declare themselves world leader. And of course the founders all fall in love with the category and their new world domination, but in the meantime, prospective customers go to the website and have no idea what the world leader in some cryptic category like "geosocial curation" actually does or why they should take the time to read more. Then guys like me have to come in and apply the NISI process in retrospect, trying to get them on a Kool-Aid-free diet for a while, with a big helping of customer data.

So don't go redefine the world as your first step. However, for Knowlix the next step was to communicate and convince the early majority that we were in fact the technology and thought leader in the new space. To do this, we focused all our resources on the relevant market infrastructure pieces that we had discovered in the earlier NISI process. Tradeshows represented an important piece of the market-communication infrastructure for Knowlix's customers. Tradeshows can be valuable tools for convincing the early majority, because you can get a large portion of the early majority in one place and create in the minds of your customers the perception of having "arrived."

When it comes to the image you create as a startup, once you start selling, go big or stay home within the niche you have targeted. This doesn't mean you have to burn all your capital, but you do want to communicate that you are established and reliable when you start trying to capture the early majority. For my time at Knowlix, this meant spending the money to obtain a moderately central space at the tradeshow their customers attended, creating a professional booth, and then pulling out all the stops to establish buzz around the booth. For starters, we had every single employee (a dozen or so) operate the booth, which helped the company look like a *big* company. And that was just the beginning. We pulled out every trick in the book to get customers sitting down, listening to their pitch, and most important, seeing other customers at the booth so that they felt that Knowlix was a legitimate and safe purchase. To do this, we set out chairs in the booth with t-shirts on every chair, and to get a t-shirt, potential customers had to fill out a brief survey and sit down for a moment to hear national stand-up comedian David Christiansen tell them more about the company and product. Then at the periphery of the booth, we hired very attractive models to catch the eye of passers-by. As soon as the IT professionals made nervous eye contact with the "booth babes," they obediently followed an invitation to come in and hear David's pitch. But if that weren't enough, they also received a clear CD case with a Knowlix demo whose backside listed five reasons to use Knowlix and on the front cover said, "Five Reasons to Use Knowlix," but also had a $5 bill on the inside, clearly visible. Soon people were dropping by asking for the demo CD, and the booth attendants would happily ask them to sit down for a minute, listen to the presentation about the company, and then they would receive their CD. Although marketing purists shrug at such gimmicks, the net effect was that we had customers standing around the Knowlix booth in droves, and as other customers and industry partners looked around, they became convinced that Knowlix had legitimate momentum and had "arrived." Not surprisingly, Knowlix consistently generated more leads than any other exhibitor at tradeshows!

Returning home from the trade show, we read through each of the thousands of detailed customer survey cards, creating a specific road map of "who Knowlix had to win over" and "in what order" in order to Cross the Chasm. The details of these and other survey cards where placed on the wall in the Knowlix war room, with corresponding objectives assigned to team members. We were confident in what we had to do in order to cross the chasm. We had to partner with 1) Remedy, 2) Bendata, and 3) Peregrine Systems, in that order. We had to deliver Microsoft and Novell content in the box. We knew which trade shows the customers attended, the version of their operating systems, and the name of the top IT industry resellers; we knew that *Service News* and *Customer Support and Management Magazine* were the top two industry publications our customers read. In the following weeks and months, we focused Knowlix's engineering, business development, and marketing resources only in the areas that customers really cared about. We took out full-page ads every single month in the key publications, featuring the testimonials of our existing customers. The goal was to be dominant in the key magazines, newsletters, and tradeshows that customers most cared about, but Knowlix remained invisible everywhere else. Our Knowlix full-page ads featured customers, professionally photographed, wearing sharp clothes, with a profile of all customers—their businesses, and their testimonials about Knowlix. Mainstream customers recognized "Bart from Autodesk" and became more comfortable that industry thought leaders were buying. Furthermore we advertised repeatedly in a targeted online newsletter and in the two core industry publications. The results was that after only 18 months we achieved #1 in aided and unaided name recognition in their space. The branding and lead generation activities generated momentum that fed our sales team. No longer were the Knowlix sales reps alone on the customer's doorstep with a just brochure in their hand, they had the backing of a sophisticated branding effort that supported their message. Not only did the early majority believe that Knowlix had arrived as a company, they started buying the product, and we soon had more seats and sites than all our other competitors combined. At its core, successfully convincing the mainstream customers required establishing key business-development relationships, creating a whole-product solution, and targeting marketing activities that communicated that the company was a safe, credible, market leader whose product would improve their business. Once we convinced the first few mainstream customers that they were legitimate, we then focused all our effort on pleasing those mainstream customers so they would go out and spread the news by word-of-mouth and act as reference customers.

PROCESS-SCALING ACTIVITIES

As a startup grows, one of the major tasks an entrepreneur faces is to begin scaling the company's processes. Whereas in the beginning, entrepreneurs and their co-founders do nearly everything in a scattered blaze of wild exploration, as the company shifts from exploring the unknown to executing on the known, most of the firm's activities need to be turned into repeatable processes that can be used by anyone in the company. Gary Kennedy, the General Manager of Oracle USA in the 1980's during Oracle's early high-growth years, was over sales, support and services as Oracle grew to almost a billion dollars. Gary was famous for saying that once you have a sales process that is working, "scale it until it breaks!" The five key activities we advocate in the NISI process to scale your processes are to 1) list 2) define, 3) externalize, 4) transfer, and 5) measure the processes.

1. LIST ALL JOBS BEING PERFORMED

Everyone in a startup wears many different hats. The first step in scaling your business is to list all the different hats you and your team members are wearing. Write down all the different jobs being performed within the company. As a new venture CEO you may be the VP of Sales, Product Manager, Director of Business Development, and Janitor. As you come across other jobs you or another team member are performing, write them down. After listing all the key roles that are performed within your company, make sure they are assigned to someone, even if it is temporary. This first process should be performed early in the life cycle of your startup so you know who has ultimate responsibility for each area. As you start to scale the business, you will look forward to handing off the various hats to someone as you decide which hats to keep for yourself.

2. DEFINE ALL JOBS BEING PERFORMED

The second step is for each employee to write a job description for each of the jobs that he or she is performing within the company. Defining the key roles and all the various hats each employee wears is key in order for the company to take the next steps of detailing responsibilities and then transferring the knowledge to new employees as the company scales.

3. EXTERNALIZE AND DOCUMENT KEY PROCESSES

Gradually you and your founding team will realize that you can't do everything anymore, and it is time to start documenting responsibilities and handing off some of the hats. There will simply be too many responsibilities, too many customers, and too many details for you to ever manage. Even when you hire a sales superstar to help you, or a bookkeeper, or another engineer, as the company grows, even they will be overwhelmed. You will need to make key hires, train those hires, and then give them the reins to begin building their own departments. But the next step is to document the responsibilities and externalize the key processes associated with each position in the company, describing them so that someone brand-new to the company can use the process, ideally without any assistance from you. Entrepreneurs often make the mistake of assuming their employees already understand these processes. It's a common mistake: research has shown that experts often have a hard time communicating with novices because they assume novices already understand what they know.[85] Even if your core team understands the process, you still need to make an effort to externalize and develop a repeatable process because soon, even your own ability to communicate this information will be overwhelmed by the number of employees joining the company. This knowledge-transfer process is a key step in the maturing of any company.

So you need to sit down and map out in detail the processes you have developed, highlighting all the relevant linkages and relationships. This requires deep understanding of the processes themselves that only comes from engaging in the process yourself. Then as you hand off the process to someone else, you need to monitor and potentially refine the process so that all the steps and relationships are maintained. The goal here is that once you have done it yourself, find a way to document and then scale what you have learned. The marriage of intimate experience with the process and then documenting to scale is a tool used by some of the very best entrepreneurs to this day. For example, Sridhar Ramaswamy, vice president of engineering over Google's AdWords, oversees the 800-plus engineers who manage the code that drives over 95% of Google's billions in revenue. You might think he would spend all his time in meetings managing such a large team. Not so. In fact, Ramaswamy spends at least 25% of his time actually coding. Why? So he understands intimately the problems and processes his engineers face and then knows how to communicate new directions and processes at scale. If Ramaswamy didn't code, his ability to develop reliable, repeatable processes for his massive team would be hindered because of his own distance from the actual problem. At the same time, if Ramaswamy didn't take what he learned and externalize that information in a scalable way, he couldn't possibly communicate it to his massive team.

4. TRANSFER PROCESSES

Once you have externalized the processes, the next step is to communicate and transfer them to your growing team, and then create a reporting and accountability system for the new process owners. There are of course many ways to do this; the most powerful method we have used employs principles of *lean manufacturing* to make the process visual. On a factory floor, this might be done by creating a single area on the shop floor where all the defective parts are brought to or outlining the process flow visually on the floor with paint, or signaling the movement of goods using cue cards (for more, read about the Kanban system). The point is to visually communicate the flow of activity so that everyone understands the big picture of that work flow and which part they own, so they can optimize their part of the process

As your startup scales and you begin to externalize processes, you will find that transferring processes requires more than just sitting down and communicating the process itself to your team members. Of course this is important, but your employees need to see how the processes you are transferring fit into the larger activities of the venture. The best way we've found to do this is to make the strategy, tactics, and processes of your company clear and highly visual.

To illustrate, Infusionsoft is a startup that develops customer-relationship management (CRM) tools for small to medium-sized businesses. In the late 1990s, CRM became a massive market for large organizations as they sought to create databases to help them manage customer relationships, but these systems, offered by companies such as E.piphany and Salesforce.com, were targeted at very large businesses. Recognizing that small businesses didn't have access to these tools, the founders of Infusionsoft developed a set of CRM tools that could be delivered at a more moderate cost to small and medium-sized enterprises. At first the Infusionsoft founders had been used to doing everything themselves, but as the company grew rapidly, it proved increasingly difficult to communicate the direction of the company and its various parts. To solve the problem, the team instituted the lean manufacturing metaphor and on a prominent wall posted all the key aspects of the Infusionsoft business. These included the intent, objective, strategy and top six priorities for that year and quarter. (see Figure 30)

Figure 30: Infusionsoft Process Transfer

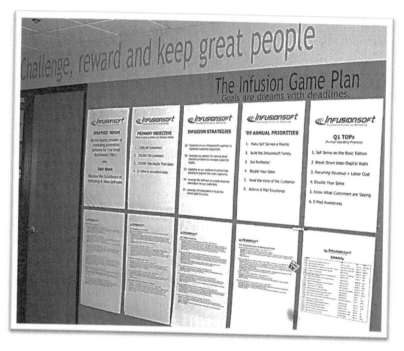

With the high-level objectives so clearly communicated, it became easy to see where the company was heading. But that is not all. Each objective was broken down into specific tasks and ownership so that each group in the company understood what specific tasks they needed to complete to meet those objectives. As a result of using the lean manufacturing communication tactic, not only does the entire Infusionsoft team understand what to do, they also understand how to do it. Not surprisingly, having already nailed their solution and now carefully managing the scaling process, the company has been growing at an incredible pace, absolutely crushing their quarterly sales goals and on their way to becoming a major player in the CRM space.

To apply the lean manufacturing metaphor as you scale, you need to do the following specific tasks:

1. Identify the big picture—establish clearly the bigger vision for your team.

2. Break it down into objectives. Focus on the top five objectives you are trying to accomplish.

3. Break down those objectives into individual ownership.

4. Keep the picture visual.

Each of the objectives should have a time frame. You may notice in the photo that below the "Infusion Soft Game Plan" is the statement "Goals are dreams with deadlines." Similarly, whatever you communicate should be tied to measureable, time-bound objectives. Without a time frame, it is hard to create accountability, and without accountability the objectives will slip through the cracks. As a side note, notice how different this phase feels than the earlier phases of the NISI process. Earlier phases were about exploration, the scale it phase is about execution and scaling that execution.

At the end of the day, the purpose of creating a visual battle plan is so that you can get everyone on your team aligned, rowing in the same direction, and believing in what you are doing. By physically creating a picture, you communicate more clearly what you are trying to do. But you should link that picture to the customer data you have, to the stories you have heard, and to the customer pain, so that your team not only see what to do but they believe in it. When we applied this process at Knowlix during the Scale It phase, our walls not only contained the strategic objectives but they conveyed the information our team had discovered during the nailing-it process. Data and testimonials on what customers wanted, the entire market infrastructure, and the target markets were all prominently displayed. Then on the adjacent wall, we listed the strategic objectives, the tactics, and the measurable steps that were driven by the customer facts listed on the first wall. The result was that team members understood what they needed to do, but they also understood how the facts gathered from customers informed those efforts and gave them extra direction and motivation.

5. MEASUREMENT AND ACCOUNTABILITY OF PROCESSES

Last, as you scale, focus on measuring your most important activities and reporting back your activities on a regular basis to your board, team, or advisors. "When performance is measured, performance improves and when performance is measured and reported, the rate of performance accelerates."[86] However, be very careful what you measure, for the old adage dictates: What gets measured gets done. Take the example of University of Utah and its technology commercialization efforts. For some time the university measured only the revenue generated from patent licenses because licenses provided the most immediate income to the university. The result was not surprising—the technology-transfer office produced modest licensing revenue and was ranked in the bottom 100 in the nation for creating university spinouts. But compare this modest revenue stream to the hundreds of millions of dollars that Stanford realized when it was able to cash in its shares of Google, which was a successful university startup. The cost-recovery mindset is a common model at universities across the country, and it leads to a starvation of innovation and a lockdown of some of the most valuable technologies in the U.S. Cost recovery leads to a short-term focus that demands cash from every deal and quashes the hopes of many an entrepreneur that can't afford the licensing and patent fees that are required of every license. Realizing that there may be greater long-term benefit to the university by encouraging the commercialization of its technology rather than just licensing revenue, President Michael Young and the University of Utah leadership led a turn-around effort that transformed the university into a global leader. By clearly stating that economic development was the driving mission of commercialization, the new University of Utah team, led by Jack Brittain and Brian Cummings, changed what they measured. Instead of measuring licensing revenue, they shifted their focus to more impactful outcomes that measured the number of new companies started, investments in those companies, job creation, and the number of students and entrepreneurs involved in the process. The University of Utah went from a short-term (cost-recovery model) to a long-term (investment model) focus, measuring things that drove higher-impact positive outcomes. The shift in thinking ignited an investment approach, which became the center of new model of economic development. By simply changing what the university measured, it literally transformed its operations and went from the bottom 100 in university spinouts to tying MIT in 2008 and surpassing MIT in 2009 to become the number one highest generator of startups using university technology in the United States.

The University of Utah is now implementing the NISI process on a large scale as a requirement in both the technology-vetting process and the startup creation process. By marrying the appropriate decision making processes with small amounts of "smart capital," the University of Utah is acting like a startup: lean and focused. Think about it: universities spent hundreds of millions of dollars protecting their intellectual property, but seventy percent of their patents will never be licensed! The federal funding agencies, Department of Commerce, and the White House are hoping that US universities will be the drivers of job creation and economic recovery. The University of Utah is leading the way and showing that a NISI methodology, tied to a systematic process that identifies technologies and products that consumers want, is delivering consistent results. Congratulations to the researchers, leadership, and the technology-commercialization team at the University of Utah. You nailed it!

In the chapter on Nailing the Business Model we talked about the importance of a business dashboard. The dashboard is a way for entrepreneurs to define and then monitor the most important elements of their business. Measurement is a critical part of understanding what is happening and one reason why Infusionsoft chose to highlight: "Goals are dreams with deadlines." The crucial task in measuring is to identify the correct things to measure and then turn them into measurable, time-bound objectives. Often the things you should measure in a startup or new business are not the obvious metrics you are taught in school or that match the received wisdom. Focusing on the financial metrics in your income statement, for example, has relatively low value. Much more important are the costs of customer acquisition, the rate of adoption, the turnover in customers, and the fully loaded cost of producing a good or service (the cost of your actual product plus all the extra costs in overhead and marketing that also cost money. Ignoring this can lead to a situation in which you make money on your product but lose money in your business).

Be sure to identify the most important measurements for your business and capture them. Also be sure that from time to time you take a step back and validate that they are the most important things to focus on. You may be surprised by something obvious that you missed. For example, in the early days of DRAM memory-chip production, Samsung focused on measuring what they believed was the key metric: die-yield. Die-yield was a measure of quality, or the amount of functional memory that could be squeezed out of one expensive silicon wafer, and Samsung invested literally millions of dollars to squeeze out a tenth of a percentage of improvement. However, because of their obsessive focus on this measure, Samsung was missing the importance of another measure: equipment utilization. Typical semiconductor fabs cost about $2 billion at the time, and while Samsung had their production lines halted to improve yields by a .01%, their $2-billion fixed asset was sitting idle. When a team of academics and consultants from Berkeley pointed this out to Samsung, the light bulb suddenly went on—simply by changing their focus to equipment utilization, Samsung could get 10%, 20%, 30%, or even higher value out of their factories. The Samsung team changed what they measured, and not only did they become radically more profitable, but when DRAM memory prices crashed and the industry experienced a shakeout, Samsung was so much more cost efficient that they not only survived but actually repositioned to become one of the dominant manufacturers in the industry.

TEAM-SCALING ACTIVITIES

We've emphasized that as you scale, what you have done in the past won't necessarily make you successful in the future. This applies equally to your market, process, and team activities. As you scale, you have to change. But how does the team change and scale? There are four key activities related to helping your team and organization scale which we focus on in this discussion: creating culture, managing communication, increasing accountability, accessing outsiders, and changing talent.

CREATING CULTURE

Most people think about the culture of the place they work as a given, if they even recognize it at all. Culture is the subtle agreement about what is important to your startup and the rules of how to do it. When a startup is three founders in a garage, culture is just as real, but it isn't as important because everyone can see what the others are doing, and changes are easy to make. As your startup scales, it becomes increasingly hard to communicate with and watch what everyone else is doing. New hires will come on board, and it will be impossible to adequately communicate all that your startup does, what to prioritize, and how to get it done. Enter culture. In the absence of you helping new and existing employees understand these important issues, they will take their cues from the culture of your startup. The culture may send messages such as "We only respond to fire drills," or "Do what your boss says," or "Experiment wildly," or any number of other combinations.

The mistake most entrepreneurs make is that they don't realize that whether they choose to consciously define and communicate the culture or not, the culture will exist. If entrepreneurs are too busy to shape the culture, it will emerge on its own and probably won't be as effective as it could be. The opportunity for you as a founder is to consciously shape the culture to be an effective tool for scaling. Shaping the culture means effectively two things. First, consciously define and then communicate what the culture is. When defining the culture it is important to keep in mind the most important activities to the success of the startup, and focus on those issues. Second, shape your rewards, communication, and other activities to reinforce, not contradict, the culture.

Mari Baker, one of Intuit's early employees and a senior vice president, argued that one of the most important things Intuit did in the early days of scaling the company was to stop and define the culture. In fact, Intuit literally stopped to do it—Scott Cook took the entire team offsite to have a discussion about what Intuit was about and what they needed to do to reach their goals. One of the important messages that emerged from this meeting was the centrality of pleasing the customer and continuing to innovate. But simply going offsite for a few days wasn't enough. Intuit had to reinforce the culture they defined with their communication and reward systems. One way that Intuit encouraged experimentation was to give an award for failure to someone who experimented in an admirable way, learned from the experience, but ultimately failed. The award acknowledged that failure is part of experimentation, and as long as you learn from the failure, it is worthwhile.

MANAGING COMMUNICATION

As the startup grows, effective communication also becomes a significant challenge. Nonetheless, a key to the NISI process is communicating the needs of customers throughout the organization. To reach your objectives you will need to communicate them and then hold people responsible. At the core, communication is critical to help your entire team to both understand what is going on and pull together in the same direction.

As you scale, effective communication will take more and more effort, but we have observed several tactics that successful startups use as they scale. The first tactic is one we discussed earlier in terms of visually highlighting your strategy, objectives, and tactics on the wall for all to see. Second, successful startups we have studied use one or more meeting types: daily synch meetings, all-hands meetings, team meetings, one-on-one meetings, and skip-level meetings.

Daily Synch Meetings: The Daily Synch Meeting is a tool that successful companies with learning cultures use to check their pulse and rapidly adapt to any changes in their environment while they are scaling. The daily sync meetings are held twice a day: a standing 15-minute morning meeting with key executives to talk about the key tasks for that day, and then a short end-of-day meeting to report back the results of that day. Promoted by Vern Harnish, in his book *Rockefeller Habits*, these daily meetings are used by many high-growth organizations to increase the quality and speed of their execution.

All-hands Meetings: Surprisingly, almost every successful startup we have observed from Facebook and Google to startups in the middle of scaling, like Xfire, Knowlix, and Fluidigm, employ all-hands meetings. Even though these companies are in the throes of scaling their business and often working round the clock, they consistently take the time out (usually on Friday afternoon) to bring every employee into a meeting and talk. This meeting usually has several key parts. First, the management team talks about the key objectives we described earlier, emphasizing them and discussing where the company stands on these objectives. Second, individual teams take time out to share what they are working on. This could include engineering, marketing, support, or any other relevant area. The purpose of these updates is to let everyone know what the others are working on and identify areas of overlap, synergy, or knowledge that can be tapped later. Third, the meetings can be a place to deal with new challenges or questions. The tone of this meeting should be to avoid competition or blame and allow everyone to understand where they are going and how to work together to accomplish the objective.

Team Meetings/One-on-one Meetings: In addition to an all-hands meetings, plan to meet with your direct reports at least weekly, or perhaps bi-weekly, in a smaller team meeting. In these meetings, insist on hearing some details of what your direct reports are working on, how well they are working with others areas of the venture, their knowledge of customer needs, and accountability of their progress on the key objectives of the company.

Skip-level Meetings: We've told the story of why Polaroid failed (because they shut down their market-leading digital camera effort and focused instead on film-based photography), but how this happened is also important. One of the reasons the top management team could justify focusing on film-based photography rather than digital photography was because at the top of the organization, they were isolated from their environment and couldn't see the changes that were coming. This is actually a pretty common problem in larger companies—the people in charge are the most removed from customers and have the worst information about customer needs. Often it is the company culture that insulates top executives from feedback. One way to fight this problem is with a skip-level meeting: every month, go meet with people in your company who are anywhere from a level down in the startup to the very front lines. Spend the time getting to understand what their needs are, and you will have a much better picture of how to operate. Customer service guru and author Gary Heil is famous for saying, "The front-line never lies."[87] Staying in touch with the front-line will not only keep you in touch with your team and customers, it will help you avoid stupid decisions that negatively impact these individuals who interact most with your customer.

In closing, the purpose of these meetings is not to create death-by-meetings. Slow startups fail, but so do startups that communicate poorly. All meetings should focus at some level on the core objectives you established earlier and on how to achieve them with your customers. Last, be sure to consider the benefits of open and honest communication. If you bring your team members into your confidence, share with them your direction, ask them about their insights, and trust them, they will reward your trust with dedication and hard work. Transparency is core to creating high-trust and highly effective organizations. Treating your employees like adults with critical company information allows them to be more effective and builds a culture of loyalty while you scale. Most often, "big secrets" quickly find their way to the rumor mill, and employees don't feel any obligation to keep it secret if they hear it on the street. At the same time, you can set an expectation that sharing confidential information entrusted directly to them inappropriately is grounds for dismissal.

INCREASING ACCOUNTABILITY

We've talked about the importance of being accountable. Your objectives need to be measurable and time-sensitive. You need to communicate to your team the objectives and hold them accountable. But as the founder and CEO, you need to be accountable too. One of the best ways to do this is to form a trusted board of directors, or at least a board of advisors, that will hold you accountable! When Knowlix began to scale, with the help of our VCs, we built a world-class board consisting of Gary Heil, Carm Santoro, and Patrick Bultema. We used our board strategically to advance the company. I was mentored in operations by Carm Santoro and in public speaking by Gary Heil and also leaned heavily on collaborator and board member Patrick Bultema, the former president of the Help Desk Institute, to provide guidance to the company as it developed (the relationship Bultema also created credibility among his customers as a fortunate by-product). But our board did more than add value by offering advice: they also held us accountable. One of the ways in which they did this was by asking for three cardinal promises—the three objectives that I as the founder would focus on every single day to ensure business success. Every time the board met, they asked us about these promises to help us stay on track. In your startup, develop a board that will help you stay accountable and focused. You will be tempted by many opportunities, but unless a real change is needed, stay focused.

ACCESSING OUTSIDERS

As you scale, don't be afraid to access outsiders for their perspective. Some of the most successful breakthroughs have been made by adding in a new perspective. When Einstein worked at his job as a patent examiner, his conversations with fellow employee Michele Besso dramatically shaped Einstein's first theory, for which he became famous: the special theory of relativity.[88] From CEOs of Fortune 50 companies to startup founders finding their way, one of the most powerful tools for seeing what you might be missing is accessing outsiders who see the world differently—even Tiger Woods has a golf coach.[89] When Knowlix was developing their sales process, the board encouraged us to bring in outside expertise to help the team better understand the systems, tools, and triggers that moved a sales lead through the process from one stage to the next. In response they brought in Jack Carroll as an outside sales mentor who helped our team discover the key tools and triggers to accelerate sales prospects through the sales process—advancing customer from being "Suspects" (raw lists of potential customers) to "Prospects" (potential customers who have made some kind of contact with the company), to "Leads" (potential customers who fit the Knowlix target-customer profile), to "Qualified Leads" (leads who have budget and expressed an interest in purchasing), and finally to customers and repeat customers. A crucial part of being an entrepreneur and scaling a company is recognizing when you don't have the necessary skills and need to find people who can fill those gaps for you.

CHANGING TALENT

As you scale, sometimes people have to change too. Some people just enjoy the early stage more than later stages and will leave the company on their own because they feel bored. This is okay; it is a matter of preference rather than something you did wrong. Other people will have a hard time adjusting to the differences between how a startup operates and how a growing company operates. In these cases, you will have to make the tough decision to replace people. In one interview, the founder told us that he had to replace some positions in the management team up to three times because the individuals were resistant to changing how they operated and so couldn't scale with the company.

As a result of scaling, you may also face one of the hardest transitions for any founder—the talent that may not scale might be you. Oftentimes founders are more capable and happier in the early, formative stages of a company but struggle when the venture starts to scale. For example, Craigslist, founded by Craig Newmark, did everything right, applying NISI principles when building the company. "Most of what we do is based on what people in the community suggest. … People suggest stuff to us, we do what makes sense, and then we ask for more feedback," according to Newmark.[90] When a big decision about how to make money came along, Newmark asked the customers, who told him to charge people who crowded the service with less effective ads, such as employers and brokers. But as the company scaled, Newmark began to struggle with the management task of the larger company. Fortunately, he had the foresight to recognize he couldn't manage a large organization: "Jim [Buckmaster] is a much better CEO. And my skills are not management skills. However, I'm a really good customer-service representative."[90] Ultimately the transition to a CEO who had experience running a larger organization was better for Craigslist and better for Newmark. However, few founders are able to recognize what Newmark was able to: the startup might need to change you to be successful. The reason is that as the company scales, the nature of the management task changes from creative exploration to stone-cold execution. These are actually remarkably different skills, and it can be hard for founders to transition from one to the other. The key is in recognizing that there is no shame in being good at creating something and handing over the reins to someone who is good at running something. If it's time to transition, find a role in the company that best fits your skills or take your success and go on to start something else.

As your company scales, your company will go through fundamental transitions that need to be managed. What you did in the past won't necessarily make you successful in the future. Your market, process, and team all need to be transitioned. The entire topic of scaling is material for another book, but you can keep these core principles in mind, and once something works, scale it till it breaks.

CHAPTER 9: CONTEXT MATTERS!

While electronic cars seem like a good idea and eventually may displace traditional vehicles, we have no idea how long it will take before they become mainstream with a majority of users. As an example of how long it can take good ideas to reach customers, take a look at the history of the light bulb. Light bulbs were a revolutionary idea, but even after the first working light bulb was developed, it still took over seventy years until Edison developed a light bulb that was commercially successful. Interestingly, to make the bulb successful he had to first put it in a format that people were willing to adopt, by dimming it down to the level of existing gas lighting and designing the distribution to mimic a gas system. The lesson to learn is that even when startups, whether the Edison Company or one of the many electric-car ventures, have come up with revolutionary solutions for market needs, the adoption of innovation still depends a great deal on the context. For example, there were many video sharing sites and tools before and after YouTube, but YouTube's timing in tackling the new market was a critical part of their success. YouTube entered the market when storage technology costs were dropping dramatically, enabling them to host videos perpetually. The combination of video uploading and viewing features was perfectly timed with the evolution of consumers' growing comfort with uploading videos and sharing them virally via social networks. In short, timing and context also mattered for YouTube's success.

> *Although the NISI process can help validate any new venture, you need to modify how you apply the NISI process depending on your context.*

Although the NISI process can help validate any new venture, you need to modify how you apply the NISI process depending on your context. In particular, you may need to modify the speed of the process, the types of customers you talk to, or your strategy for attacking the market and scaling your business. Although there are many ways to describe different contexts, we will keep it simple and focus on the division between new and established markets. How do you know whether you are tackling a new or established market? It all depends, but it doesn't actually depend on your technology or product. Most people, when trying to decide whether they are tackling a new or established market, focus on the technology or product itself. But what determines whether you are in a new or established market is how you *apply* the technology or solution. Any single solution can often be applied in either new or established markets, and you need to decide which market you are tackling. For example, the HP Kittyhawk project developed a 1.3-inch hard drive which was two generations ahead of competitors. At the time, the project managers were trying to decide where the technology could be applied. It could be used in the emerging PDA market (new market) or the video-game market (established market). Unfortunately, because the management team didn't recognize the difference between the market types and how to adjust based on market type they ultimately stumbled, bringing down the entire hard-drive division with them.

NEW MARKET CONTEXT

New markets are often created by a disruptive technology that serves new customers or an opportunity that was previously unnoticed or underserved. New markets are exciting for entrepreneurs who eagerly interpret the lack of competition as a wide-open opportunity waiting to be captured. While it is true that new markets can be very promising, they can also be dangerous. For example, in their book *Fast Second*, Costas Markides and Paul Geroski of London Business School argue that most new markets are won by later entrants who learn from the mistakes of the early entrants. Similarly, although Clayton Christensen is best known for identifying the dangers posed by disruptive innovations to established firms, Christensen also spent time discussing the challenges that new firms face in bringing disruptive innovations to new markets. Although the risks are high, the rewards are great. If you are tackling a new market, you might take into account some special considerations while you adapt the NISI process to your specific industry.

MOVE DELIBERATELY WHILE MOVING FAST

New markets are dangerous for startups because you are exploring uncharted territory, defining a new category, educating consumers, and trying to change behaviors. All these activities are time-consuming, costly, and risky. First and foremost, counter to the logic of "get big fast" strategies of the dot com era, in new markets you often need to keep your resources aligned with the pace and stage of the market to avoid spending all your resources before your market actually takes hold. Consider the patience of Pierre Omidyar when founding eBay, which blazed new territory with the idea of online auctions. It took several years for the eBay concept to catch hold while users slowly adopted the new website. It was only after the website traffic became so voluminous that Omidyar's internet service provider began charging him for a business account that he considered charging for the service. Even then, it was only when there were so many checks coming in that he had to hire someone to open them that he realized he had a real business and quit his job to focus on eBay. Obviously, most entrepreneurs want to move faster than Omidyar, but the point is that if you try to move too fast, the new market might not keep pace with your expectations, and you will run out of runway before takeoff. Capturing new markets takes time, patience, and resources because consumers have to be educated about the new market.

CONSCIOUSLY DEFINE THE MARKET

Another critical activity many entrepreneurs overlook in new markets is the process of defining the new category and market. Most of the time in a new market, customers may be uncomfortable with exactly what the business is—they don't see where you fit. And the problem for you as an entrepreneur is that people tend to ignore or even reject things that don't "fit." For example, in one study, researchers looked at the emergence of financial cooperatives in Singapore during the 1920's. They observed that these new "cooperatives" failed because people had a hard time understanding what they were and how they fit—they didn't seem legitimate. Later, when large commercial banks moved into the space and offered similar cooperatives, they were adopted, but only because several banks moved at once (which added legitimacy to the new market category) and because the large banks were already seen as legitimate, and this ultimately gave consumers enough comfort to jump into the new market.[91]

As an entrepreneur with a new product in an existing market or when creating a new market, your challenge is to define new categories and then find a way to make them seem legitimate so that the vast majority of customers are comfortable adopting your product. So how do entrepreneurs define categories and then make them legitimate? As it relates to market positioning, entrepreneurs do three things: define, claim, and legitimize new market categories. In short, successful entrepreneurs first define which market they are operating in. Defining the market should begin with a focus on the problem, not the solution. As an entrepreneur you can gain traction by focusing on the language of the problem and then subtly define the solution around yourself. So for example, Knowlix entered the IT Help Desk Industry with the recognition of a key pain point: knowledge about how to solve IT problems was poorly managed. We spent our time talking about the core problem and then defined ourselves as being in the subcategory of "knowledge management" by giving it a new label and then positioning Knowlix as the leader in that space. To define a space, look for the pain, discuss the pain in the language of the pain, then define the solution and the labels used to solve the problem around your firm.

As you try to legitimize your claim, there are many tools you can use to claim and legitimize a category. This might include using analogies to other established markets that make the new category seem legitimate. So for example, Rhomobile described themselves as the Ruby on Rails of mobile applications. This analogy helped their customers understand where the business "fit" and made the company seem like the next step or a natural evolution. Similarly, the Web 2.0 label defined an entirely new space for web startups separate from their competitors, but the analogy to a version 2.0 of software helped people understand not only where the company fit but that Web 2.0 companies were the next big thing in the online space. Alternatively, entrepreneurs will often associate themselves with others who transfer legitimacy to the startup. At Knowlix we persuaded Patrick Bultema, the former president of the Help Desk Institute, to join their board, which increased our legitimacy. Alternatively, forming alliances with corporate partners or taking money from high-prestige investors can transfer legitimacy to a startup. For example, Dominic Orr, founder of the now public company Aruba Networks, argues that one of the purposes of venture capital is to give a new company legitimacy.[47] Last, entrepreneurs tell and disseminate stories about their company and the industry that increase their legitimacy.[84] When Knowlix took out full-page ads profiling how our customers' businesses had been transformed by using the Knowlix software, we were telling stories that legitimized our business. Similarly, when O'Reilly and MediaLive hosted the first Web 2.0 conference, the very existence of a conference not only legitimized the label but provided the vehicle for story telling about the new category.

CONSCIOUSLY SHAPE THE MARKET

In addition to defining the market around themselves, successful entrepreneurs also proactively shape the boundaries of new markets. These strategies include co-opting competitors, connecting distant partners, and controlling the market. For one, successful startups often shape the market by co-opting potential competitors to eliminate the potential threat they pose. In recent research by Filipe Santos (INSEAD Business School) and Kathleen Eisenhardt (Stanford University), they observed that one startup in the emerging intersection between networking and telecom was concerned that competitors from either market could enter and attack the startup's core business. So the startup pursued equity partnerships with its potential competitors in both markets, using two tactics. First, the entrepreneurs convinced their potential competitors that a partnership with the startup would allow the big company to focus on its core business while still having a stake in the emerging market in case the market became a valuable source of growth. Second, the entrepreneurs positioned themselves as the anti-leader, or the enemy, of the market giant who all the competitors wanted to defeat. The result was that the five potential competitors they approached all invested money in an equity partnership.[84]

Second, some entrepreneurs shape the market by trying to serve as the connection point for partners. So, for example, while the mobile-phone gaming industry is fairly well established today, at the beginning of the wireless-gaming industry, startups were in a difficult predicament. On the one hand, mobile carriers, such as AT&T or Verizon, were behemoths with little interest in talking to a startup. On the other hand, mobile handset producers were also mega firms, such as Motorola or Nokia, that were equally uninterested in upstart companies. To effectively produce a mobile game, startups needed the cooperation of both the handset producers and the wireless carriers. One strategy that successful startups used to shape their industry was to position themselves as the middleman in the process.

A startup would approach AT&T and suggest that the startup was currently in talks with Nokia for a hot new mobile game and that it was searching for the right mobile carrier as a partner. Instantly, AT&T was paying attention. Then the same startup would approach Nokia and suggest they were in talks with AT&T for the next exciting mobile game, and they were looking for the right handset producer as a partner. Again, Nokia was paying attention. On the surface it might seem duplicitous; however, the startup was in fact talking to both companies at the same time. By moving in parallel rather than first securing one partnership and then trying to secure a second partnership, the startup was able to move quickly and effectively close a major deal![92] This same strategy can be applied in other contexts in which entrepreneurs shape the market by positioning themselves as the go-between to forming a deal.

Third, entrepreneurs often actively try to control their market, either by gobbling up market-share, blocking competitors, or eliminating business models that are threatening to them. Once a startup grows sufficiently large, it may acquire smaller competitors to increase its market coverage and eliminate the emergence of stronger competitors, or it tries to block the entry of new firms. One company in the virtual marketplace space actually acquired a small but rather insignificant rival simply because it didn't want another business to acquire the rival and use it as a stepping-stone into their business. Some entrepreneurs will seek to get legislation, form industry groups, control key intellectual property, or define industry standards to block the entry of competitors. Finally, entrepreneurs will often eliminate business models that threaten them. You can observe this pattern recently in the VOIP industry, where most players in this space live on a recurring revenue business, whereas competitors like Ooma and Magic Jack sell solutions that are flat-fee solutions. One particular strategy might be to acquire these competitors in an effort to eliminate or control their business model.

BEWARE OF THE ECOSYSTEM: SUBSTITUTES AND COMPLEMENTS STILL MATTER

Last, as you enter the new market, beware of the ecosystem. Because they are entering what seems a new market, most entrepreneurs don't realize they have to deal with substitutes and complements. But both can be very important to the success of a new venture. Substitutes are the alternatives to your product and in new markets substitutes usually represent the old way of doing things. Complements are all the pieces of the puzzle that need to come together for your product to work. Both can create barriers and switching costs that limit the adoption of products in new markets.

Substitutes: Switching Costs and Hidden Incentives

For most new markets, substitutes, or the old way of doing things, represent the most dangerous threat. Despite the fact that you may have invented something that is an order of magnitude better or cheaper, often there are vested interests and habits in the old way of doing things that can be difficult to break through. One of the best-known examples of old habits dying hard is the traditional keyboard in use today, known as the "QWERTY" keyboard. This keyboard was designed to keep the keys on manual typewriters from sticking, but it does not represent the optimal layout of keys to increase typing speed. However, attempting to change the keyboard layout would be nearly impossible today, given the switching costs involved for customers. Furthermore, a QWERTY keyboard represents a pain almost no one feels. So be careful to assess the costs to your customers of switching to your product.

Closely related to these switching costs are the hidden incentives of the existing market structure and the decision makers in a market that will be disrupted by the new market. Often, the people or structures of the substitute market may have incentives that can hamper the growth of a new market. Clayton Christensen tells the story of an innovator who developed higher-resolution radiology film that was dramatically cheaper than existing solutions. The film was so clear and so much cheaper that in many ways it eliminated part of the job of radiologists, who are paid large salaries to interpret the results of fuzzy radiology films. Although the entrepreneur assumed that he could create a new market in radiology that would be enthusiastically embraced by the medical industry, he discovered that radiologists were highly reluctant to adopt the new technology, perhaps in part because it partially eliminated their jobs. Similarly, we worked with a startup that delivered distance-interviewing solutions for human resource departments in large corporations. This startup allowed hiring professionals to interview candidates via video quickly and inexpensively from a distance. As the startup began to grow, its developers discovered that many of its customers became increasingly uncomfortable adopting or using their product. Why? Because the product was so effective at saving time and cost that it actually eliminated jobs in the HR department! Because customers were HR departments, some customers decided they would rather keep their jobs than adopt the new technology.

Complements: Asynchronous Development and Co-Opting Value

For many new markets, complements can also be a hindrance in developing a new market. Complements are the related components that make up a whole-product solution. The classic example in economics of complements is hot dogs and buns or peanut butter and jelly. While a cute comparison at an abstract level, in many new markets, complements are a critical component of any successful startup strategy. The key challenges when dealing with markets affected by complements are timing and capturing value. In terms of timing, the key challenge in a new market is ensuring that the related complements are ready to go to market at the same time that you are. If the timing is off, or asynchronous, your product may be ready, but because the complementing technologies are not, the market never materializes.[93] For example, the HP spinoff project we mentioned earlier developed a revolutionary 1.3" hard drive targeted at the PDA market, but although the HP team delivered the hard drive on time, many of the other complements, such as handwriting software, were woefully inadequate, and as a result the new market never materialized. As a result, in a new market, take a good hard look at the complements, related technologies, and market structure and decide whether they will also be ready at the same time you are. If not, consider alternatives. In case of the HP hard drive, Nintendo had been knocking on their door to develop a cheaper version of the new drive. Although it was an established market, all the Nintendo components were in place and ready to go and might have been a market where HP could have succeeded.[94]

In addition to timing, also pay attention to who captures the value among the complements. Although many components often make up a technology product, not everyone captures the same amount of value. For example, although both microprocessors and hard drives go into a laptop,

Intel makes far more money than the disk-drive producers or even the makers of the laptop itself. The reason Intel captures far more of the value relates to strategic, competitive, and structural characteristics of their industry. Therefore, when entering any industry, whether new or old, it is always a useful exercise to examine where the money is made and by whom (we recommend the article "Profit Pools" by Orit Gadiesh and James Gilbert).

ESTABLISHED MARKETS

In contrast to new markets, established markets are markets where products exist and where you intend to compete by offering a product that serves a niche within the existing market or is a complement to an existing product. A good deal has been written about competing in existing markets, so we won't spend as much time reviewing these principles. Instead we will just highlight a few key points.

SPEED MATTERS IN ALL MARKETS, BUT ESPECIALLY ESTABLISHED MARKETS

In all markets, speed is important. In a new market you need to be faster than your competitors but not too fast, or you will overshoot the market. In contrast, in an established market, speed is one of your primary competitive advantages. Established markets are often inhabited by big companies with lots of resources, significant brands, captive distribution channels, and a host of other advantages. However, the two things big companies rarely have are innovation and speed. In the words of Dominic Orr, founder of Aruba Networks, "I've done enough startups now, so if you ask me to distill the formula of success of a small company competing against a big company, it all boils down to one factor: that is speed. Speed of execution, and speed of innovation."[47]

While we cautioned that in new markets you have to proceed at a more measured pace because the market takes time to define and educate, in established markets, customers are often already educated. Because you are a startup, your customers will more quickly recognize "what" you are as well as how to use your solution to solve their pain. As a result, you can move much more quickly because you don't need to take as much time to educate and legitimize the market—it already exists. You need to move quickly; otherwise your competitors, large or small, may recognize the opportunity and beat you to the prize. This doesn't mean you should neglect the NISI process. If you take out the time to run the NISI process and really deeply validate your solution, go-to-market strategy, and business model with customers, you will ultimately save time and beat your competitors. The point is that you should move more quickly in established markets than in new markets.

ATTACK THE FLANK, NOT HEAD ON

One of the interesting characteristics of established markets is that over time they tend to consolidate. As markets mature, the needs of customers are often better served through efficiency, and as a result, market players slowly consolidate, and eventually several large firms come to dominate the market. These large firms do an excellent job of serving the bulk of customers with an efficient solution, manufactured at scale, and delivered with as few errors as possible. But the very nature of the consolidation process means that as the large firms move to the middle of the market, the edges of the market always remain underserved. From soft drinks to social networks, large, dominant players like Coke or Facebook emerge, but the edges of the market are open to new entrants, like Red Bull or Chess.com. This process of consolidation at the middle of the market presents significant opportunities for entrepreneurs to serve the needs of customers at the edge of the market, which is often called a *market niche*. The beauty of tackling an established market with a niche strategy is that because of the way large firms are structured, rarely do they have the speed or ability to serve a niche as well as the entrepreneur who focuses on the niche. For example, airlines like Southwest Airlines in the U.S., Ryan Air in Europe, and Kiwi Airlines in New Zealand have carved out very profitable businesses by tackling the low-cost traveler niches that big airlines have been unable to serve (and the large airlines have failed every time they have tried). In contrast, if you try to attack an established player head-on, say, for example, a Microsoft, Intel, Intuit or Google, you will be crushed. Simply put, the big player will defend its territory with great vigor, and your chances of success are very low.

MOVE FROM THE LOW TO HIGH END

An alternative way to attack an established market with big players is to tackle the low end of the market and move up to the high end. The reason is that customers at the top of the market often aren't willing to risk their business on an unproven startup, no matter how innovative the idea. In contrast, customers who are fighting the big players in an industry are constantly looking for an edge and are more willing to work with a scrappy startup who could give them an advantage. Over time, as the product gets better, that same scrappy startup becomes a resourceful, trusted industry partner with a robust solution and can gradually move up the market to the high end. So for example, one startup that was developing software for investment banks had a strategy of selling to the tier-1 players, such as Goldman Sachs and Citigroup first, with the belief that after closing tier-1 customers they would then have the credibility to easily sell to tier-2 and tier-3 customers. Unfortunately, the tier-1 customers weren't interested in working with an unproven startup. Frustrated and confused, this software startup tried to target tier-3 customers and successfully closed several customer deals. From there, as it developed more experience, refined its product, and became more well-known in the industry, it was able to move up to tier-2 customers, and from there eventually tier-1 customers. This basic idea plays out at the level of entire industries, which was the basis of Clayton Christensen's *Innovator's Dilemma*, but also in the lives of individual startups. Most often for young startups, it makes the most sense to go from the low end to the high end rather than vice versa. Of course, there are always exceptions to the rule, and if you can start from the high end, there are clear advantages.

BE AN ECOSYSTEM PLAYER

An alternative strategy to targeting a niche is to target the core of the market but with a solution that is symbiotic to the business of the market leader. Add-ons to the Microsoft Windows operating system or applications for the iPhone are examples of ecosystem strategies. Rather than attacking the big firms in the market, you develop a solution that works with and even enhances the value for the big firms in the market. The advantage of this approach to an established market is that you leverage off a bigger firm's established market, and the big firm most likely won't attack you. In fact, the big firm will often help you by providing assistance or marketing dollars. The key to successfully executing this strategy in an existing market is to create a solution that co-exists with and hopefully increases the value of the solutions provided by the 800-pound gorillas already dominating the market.

DON'T MIX YOUR COMPETITIVE LOGIC: LOW COST VERSUS DIFFERENTIATION

As entrepreneurs tackle an established market, sometimes they try to be all things to all people, but this can lead to the entrepreneur's demise. We've discussed the importance of focusing on a core market, but it is also important to focus your strategy. At its simplest, there are two basic strategies: low cost and differentiation. Low-cost strategies focus on delivering products at as low a cost as possible, whereas differentiation strategies focus on providing solutions that distinguish themselves by the value-added features they provide. Wal-Mart clearly pursues a low-cost strategy, whereas Nordstrom follows a differentiation strategy by trying to provide incredible customer service and attention. The mistake many businesses make is trying to do both things at once, but the strategies are like oil and water—they don't mix well. If Nordstrom tried to offer Wal-Mart-style prices, they would quickly go out of business, because the cost of high-customer service (sales representatives on commission, liberal return policies, and attractive stores) would quickly destroy their profit margin. However, the same is also true for Wal-Mart. Despite all Wal-Mart's many capabilities, if they tried to provide Nordstrom-level service, the costs to do so would soon leave Wal-Mart open to attack from low-cost competitors seeking to displace them. For many entrepreneurs, this advice is difficult to put into practice—it is so tempting to try to be all things. Failing to settle on a competitive logic (low cost or differentiation) can destroy your core-value proposition.

IN ANY MARKET, LEARN TO CHANGE

At the heart of it, to be a successful entrepreneur you have to learn to change and adapt. You may need to adapt the NISI process slightly, depending on the market you are trying to win. You will certainly need to learn to adjust your hypotheses about the customer pain and the solution.

And as you move forward, you may need to change in other ways you didn't see in advance. At the beginning of this book we highlighted some of the myths that surround entrepreneurship, including the characteristics that make an entrepreneur successful. One of these myths is that determined entrepreneurs persist no matter what anyone tells them. While it is true that entrepreneurs have to keep working hard, the reality is that persistence is often misconstrued. Many of the most successful entrepreneurs are quick to change and adjust, depending on what they discover.

Our research on change and cognition revealed that many startups make dramatic changes to almost every aspect of their business model. But why are some startups willing to change when others were not? The reason came down to how the entrepreneurs viewed the world, or what we call *cognitive flexibility*.[11] Cognitive flexibility is the ability to recognize new information and then change the way you view the world. It can help you be more agile and beat out your competitors who are stuck in the old way of doing business. Many things can increase your cognitive flexibility, such as experiencing different things (either in the industries, organizations, or cultures in which you work), listening to outsiders, framing the world as an opportunity, drawing on multiple analogies, and so forth. The central idea is to be flexible in how you view the world and be prepared to change. As an entrepreneur you will face many surprises, and being flexible enough mentally is the key to being able to adapt successfully!

> *Cognitive flexibility is the ability to recognize new information and then change the way you view the world. It can help you be more agile and beat out your competitors who are stuck in the old way of doing business.*

CHAPTER 10: CRISIS AND FOCUS

Remember the story of how Intuit almost failed early on by overlooking their assumptions about the go-to-market strategy? The result was a crisis that should have killed Intuit but instead saved it. When the money ran out, a few crucial things happened. First, Intuit radically cut their burn rate (the amount of money spent every month). When Cook announced they couldn't pay salaries, about half the employees left. Surprisingly, four employees stayed—the two founders as well as Virginia Boyd and Susan Schlangen, who believed in Quicken. The team took other radical measures as well. They returned all the rental furniture, and for desks they used empty Quicken boxes to prop up pieces of plywood. For paper, they used the discarded stationary from the bank where Proulx's girlfriend had worked before it was acquired by Wells Fargo. In addition, the team redesigned Quicken's packaging to eliminate boxes altogether and instead inserted the disk in the instruction manual and then shrink-wrapped the manual—it cut cost of goods sold by 50%. And when the landlord began nosing around, asking whether Intuit could really pay rent, Boyd simply said that they were redecorating and waiting for new furniture. As they juggled payments, at times the bank account got as low as $52.

As a direct result of this crisis, several important things happened. The lower burn rate meant they bought themselves extra time. This extra runway also gave Proulx the time and focus to finish the Apple version of Quicken (the PC version had already been launched). Also, the extra time allowed Intuit to discover that although they had used the right process to nail their product, they had the sales channel completely wrong. Initially, Cook had believed they could push a PC version of Quicken through software retail stores. But as Cook personally visited the retail stores, he discovered that software stores didn't want to carry Quicken unless customers asked for it, and without a big marketing budget, Intuit couldn't make customers aware of the product. As a next step, Cook had tried to stir up free press by talking to industry analysts and other influencers. But although this did generate some press, it didn't seem to stick. As Cook and his team grew more desperate they decided that maybe banks might sell the software to their customers, as part of a home-banking solution. Through a personal relationship, Cook was able to make one sale to Wells Fargo and eventually one more to Bank of Hawaii. But after closing the contracts, software sales were sluggish, and no additional banks signed up to sell Quicken.

At this point, if Intuit had maintained a higher burn rate, the company would absolutely have failed. However, because the team had time, they stayed afloat long enough to finish the Apple version of Quicken. Although no one expected much from the new version, surprisingly, sales began to pop. What's more, suddenly several media outlets began to talk about the Apple version, and Intuit began to sell even more copies directly to customers. Then Intuit discovered the critical flaw in the sales model. PCs at the time were generally for business use, and the media outlets that covered PC-related products focused on business applications. In contrast, Apple computers were being used at home, and the media outlets that covered Apple-related products focused on things that home users might want, such as personal finance software.

In the end, the crisis at Intuit forced changes that created the focus and time to discover the right sales model for Quicken. Had Intuit raised a big round of funding from a venture investor, they might have burned several million dollars advertising a PC version and driven the company to bankruptcy, only to discover the same lesson. The crisis taught Cook and his team other important lessons. By learning to cut corners they hadn't seen before—such as the product packaging—they actually became profitable by the end of the same year. Even more important, Cook's experience pounding the pavement, trying to sell to retail outlets and reluctant banks, taught him an important lesson: he couldn't hire enough sales reps to make the product successful. Instead, Cook would have to turn his customers into his sales reps. Months later after Intuit had begun to revive, Mari Baker, who would eventually become an Intuit senior vice president, asked Cook how in the world Intuit could be successful with only three sales reps. Cook replied, "We actually have a million sales people because our goal is to make those customers so excited they'll go out and tell their friends."[95] The strategy proved as successful as it was low-cost. In the end, Intuit crushed all their competitors—42 in total.

That's the value of a good crisis— it forces the company to focus. Focus is the key to successfully running the NISI process and success as an entrepreneur. And ultimately, many investors and entrepreneurs will admit that most successful companies face a crisis before they succeed. Even companies that appear like

> *Focus is the key to successfully running the NISI process and success as an entrepreneur.*

they have had an uninterrupted rise to success have often had crises that make them successful. Take Dell Computer, for example. Michael Dell describes how only one year after going public, they almost failed because they missed a technology transition in the industry. As a result, the entire inventory system broke down, and Dell had to fundamentally rethink how they did business. But Dell believes that because of the crisis, they "arguably became the best in the world at managing inventory and dealing with technology transitions after that near-death experience."[96] Ultimately, a good crisis can reshape your views, business, and success. But is a crisis really necessary for success? When it comes to the NISI process, the answer is yes! Or more accurately, the focus that a crisis will force on you is necessary for success.

A BARN WITH ENGINES: WHY A CRISIS CAN HELP YOU RUN THE NISI PROCESS

When it comes to startups, people want to invest in companies, join companies, and buy product from companies that are taking off like a rocket. The speed and momentum of a great idea taking off naturally attracts money, employees, sales, and carries everyone along for the ride. But the startup process can be unkind to rocket ships. Even when entrepreneurs start a company right and begin with a simple, sharp, focused idea akin to a shiny rocket, their guidance systems can become corrupted as the team gets distracted by their success. As a result, companies often lose their focus and shift from becoming a market-driven company to be driven by sales or engineering or other factors. Losing connection to the market, the entrepreneur makes changes that add significant friction to a once sleek machine. Eventually the idea becomes an amalgamation of ideas; and as the features and markets expand, the company is no longer a rocket ship capable of breaking orbit but rather resembles a barn with engines on it—burning fuel, but unable to achieve a sustainable orbit. In this state, it takes every last ounce of energy and sweat for the entrepreneur to levitate the barn a few hundred feet in the air. And no matter how determined the entrepreneur, the barn will never break free of gravity and reach orbit. Not unless it is transformed into a rocket ship again.

The value of a crisis is that it forces you to focus, and provides renewed commitment to make the time to really nail the product or service and reshape the company. It is the crisis that gives entrepreneurs the dire resolve required to transform their levitating barn into a rocket ship. Either that, or the company fails. But why is a crisis even necessary in the first place? Can't entrepreneurs, through willpower alone, do the same thing? Yes, but it requires a relentless focus.

> *The value of a crisis is that it forces you to focus!*

Take the example of MyFamily.com (today known as Ancestry.com), one of the companies where I had a front-row seat as it went through their crisis. MyFamily.com was founded as Ancestry.com in the mid-1990's to bring family history searches online. For the devoted niche of genealogists interested in family history, Ancestry.com was a huge innovation, offering time savings of 100 times over the laborious process of digging through paper or microfiche records. Thanks to their focus and value proposition, the founders quickly grew the company into a profitable operation, doing close to $1M in sales per month. As Ancestry.com continued to grow, the dot com market was in full swing, and the small company was no longer satisfied with its small-niche business. The team decided to pursue a "bigger idea" of using the Internet to connect family members and enable them to share stories, photos and information—essentially social networking for families. The company changed its name from Ancestry.com to MyFamily.com, raised $75 million dollars of investor capital, and began to build a social-networking site for families. Initially, the execution of the idea sounded good, but as the dot com bubble began to pick up, MyFamily.com had too much cash and too little discipline. As with many dot coms, they began to lose their focus and went looking for more "eyeballs" to fuel growth, acquiring other companies to add to their portfolio, some of them largely unrelated. With the new war chest of venture funding, they began building a massive headquarters in Northern California to complement their offices in New York and Utah. At its height, the rumors of the company's multi-billion dollar IPO fueled by Mary Meeker and other Wall Street "luminaries" led the company to increase their burn just as the dot com bubble burst.

The distracted board and management team couldn't see that their sleek rocket ship had been lost in the continuous addition of features, customers, and other companies. It had become a barn with engines, but not capable of leaving orbit or sustaining its own momentum. The core-value proposition was still there, but hidden and suffocating under a lot of other features and infrastructure that had been tacked on. Then the bubble popped. Not surprisingly, the company began to scramble. MyFamily.com was burning millions a month, revenues weren't on track, and management was being whipsawed by the market and investors as to what really mattered: one day it was page views, the next it was top-line revenue, the next day it was something else. As the company began to run low on cash, they raised a $15 million series E round of venture capital co-led by Dave Moon (Esnet Capital) and myself (vSpring Capital), this time at a valuation less than 15% of its peak. After investing the first tranche of $10M, a funny thing happened. Nothing! Although management tried to tighten their belts a little, business as usual continued. The real crisis had been averted. That is, until 45 days later when the CEO, Greg Ballard, called investors to let them know that the company was out of money again. Through a combination of bad luck, prior commitments, and mismanagement, somehow MyFamily.com had burned through $10M of the Series E financing in just 45 days. During an emergency board meeting, the investors gathered to make the hard decisions. On the emergency board call, I agreed to lead the investment of an additional $5 million if immediate changes were adopted. Some of these changes included immediately replacing the CEO with an interim CEO, focusing the entire company on the core business of genealogy, reducing staff, spinning off the non-core acquisitions of Ah Ha and Third Age, shutting down the New York and Northern California offices, and consolidating to the company headquarters in one location. Although incredibly hard to do, the value of the crisis was that MyFamily.com was able to make changes that helped it rediscover its value proposition and save the company. When things were merely urgent, the company made few changes.

Only the crisis created the resolve to align the company and the board with its core customers, fire non-core customers, abandon non-core business, trim staff, and re-see the world. And it worked. In the words of Mike Wolfgramm the CTO of Ancestory.com,

> *The transformation at Ancestry.com began after a meeting with Paul Ahlstrom shortly following the Series E investment. Paul sat down with V.P. of Product Gary Gibb, Steve, the V.P. of Marketing, and myself to help us understand a portion of the model\concepts described in this book. That was the catalyst behind the change at Ancestry.com that turned out to be one of the greatest learning experiences for Gary Gibb, Steve, and myself."*

> *After the Series E investment Dave Moon came in as the interim CEO and we scaled the organization down to a minimum set of key people, "FOCUS" became the central theme of the organization. We shifted from a focus on increased page views to a focus on increased revenue. We went from a focus on MyFamily.com and numerous other products and businesses to exclusively focusing on Ancestry.com. We entered a phase where we began to focus on not only the pain points of customers but more importantly those pain points that would ultimately give the company a return on investment. We began to change the way we thought about product development. We decided to create a weekly meeting where the head of product, marketing, and development gathered to review new product and marketing initiatives in conjunction with infrastructure. We began to create an environment within the organization that had a laser beam focus on customer needs that would give a ROI. We also became very good at saying "no" to initiatives that had no substance. Our goal was to ensure that every minute that a resource was working, that person was working on something that was going to increase the bottom line. Each week the owner of the initiative would present his/her case justifying why the initiative was critical to the customer and*

ultimately how it was going to make us money. Once the initiative was approved and delivered to the marketplace, we would meet frequently to review results, key learnings, correct course and iterate quickly based on customer feedback / financial data or terminate the initiative when obvious. As time passed our product and marketing teams became very good at understanding how to measure which of the customer's pain points were ultimately giving the company a positive return. An amazing thing happened, as the months and years went by: we found ourselves doubling revenue every year. The culture of the company had changed from a "living high on the hog" mentality to a startup mentality where focus and efficiency were paramount. The team became much more attuned to assessing customers' pain points and determining which pain points translated into real dollars.

As the company refocused and rediscovered its market, the company not only turned profitable but under the leadership of new CEO Thomas Stockham, it began to grow. Over the next 18 months the company grew at an increasing rate month over month. Eventually the company changed its name back to Ancestry.com and through new leadership went public. Today Ancestry.com has a market capitalization approaching $2 billion (NASDAQ: ACOM) but they could easily have become another failure if they had not learned to focus. At the heart of it, the crisis helped Ancestry.com learn to focus in order to discover the Monetizeable pain points within their core business.

MODELS, PACKRATS AND JUNKIES

These examples highlight the value of a good crisis to transforming your business. But don't be mistaken. The inherent value is not in the crisis but in the process that is forced on management to make the necessary changes—to run the NISI process and *focus* on understanding and satisfying the Monetizable Customer Pain. It can be surprisingly hard for entrepreneurs to develop the resolve, focus, and unity to undertake the NISI process. Time and again, CEOs and entrepreneurs nod in agreement upon hearing the steps that we outline in the NISI process, yet most lack the resolve to actually run the process. It is the crisis that leaves them no choice. The entrepreneurs who lack the resolve to run the NISI process properly usually fall into three buckets—models, packrats, and junkies.

Models. Models, as their name would suggest, are model entrepreneurs or CEOs who are well-spoken, intelligent, and successful individuals who pay lip service to the process but under the surface believe they already have the answer. Usually they have experience at a big-brand company like IBM, Google, McKinsey or Microsoft, and they believe they already understand how to be a great product manager or build a company. These types of entrepreneurs don't have the resolve to run the NISI process because in the back of their minds, they already know the answer. We find that they either never start the NISI process or they run it half-heartedly. Model CEOs might send a team out to investigate for a few weeks, but they don't block out the time to do it themselves. Or if the model CEO does engage in the process himself, he or she usually cuts the process short, failing to ask the really big questions—the breakthrough questions— that determine whether their company will be a blowout success or a crater. At other times, the model CEO substitutes his or her own preconceived answers for the discovery of new insights which the process would generate if given the time.

It is not only normal but admirable for an entrepreneur or CEO *not* to have all the answers. A more enlightened CEO or entrepreneur doesn't seek to be the hero but recognizes that there is no such thing as a model entrepreneur who knows all the answers. We agree with Michael Goguen, a partner at the venture capital firm Sequoia, that great entrepreneurs are

- Very sharp, scrappy, frugal

- Obsessively driven, inquisitive, never satisfied

- Fixated on thrilling customers

- Not distracted by ego or title envy

- Focused on constantly iterating and improving

- Not necessarily experienced

Great entrepreneurs start out searching for, rather than knowing, the answer. As serial entrepreneur Mike Cassidy argued, what makes him successful is precisely the fact that he knows he doesn't know everything.

Packrats. Packrats also live up to their name—they can't abandon a customer. They relentlessly chase down every opportunity and every customer, hoping that, by playing the odds, they will strike gold. But when packrats run a company, they end up building a barn with engines rather than a rocket ship to accommodate the needs of all their customers. These entrepreneurs are willing to engage in the NISI process, but as they go through the process, they see every statement made by every customer as a need they must fulfill. They fall into the trap described by Mari Baker— they listen to everyone and by doing so satisfy no one.[95] Often the hardest decision is the one to decline or even fire a customer in order to focus on the real value proposition.

Jeff Miller, former CEO of Documentum, a document management company that eventually was acquired by EMC for $1.7B, described how he faced this challenge in Documentum's early days. After taking the reins, Miller found that the company had spent a good deal of time and money unsuccessfully chasing customers in several industries. Miller came to believe that for Documentum to succeed, the company had to focus on providing value to one customer vertical rather than many. In other words, Documentum must build a rocket ship that could break orbit rather than a barn with engines, as the company had been doing. But Miller faced his share of pressures. He had promised his venture investors that he would triple revenue and hit a lofty sales goal of $2M the next quarter. As the research poured in and the team debated, it became clear to Miller that the company should focus on pharmaceutical companies, an area where Documentum could provide clear customer value. By using Documentum, big pharmaceutical firms could save almost $1M a day during the patenting process. But then the top salesperson phoned in with a big win: he had closed a nearly $1M contract with the big insurance company Marsh & McLennan. Most of the team wanted to take the contract and Miller did too—Miller's sales pipeline was pretty much empty, and this deal would allow him to get close to his quarterly sales goal.

Looking back on it, Miller described this decision as the difference between a difficult decision (one where you don't know what to do) and a painful decision (one where you know what to do but it will be painful). Much to his credit, Miller made the painful decision and turned down the Marsh & McLennan deal to focus on pharmaceutical firms. At the time, Miller used to jokingly say, "We may not be right, but we're not confused."[97] And ultimately he was right—by focusing on the customer segment where Documentum's research indicated they provided the most value, Documentum was able to close sale after sale, and ultimately they came to dominate its market niche and finally had a very successful exit. Ultimately, Miller achieved what few entrepreneurs achieve without a crisis: the ability to discover where the most value is created and the focus to ignore all the other customers that might distract you. Often the entrepreneurs we meet can't let go of customers because they are needed to keep the company afloat. The decision in this case is often the painful decision: cut expenses and focus. The Documentum example demonstrates that a barn can be turned into a rocket ship, and the rewards of reaching orbit can be big.

Junkies. Last, venture junkies are the third type of entrepreneurs who forego the NISI process until a crisis forces them to do otherwise. Such entrepreneurs are often enthusiastic and driven, but they focus all their energy on pleasing potential investors, investment bankers, or analysts, telling them what they want to hear instead of focusing on the customer and building real value. Like junkies, they spend all their energy in pursuit of the next fix, which in this case is money from investors. Although the venture junkies almost always pretend to listen and to be supremely open to feedback, the money makes them internally focused and for some reason hinders them from truly listening to the customer or feedback from anyone except investors. It is as if they have cotton stuffed in their ears which they pull out only when the investors, analysts, or investment bankers come into the room. When investors do come into the room, they weave a great story, dropping words like "India," "China," and "social networking" that make the investors drool. And with the cotton out of their ears, they will listen to and do whatever investors seem to suggest. But when the check is written, the cotton goes back in their ears and the entrepreneur races to the next pseudo-milestone needed to squeeze out some more investment money. In many ways, part of what got MyFamily.com into trouble was the distraction created by millions of dollars of venture money. For a season, management listened almost exclusively to the conflicting voices of the industry analysts, investment bankers, board members, and investors and completely ignored the real customer. When it comes to running the NISI process in a startup, if investors request that the company run the NISI process, junkies will nod their heads and pretend to run the process, but really they are busy searching for the path of least resistance to more money.

How do you avoid becoming a model, pack rat, or junkie? You can develop the intellectual honesty required to run the process we described earlier. Also, you just might need a good crisis—one that will force you and your company to get aligned with creating the most value for the most valuable customer. This process will force you to transform your lumbering barn in to a rocket ship. Alternatively, you may be able to choose it, even use the NISI process to do it, rather than have it forced upon you.

THE VALUE OF A GOOD CRISIS

Initially, Aeroprise had been founded to mobilize corporate software and, like good entrepreneurs, they realized they needed to focus in order to be successful. So the founders decided to focus on the IT service management niche as a beachhead. IT service management seemed like the right market because of the shirt tug problem.

The shirt tug problem occurs whenever an IT service person goes out in the field to solve one problem but is then inundated with multiple problems. Although the technician, we'll call him Tim, might have been called out to fix a PC in the accounting department, inevitably, while Tim is fixing the PC, someone else tugs Tim's shirt to ask about their printer that won't print in color. Then, while Tim is fixing the printer, somebody else asks about why Outlook keeps crashing, and so on. By the end of the day, Tim is juggling a dozen requests beyond his typical workload, can't remember what he finished and what he didn't, and certainly didn't have time to submit tickets for the shirt tugs. So Tim's other customers suffer (the ones still waiting for help), the business suffers, and at the end of the quarter, as productivity reports are put together, suddenly it looks like neither IT nor Tim were very productive. The system reports only a fraction of the work Tim completed, and management has no idea how many or what type of problems were fixed.

How to manage IT trouble tickets and resolve them on the go represented a major pain point that Aeroprise felt they could solve. To solve the problem, Aeroprise built relationships with each of the major IT service management companies such as IBM, HP, FrontRange and BMC Software—the firms that provide the software IT professionals use. Aeroprise's pitch to these software makers was that Aeroprise would work as their partner to mobilize their core IT applications. Because an HP or IBM or BMC sales rep could go into potential customers and sell not only their own core software product but a mobilized version of that same software, Aeroprise hoped that partners would get excited and help sell Aeroprise's product. But it didn't work out that way. Despite having built partnerships with several of the major software providers and wireless carriers, Aeroprise was doing all the legwork and often still paying a hefty revenue-share to partners.

As a result, although Aeroprise software sales people were running around generating leads, following up on sales, and delivering the product it was as if their partners didn't care or didn't see any value in the Aeroprise offering. As the money began to run out and the broader mobile enterprise market limped along, crisis set in. Aeroprise had already raised venture capital but they hadn't hit a solid milestone yet which made going back to raise more money virtually impossible. As an alternative, the company considered a Hail Mary play, raise more money and find a different market.

As the heat increased, the crisis began to transform Aeroprise. First, management cut down the team to reduce the burn rate. Next, the management team became unified in the need to find the answer and save their company. With the focus, commitment, and time devoted, the Aeroprise team ran the NISI process. As the team worked through the steps of the process and talked to members of the ecosystem—customers, partners, channel partners and other stakeholders, a surprising answer emerged. The answer wasn't to go broader and find another market. The answer was to go even narrower! Specifically, Aeroprise discovered that although on a surface level their software partners were cooperating, beneath the surface they worried that if they worked with Aeroprise too closely, or tried to sell their products, Aeroprise might interfere with their own deals or, worse, introduce customers to competitors who had also partnered with Aeroprise.

With the focus and unity created by the crisis, the Aeroprise team committed to the counter-intuitive answer generated by the NISI process: in this narrow market, go even narrower. To this end Aeroprise terminated all partnerships except the only one that really mattered: the market leader, BMC Software, owner of the Remedy IT Service Management product. Furthermore, they took the bold step of focusing first on the mobile platform their customers cared about most: BlackBerry. What resulted was incredible.

Recognizing that Aeroprise was a serious and trusted partner, BMC made a similar commitment to Aeroprise by giving its sales team the ability to sell Aeroprise as one of their own products – including full commission and quota credit. That bonus was just the beginning. RIM, maker of the BlackBerry, upon seeing Aeroprise's momentum, also increased its commitment level and provided Aeroprise with special access to marketing programs and funding unavailable to other companies supporting RIM competitors.

RIM wanted exclusive access to BMC's treasure chest of Remedy customers, BMC wanted access to RIM's treasure chest of enterprise customers, and Aeropris—so close to being irrelevant before NISI—was the capstone that made it all work. The partnership took off almost immediately. BMC, seeing that RIM was putting more money behind Aeroprise also increased their budget and effort to push the application. As RIM got even more excited, they committed yet more money to market Aeroprise's software, giving away free phones to Aeroprise customers and introducing the small Aeroprise team to global customers and resources they never could have received otherwise.

As the positive loop continued, on BMC's next earnings call they highlighted mobile as one of their core sources of growth. Better yet, by the end of the first quarter of 2009, when the worst recession since the depression was in free fall, Aeroprise not only met their quarterly sales goal for BMC, but the goal for the entire year! In the end, Aeroprise had taken a sinking ship and turned it around: they had picked up several thousand free sales reps through their partners, hundreds of thousands in marketing dollars, and created an expanding pipeline of sales. All of this led to the founders eventually selling the company to BMC. The Aeroprise turnaround was successful precisely because the earlier crisis gave them the focus, commitment, and time to run the NISI process, which provided the counter-intuitive insight not to switch markets but to go narrower. Many times entrepreneurs are tempted to switch markets because they can't find customers, but the truth is that often they just haven't had the discipline to run the NISI process and understand their customers. Once they have run the process, then they can answer the question: should we go narrower or should we switch markets? In either situation the key ingredients are understanding the customer and focus—the kind of focus created by crisis. Andy Grove, the CEO of Intel, said,

> *A question that often comes up at times of strategic transformation is, should you pursue a highly focused approach, betting everything on one strategic goal, or should you hedge? ... Mark Twain hit it on the head when he said, "Put all of your eggs in one basket and WATCH THAT BASKET."*[98]

The turn-around stories of Intuit, Aeroprise, and Ancestry.com all provide insight into the value of a good crisis: when managed properly, the crisis creates the focus, unity, and creativity to find a successful path forward. A crisis aligns company executives and team members with the principles and processes required to save the company. As leadership recognizes the peril and the dire need to save the company, some very visible changes happen: people are let go and the firm gets cut to a fraction of its former size, expenses are cut to the bone, and the burn rate drops. But it's below the surface where the real transformation is taking place. It is the laser-focus on the core business, renewed commitment, and additional time the crisis offers that have the most impact. We've discussed these essential qualities briefly during the discussion of each case study, but here's a further explanation of how these things ultimately saved each company from ruin. First, when a crisis hits, the team becomes laser-focused, hopefully on saving the company by understanding the real customer need. In the past, an entrepreneur was focused on his or her own agenda or worse, the team was focused on pleasing every customer, and as features were added to please everyone, the company began to resemble a barn with engines. In a real crisis, the direction of the company often becomes focused on finding the real customer and understanding what that customer really wants. This kind of focus is critical to the NISI process in two ways. One, while running the process, the team needs to focus on the process and find an answer. Two, after the team runs the process, the company also must focus to execute on what it discovers—to narrowly solve a single customer group's problem: to build a rocket that can break into orbit.

Second, when a crisis hits, the team gets commitment and urgency. The imminent failure of the company shatters the half-truths, guesses, biases, and politics that cripple all organizations. Suddenly everyone realizes that nothing else matters except saving the company; and to save the company, the truth must be known. The urgency and commitment from the crisis is crucial to the NISI process in several ways. For one, the stripped down humility created by near failure allows people to leave their pride, opinions, and games at the door and focus on the intellectually honest truth. Just as important, a crisis creates the commitment to muster the time and energy required for the NISI process. Without the commitment, the founder or CEO will hand off the NISI process to a junior person, who will be allowed to run it for a few weeks, and then, when the process seems to slow compared to the startup's other real needs, will have the plug pulled and be declared a failure. Again, unless the entrepreneur, CEO, team, and investors are committed and urgent, and participate, the process will be cut short and the results will be disappointing.

Third, ironically, the crisis creates time. In cutting the team, expenses and burn rate are cut down to a fraction of what they had been, two months of runway can be transformed into twelve months, and something crucial happens. Suddenly the entrepreneur and the team have more time to experiment and find the right market. Whereas previously, at a higher burn rate, the startup really only had one swing at the plate, suddenly the team can take two, three, four, maybe even twelve exploratory swings. Then when the team have found the real market for their product or service, and they have validated everything, then they can scale up and take a big swing. Because the NISI process relies on low-cost experimentation to validate all the facts, taking several swings at the plate and having several strikes is all part of the process before hitting it big.

In closing, the value of a good crisis is that it can create focus, commitment and time—all three of which are crucial in the NISI process. Without the focus, commitment, and time, as an entrepreneur or CEO, you will not be able to resist shortchanging the process by not participating, cutting it short, or substituting preconceived opinions for the facts that the NISI process should generate. Politics will get in the way. Opinions will get in the way. Demands will get in the way. If you allow this to happen, you will find that the process really only produces modest results and basically tells you what you already knew. But that is an operator error, not a problem with the process.

HAVE YOU HAD A GOOD CRISIS?

To be fair, you can run the NISI process without having had a crisis. The important precursor characteristics are the focus, commitment, and time. But how do you know if you are ready and if you have these? We have developed some self-awareness questions to help you assess whether you are ready or whether perhaps you need a good crisis. As you answer the questions, try to just give the answer that pops into your mind rather than second guessing yourself or the question. Remember, the goal isn't to "pass," it is just to get a candid peek at where you are on the NISI readiness scale.

Figure 31: Nail It then Scale It Self Awareness Quiz

Nail It then Scale It Self-Awareness Quiz			
Answer questions on a scale of 1-3 (3 = agree, 2= neutral, and 1 = disagree)			
When talking to others about your business idea, most of the time is spent explaining your idea.	1 Disagree	2	3 Agree
Feedback about something I am doing poorly is challenging for me to take.	1 Disagree	2	3 Agree
The point of school was to get a rubber stamp, not necessarily learning.	1 Disagree	2	3 Agree
When talking to others about your business idea, you spend most of your time selling them on the merit of the idea.	1 Disagree	2	3 Agree
At this point in my life I'm fairly independent financially.	1 Disagree	2	3 Agree
I relish positive feedback. You might even say I'm a people pleaser.	1 Disagree	2	3 Agree
I like starting projects but find it hard to finish them.	1 Disagree	2	3 Agree
I tend to be pretty opinionated and prefer to prove to people that I am right.	1 Disagree	2	3 Agree
I have a great business idea and am looking for investors because I don't want to risk my own capital.	1 Disagree	2	3 Agree
When someone disagrees with me, I like to defend my position.	1 Disagree	2	3 Agree
People have very strong opinions in my team and sometimes get political about them.	1 Disagree	2	3 Agree
Currently I have a lot of potential customers that I am trying to satisfy.	1 Disagree	2	3 Agree
I have a good guess about who my customer is and that should be a good enough starting point to get going.	1 Disagree	2	3 Agree
Any money from customers is good money. It doesn't matter where it comes from.	1 Disagree	2	3 Agree
At home or with friends, I tend to be in the limelight and lead the conversation.	1 Disagree	2	3 Agree
Things are so hectic, there is really no way to spare the time, let alone several weeks to go gather a bunch of data.	1 Disagree	2	3 Agree

As you took the self-assessment or glanced over the questions, how did you do? Did you score above 30? If so, don't feel bad or be offended. Most of us are right there with you—these kinds of habits are created largely by the very fact that you have been successful. Regardless, you probably are wrestling with some focus, commitment, or "intellectual honesty" issues that might get in the way of getting the most value out of the NISI process. Again, don't let that discourage you. It can be remedied, and the ideas discussed in this book can help you do it. The important point is that if some of these questions stuck out to you or rang true, you probably need to stop and assess your commitment to nailing your product or service so you can build a rocket ship. This self-assessment is only a rough indicator that precedes a deeper soul-searching about what you really want. Do you want to know the truth, or do you just want to be right—or at least to feel you are right? Are you so in love with your own idea, and your dream, but underneath it all you are terrified that it could all be smoke and mirrors? Is your primary motivation the pot of gold at the end of the journey? Everyone struggles with these kinds of issues, but to run the NISI process you need to really look at your motivations and get to the place that a crisis will bring you: honest, focused, and committed, with time to experiment. You can get there.

HOW TO CREATE A GOOD CRISIS

Entrepreneurs don't have to wait for a crisis to be able to run the NISI process. If an entrepreneur recognizes the challenges he or she will face and commits to fully engage the NISI process, he or she can reap the benefits. It isn't impossible, it just takes awareness. You may be able to reap the benefits of having a crisis without actually going through one by creating an artificial crisis. One way to create an artificial crisis is to constrain the amount of money invested in your startup by staging the investment into smaller tranches. If you have the opportunity to take investment money, you may consider constraining how you receive the money and how you use it. Use milestones and budgets to simulate a cash crunch as you would in a crisis. It will help your team get focused and give you more time. Or you may also want to set a deadline and mentally simulate the future. Give yourself two months before the imagined doomsday and commit to "save" the company by staying fully invested in the Nail It then Scale It process. Researchers have shown that thinking about how future events will occur actually lays the foundation for such events to occur. But your thinking about the future has to be concrete. In one study about the effect of thinking about the future, one group of students was asked to imagine the happiness of doing well on a test under the premise that envisioning this happy outcome would motivate students to study. A second group was asked to imagine studying hard before a test but were not told to think about how it would feel. Finally, a third group was told nothing (the control group). After taking the test, the students who envisioned studying hard (the second group) actually performed the best of all groups. The students who were supposed to be motivated by envisioning the joy of performing well actually performed the worst. So effective thinking about the future relies not on imaging a successful firm but on thinking about the concrete steps to get you there. In this case, that means thinking about running the Nail It then Scale It process with focus and commitment. The good news is that even by simulating a crisis, laying the groundwork for how to overcome it, and committing to run the NISI process can actually increase your ability to not only complete the process, but find a big discovery.

In Closing

As we finish introducing you to the Nail It then Scale It process, we want to encourage you by reminding you that entrepreneurs and innovators are the creative geniuses that transform the world. They create value for society and themselves by solving fundamental problems of all kinds. However, they only create that value when they focus on solving real pains in sustainable ways. The NISI process can help you discover the real opportunities and they are abundant. Thomas Edison argued that we are surrounded by opportunities: "We don't know one millionth of one percent about anything," and as a result "there's a better way to do it. Find it." Once you are on the right track, "scale it until it breaks." We would love to hear about your success and failures as you follow the NISI process. Send us your war stories and feedback info@nailthenscale.com or visit us at www.nailthenscale.com.

APPENDIX: NAIL IT THEN SCALE IT CHECKLIST

Below you will find a detailed checklist for the steps described in the book. Use it as a reminder and a guide as appropriate.

NAIL THE PAIN

Objectives

Clearly define and understand the customer pain.
Determine whether the customer pain is a market opportunity.
Shut it down or move to the next phase.

Steps

Step 1	Write down the Monetizable Pain hypothesis.
Step 2	Write down the Big Idea Hypothesis.
Step 3	Quick test of the Monetizable Pain and Big Idea Hypotheses.
Step 4	Quickly Explore Market Dynamics and Competition

NAIL THE SOLUTION

The Pre-Test: Develop Minimum Feature Set

Objectives

Discover the minimum feature set that drives customer purchase.

Discover key driver of customer purchase.

Keep solution set at absolute minimum—extreme simplicity.

Steps

Step 1 | Write down a minimum feature set hypothesis.

Test 1: The Virtual-Prototype Test

Objectives

Remove personal bias.
Develop a profile of relevant customers.
Develop, refine and test initial hypotheses about market solution.
Outline a customer-defined solution with value added to all stakeholders.
Define the best market segment for an initial beachhead.
Decide to shut it down quickly or move to the next test.

Steps

Step 1	Develop a customer profile.
Step 2	Choose a rapid prototyping technology and develop a virtual prototype.
Step 3	Make phone calls and visits to understand how the solution solves the pain.

Test 2: The Prototype Test

Objectives

Remove personal bias.
Take feedback from first test and develop a rapid, cheap prototype.
Focus on minimum feature set.
Use as little cash as possible.
Develop a prototype that gives customers a real feeling of how it works.
Validate your solution hypotheses by learning, not selling.
Have customers refine features of the product.
Get advised of potential competition and roadblocks.
Start to create a credible company brand and image.

Steps

Step 1	Develop an inexpensive, rapid prototype.
Step 2	Do a prototype roadshow.
Step 3	Refine the minimum feature set.
Step 4	Check the crucial tests of your hypotheses.

Test 3: The Solution Test

Objectives

Remove personal bias.
Make sure you are interpreting correctly and truly listening to the market.
Refine the solution to be an exact match of your customers' needs.
Test the price point and Breakthrough Questions.

Steps

Step 1	Validate the solution.
Step 2	If you get it wrong, adjust or move on.

NAIL THE GO-TO-MARKET STRATEGY

During the First Test (the Virtual-Prototype Test): Customer-Buying Process and Sales-Model Discovery

Objectives

Focus on the job your customer is trying to get done.
Understand the customer-buying process from beginning to end.
Develop a repeatable sales model customized for your company.
Explore price points with customers.

Steps

Step 1	Explore customer-buying process from beginning to end.
Step 2	Discover a repeatable sales model.

During the Second Test (the Prototype Test): Market Infrastructure Discovery

Objectives

Develop a robust understanding of the market ecosystem.

Frame a strategy to influence and leverage the market ecosystem.

Explore price points and IPO questions with customers.

Nurture early-stage customers.

Steps

Step 1	Map and understand the market-*communication* and -*distribution* infrastructure.
Step 2	Define a market infrastructure strategy for your startup.
Step 3	Plant seeds for early customers and pilot deals.

During the Third Test (the Solution Test): Pilot Customer-Development

Objectives

Validate your solution and go-to-market strategy with customers.
Validate key go-to-market assumptions with paying pilot customers.

Steps

Step 1	Close pilot customer relationships and develop reference customers.
Step 2	Revisit price points and crucial tests.

NAIL THE BUSINESS MODEL

Objectives

Conduct rigorous financial analysis of business viability.

Launch product and go-to-market strategy.

Drive early stages of company growth.

Decide quickly to shut down or move to next stage.

Steps

Step 1	Leverage customer conversations to predict the business model.
Step 2	Validate the financial model.
Step 3	Iteratively launch the product and go-to-market strategy.
Step 4	Develop a business dashboard with continuous data flow.

Appendix: Nail It then Scale It Sample Interview Guide

There are many ways to conduct a Nail It then Scale It interview, and each interview should be adapted to your specific purpose. For your introductory conversations about the customer pain and conceptual prototype, we suggest focusing on the following three questions.

1. "Do you have this problem?" Describe the problem to your customer in words like "We see this problem. Does that match your experience?"

2. "Tell me about it." Ask your customers to share their concerns, their experience, and their current solutions. Again, focus on listening, not selling.

3. "Does something like this solve the problem?" Describe the outline, or framework, of your problem. Again, don't get into the specific details but do give something customers something they can respond to, and ask for their feedback on whether it solves the problem.

As you progress and begin testing your virtual prototype, you might try on your own version of the following sample interview guide:

1. Include the person or people who will actually be using the product. Specifically, try to assemble the buying panel in one room

2. Set up a "moment-in-the-life" scenario for the monetizable pain. (You should have learned by now from the earlier interviews about the pain what a realistic use case would be.) Ask the panel if they have this pain or they see the world differently. Observe the response.

3. Walk the customer through the virtual prototype/prototype, step by step, taking careful notes on what they say (you should be recording the entire conversation as well for later transcription).

4. Ask the $100 question. Depending on the panel's response, it might be interesting to force a little prioritizing by saying each feature costs $25.Now how do you spend your money?

5. Of everything I have showed you, what else should it do?

6. What are the top two (or three) things this needs to do well?

7. What features are missing that you need in order to purchase?

8. What does it take to deploy something like this? (look for internal process, other departments, training, deployment, integration, etc.).

9. Begin exploring the customer-buying process or market and distribution infrastructure

   a. (Customer Awareness) How would you expect to hear about this product? How do you hear about products like this?

   b. (Customer Evaluation) How would you decide whether something like this fits your needs? What information would you need? Who would you want to talk to? Are there any magazines, blogs, conferences or anything else that helps you evaluate something like this?

   c. (Customer Purchasing) What goes into the purchase-decision process for something like this? Who has to approve the decision, and at what price points? How long does approval usually take? How would you expect to buy it? What else affects the decision to purchase?

   d. (Customer Use) Once you buy it, what kind of support would you normally expect? What other features would you need?

10. Crucial Tests (Note that the crucial tests are meant to be selling customers, although a sale can be a good thing. Instead, the crucial test questions are meant to provide a window into the customer's real desires and a conversation opener to discover them.)

    a. What price would you expect to pay for something like this? Would you expect to pay on a one-time or recurring basis? Other approaches?

    b. Given our conversation, would you be willing to preorder this today? Would you be willing to install this system-wide?

        i. If the answer is no: What is standing in the way of a preorder? What would we need to do to secure a preorder?

Clearly, the above interview guide represents but a sample of the types of questions you can ask. They would need to be modified, depending on your application (for example, the questions in this guide focus more on business-to-business purchases, so a business-to-consumer business would need to modify this guide).

END NOTES

1. Blank, S., *Retooling Early Stage Development*, in *Entrepreneur Thought Leader Lecture Series*. 2008, Stanford University: USA. p. 56:52.
2. Busenitz, L.W. and J.B. Barney, *Differences between entrepreneurs and managers in large organizations: Biases and heuristics in*. Journal of Business Venturing, 1997. 12(1): p. 9.
3. Ross, L. and R.E. Nisbett, *The Person and the Situation*. 1991, New York: McGraw-Hill.
4. Cavarretta, F. and N. Furr, *Too Much of a Good Thing? Extreme Outcomes and the Resource Curse*. Working Paper, 2010.
5. Thompson, C., *Learn to Let Go: How Success Killed Duke Nukem*, in *Wired Magazine*. 2010.
6. Maples, M., *Angel Investing Revealed*, in *Entrepreneur Thought Leader Lecture Series*. 2010, Stanford University.
7. Kawasaki, G., *Art of the Start*, in *Entrepreneur Thought Leader Lecture Series*. 2004, Stanford University: USA.
8. Mayer, M., *Creativity Loves Constraint*, in *Business Week*. 2006.
9. Seelig, T., *What I Wish I Knew When I Was 20*. 2009, New York: HarperOne.
10. Metcalfe, B., *Invention Is a Flower, Innovation Is a Weed* in *BerliNews*. 1999.
11. Furr, N., *Cognitive Flexibility and Technology Change*. Working Paper, 2010.
12. McCullough, D., *Interview with David McCullough*, P. Ahlstrom, Editor. 2004.
13. Greenspan, A. *Structural Change in the New Economy*. in *National Governors' Association*. 2000. State College, Pennsylvania
14. Katz, G., *The Sometimes Curious Language of NPD*. PDMA Visions Magazine, 2008. March.
15. Hamel, G., *Strategy as Revolution*. Harvard Business Review, 1996. July-August.
16. Hargadon, A., *How Breakthroughs Happen: The Surprising Truth about How Companies Innovate*. 2003, Cambridge, MA: Harvard Business School Press.
17. Walton, S. and J. Huey, *Sam Walton: Made in America*. 1993, New York: Bantam.

18. Barthelemy, J., *The Experimental Roots of Revolutionary Vision.* Sloan Management Reivew, 2006. 48(1).

19. Hargadon, A. and R.I. Sutton, *Technology Brokering and Innovation in a Product Development Firm.* Administrative Science Quarterly, 1997. 42(4): p. 716-749.

20. Lemley, M.A., *Are Universities Patent Trolls?* Stanford Public Law Working Paper, 2006.

21. Leonard, D., *The Limitations of Listening.* Harvard Business Review, 2002. January.

22. Christensen, C., *Discovering What Has Already Been Discovered.* Harvard Business School Publishing, 1999.

23. Berner, R., *Why P&G's Smile Is so Bright,* in *BusinessWeek.* 2002.

24. Kirzner, I., *Competition and Entrepreneurship.* 1973, Chicago: University of Chicago Press.

25. Kirzner, I., *Entrepreneurial Discovery and the Competitive Market Process: An Austrian Approach.* Journal of Economic Literature, 1997. XXXV: p. 60-85.

26. Dweck, C., *Mindset: The New Psychology of Success.* 2006, New York: Random House.

27. Dyer, J., H. Gregersen, and C. Christensen, *The Innovator's DNA.* Harvard Business Review, 2009. December.

28. Rogers, E., *Diffusion of Innovations.* 1980, New York: Free Press.

29. Ries, E., *Evangelizing for the Lean Startup,* in *Entrepreneurial Thought Leaders Lectures Series.* 2009, Stanford University. p. 58:03.

30. Blank, S., *Four Steps to the Epiphany.* 2005, San Francisco: Cafe Press.

31. March, J. and H. Simon, *Organizations.* 1958, New York: Wiley.

32. Blank, S., *The Path of Warriors and Winners.* 2010.

33. Christensen, C., *Personal Interview.* 2005: San Jose, CA.

34. Livingston, J., *Founders at Work.* 2008, New York: Apress.

35. *World Development Report.* 1994, World Bank: New York.

36. Loftus, E.F. and J.M. Doyle, *Eyewitness Testimony - Civil and Criminal* 1992, Charlottesville, VA: The Michie Co. .

37. Tripsas, M. and G. Gavetti, *Capabilities, Cognition and Inertia: Evidence from Digital Imaging.* Strategic Management Journal, 2000.

38. Christensen, C., *The Innovator's Dilemma.* 1997, Boston: Harvard Business School Press.

39. Plous, S., *The Psychology of Judgment and Decision Making* 1993: McGraw-Hill

40.   Arkes, H.R. and C. Blumer, *The Psychology of Sunk Cost.*
       Organizational Behavior & Human Decision Processes, 1985.
       35(1): p. 124-140.
41.   Staw, B.M., *Knee-deep in the Big Muddy: A study of escalating*
       commitment to a chosen course of action. Organizational
       Behavior & Human Decision Processes, 1976. 16(1): p. 27-44.
42.   Goldberg, L., *The effectiveness of clinicians' judgments: The*
       diagnosis of organic brain damage from the Bender-Gestalt test.
       Journal of Consulting Psychology, 1959. 23(25-33).
43.   Furr, N. and F. Cavarretta, *The Dangers of Deep Expertise: New*
       Ventures in the U.S. Solar Industry. Working Paper, 2011.
44.   Tripsas, M., *Unravelling the Process of Creative Destruction:*
       Complementary Assets and Incumbent Survival in the Typesetter
       Industry. Strategic Management Journal, 1997. 18(Special
       Issue): p. 119-142.
45.   Malone, M., *John Doerr's Startup Manual*, in *Fast Company.*
       1997.
46.   Rock, A., *Strategy versus Tactics from a Venture Capitalist.*
       Harvard Business Review, 1987. November.
47.   Orr, D., *Startups: The Need for Speed*, in *Entrepreneurial*
       Thought Leaders Lecture Series. 2007, Stanford University. p.
       57:57.
48.   Perez, R.C., *Inside Venture Capital: Past, Present, and Future.*
       1986, Westport, CT: Praeger Publishers.
49.   Dane, E., *Reconsidering the Trade-off Between Expertise and*
       Flexibility: A Cognitive Entrenchment Perspective. Academy of
       Management Review, 2010. 35(4): p. 579-603.
50.   Kelley, T., *Cultivating an Attitude of Wisdom* 2008, Stanford
       Technology Ventures Program.
51.   Burgelman, R.A., *Fading Memories: A Process Theory of*
       Strategic Business Exit in Dynamic Environments.
       Administrative Science Quarterly, 1994. 39: p. 24-56.
52.   Iyengar, S. and M.A. Lepper, *When Choice is Demotivating: Can*
       One Desire Too Much of a Good Thing? Journal of Personality
       and Social Psychology, 2000. 79(6): p. 995-1006.
53.   Khosla, V., *Any Big Problem Is a Big Opportunity*, in
       Entrepreneurial Thought Leaders Lecture Series. 2002, Stanford
       University. p.:27.
54.   Rip, P., *The Teqlo Adventure.* 2008.
55.   DeSimone, B., *Rewarding Recyclers, and Finding Gold in the*
       Garbage, in *New York Times.* 2006: New York City.

56. *New Recycling Program Like Money in the Bank*, in *Nashua Telegraph*. 2008: Nashua, NH.

57. Walsh, B., *Making Recycling Really Pay*, in *Time*. 2008: New York City.

58. Siebel, T., *Emerging Opportunities in a Post IT Marketplace*, in *Entrepreneurial Thought Leader Lecture Series*. 2009, Stanford University. p. 1:00.

59. Eisenhardt, K.M. and C.B. Schoonhoven, *Organizational Growth: Linking Founding Team, Strategy, Environment, and Growth among U.S. Semiconductor Ventures*. Administrative Science Quarterly, 1990. 35(3): p. 504-529.

60. Markides, C.C. and P.A. Geroski, *Fast Second*. 2005, San Francisco: Jossey Bass.

61. March, J.G. and J.P. Olsen, *Ambiguity and Choice in Organizations*. 1976, Bergen: Universitetsforlaget.

62. Ulwick, A., *Turning Customer Input into Innovation*. Harvard Business Review, 2002. January.

63. Kirkpatrick, D., *Intuit's Innovation Intuition*, in *Fortune*. 2005: New York.

64. Goldenson, M., *Ten Lessons from a Failed Startup*, in *VentureBeat*. 2009.

65. de Saint-Exupery, A., *Wind, Sand and Stars*. 1992, Boston, MA: Houghton Mifflin Harcourt.

66. Lewis, L., *Trader Joe's Adventure: Turning a Unique Approach to Business into a Retail and Cultural Phenomenon*. 2005, Chicago, IL: Dearborn Trade.

67. McGregor, J., *Leading Listener: Trader Joe's*, in *Fast Company*. 2007.

68. Covey, S.R., *The Seven Habits of Highly Effective People*. 2004, Free Press: New York.

69. Maples, M., *Interview with Mike Maples Jr.* 2010.

70. Rayport, J., M. Iansiti, and M. Hart, *Motive Communications*. Harvard Business School Publishing, 2001.

71. Blank, S., *Victory from Adversity*, in *Steve Blank*. 2010.

72. Dewalt, K., *Customer Development with Microsoft Visio*, in *From the Start-up Trenches*. 2009.

73. Dewalt, K., *Many Wheels: A Lean Startup Case Study on Vetting Opportunities*, in *From the Start-up Trenches*. 2009.

74. McNichol, T., *A Startup's Best Friend? Failure*, in *Business 2.0*. 2007.

75. MacMillan, I. and R.G. McGrath, *Discovering New Points of Differentiation.* Harvard Business Review, 1997. July-August 1997.

76. McKenna, R., *Relationship Marketing.* 1993, New York: Basic Books.

77. Taylor, S.E., *Inside Intuit: How the Makers of Quicken Beat Microsoft and Revolutionized an Entire Industry.* 2003, Boston, MA: Harvard Business Press.

78. Griffin, A., R. Price, and B. Vojak, *How Serial Innovators Understand Customer Needs.* Working Paper, 2010.

79. Novitsky, D., *Personal Interview.* 2007: Stanford University.

80. Glasner, J., *Why Webvan Drove Off a Cliff,* in *Wired.* 2001.

81. Mullins, J.W., *The New Business Road Test.* 2004, New York: FT Press.

82. Wasserman, N., *Founder-CEO Succession and the Paradox of Entrepreneurial Success.* Organization Science, 2003. 14(2): p. 149-172.

83. Moore, G.A., *Crossing the Chasm.* 2002, New York: Harper Paperbacks.

84. Santos, F.M. and K. Eisenhardt, *Constructing Markets and Shaping Boundaries: Entrepreneurial Power and Agency in Nascent Fields.* Academy of Management Journal, 2009. 52(4): p. 643 - 671.

85. Hinds, P.J., M. Patterson, and J. Pfeffer, *Bothered by Abstraction: The Effect of Expertise on Knowledge Transfer and Subsequent Novice Performance.* Journal of Applied Psychology, 2001. 86(6): p. 1232-1243.

86. Monson, T.S., *Favorite Quotations from the Collection of Thomas S. Monson.* 1985, Salt Lake City, UT: Deseret Books.

87. Heil, G., *Personal Interview.* 2000.

88. Isaacson, W., *Einstein: His Life and Universe.* 2008, New York: Simon & Schuster.

89. Joni, S.-n., *The Third Opinion: How Successful Leaders Use Outside Insight to Create Superior Results.* 2004, New York: Portfolio Hardcover.

90. Weiss, T.R., *Craig Newmark,* in *Computer World.* 2008.

91. Dobrev, S.D., S.Z. Ozdemir, and A.C. Teo, *The Ecological Interdependence of Emergent and Established Organizational Populations: Legitimacy Transfer, Violation by Comparison, and Unstable Identities.* Organization Science, 2006b. 17(5): p. 577-597.

92.   Ozcan, P. and K. Eisenhardt, *Origin of Alliance Portfolios: Entrepreneurs, Network Strategies, and Firm Performance.* Academy of Management Journal, 2009. 52(2): p. 246 - 279

93.   Adner, R. and R. Kapoor, *Value creation in innovation ecosystems: how the structure of technological interdependence affects firm performance in new technology generations,* in *Strategic Management Journal.* 2010. p. 306-333.

94.   Christensen, C., *Hewlett-Packard: The Flight of the Kittyhawk.* Harvard Business School Publishing, 1997.

95.   Baker, M., *Building an Organization, Building a Team,* in *Entrepreneurial Thought Leader Lecture Series.* 2009, Stanford University. p. 55:52.

96.   Dell, M., *Overcoming Some Early Mistakes of Dell Inc.,* in *Entrepreneur Thought Leader Lecture Series.* 2007, Stanford University.

97.   Miller, J., *Personal Interview.* 2007: Stanford University.

98.   Grove, A.S., *Only the Paranoid Survive.* 1996, New York, NY: Currency.

Made in the USA
Lexington, KY
07 April 2014